AL MARTINEZ

REFLECTIONS

COLUMNS FROM THE LOS ANGELES TIMES

Los Angeles Times
BOOKS

Editor: Carla Lazzareschi
Designer: Catherine Vandecasteele
Copy Editor: Stephanie Goodman
Cover Illustration: John Robertson

ISBN: 1-883792-72-X
Copyright 2003 Los Angeles Times
202 W. 1st St., Los Angeles, CA 90012

First printing June 2003
Printed in the U.S.A.

Los Angeles Times

Publisher: John P. Puerner
Editor: John S. Carroll
Book Development General Manager: Carla Lazzareschi

**FOR CINELLI
AND FOR YOU**

CONTENTS

PROLOGUE   1

CHAPTER ONE   THE PEOPLE, YES   5

CHAPTER TWO   ANYTHING FOR A LAUGH   45

CHAPTER THREE   CAUSES, CONCERNS AND CALAMITIES   81

CHAPTER FOUR   A FAMILY OF FRIENDS   109

CHAPTER FIVE   ON THE ROAD AGAIN   149

CHAPTER SIX   SUNSETS AND WINDS OF FIRE   183

CHAPTER SEVEN   WAR AND REMEMBRANCE   207

CHAPTER EIGHT   ENDINGS: JUST PASSING THROUGH   235

                   INDEX   273

❖

PROLOGUE

SOUTHERN CALIFORNIA IS MY HOME, MY BEAT AND MY OBSESSION. I have wandered its valleys and its canyons, its beaches and its city streets for 30 years, 10 as a reporter and 20 as a columnist, all for the Los Angeles Times.

I've been driven to frustration on its tangle of freeways, ridden its crawling buses and limited subways, and walked its many streets, from Cesar Chavez Avenue to the ocean, and from Martin Luther King Jr. Boulevard to Rodeo Drive.

I have marveled at the variety of its people, the melody of its many languages and the dichotomy of its cultures. In years of traveling the world, I have never seen a place quite like L.A., quite as big and quite as diverse. With some notable exceptions, we manage somehow to get along, to hold it all together, to make it work.

Writing a column in such a place is both a chore and an honor. There's so much going on at the same time that to concentrate, research and illuminate one element of this sprawling place requires an effort beyond any work I've ever undertaken. But there's a joy to it too, an exhilaration that makes you want to see more, to hear more and to know more about this phenomenon called the City of Angels or, even better, the City of Angles.

In just the relatively short time I have been here, L.A. has grown from a listless, scattered set of suburbs to a place of energy and identity. We are a metropolis to be dealt with now, a player on the world stage, a giant on the western rim of the Pacific. When we speak, New York listens. When we move,

Chicago moves with us. Dallas knows we're here, and so do Miami and Omaha and San Francisco.

Included in this book are columns spanning my decades and my interests. I sing the people, as Walt Whitman sang the people, and I observe the foibles of the people, as Mark Twain once observed them. I'm not comparing myself, God forbid, only acknowledging them for what they did first and so magnificently. The book also contains observations on war, politics, nature, travel and life's passages, the deaths of those I knew and others I wish I had known. And it talks of my family because it is your family too: Cinelli, the dogs Hoover and Barkley, and the others. It's a universal family with universal dogs.

I am indebted to Carla Lazzareschi for seeing this book through to fruition, to my good friend Russ Manzatt for solving all my computer problems and to you, for just being there. But the day is late. Shall we begin?

CHAPTER ONE

THE PEOPLE, YES

"I am the people, the mob, the crowd, the mass
Do you know that all the great work of
the world is done through me?"

—CARL SANDBURG

A POET OF THE STREET

SHE CALLS HERSELF FRANCEYE, WRITES POETRY AND LIVES ALONE in a small apartment in Venice. Well, not totally alone, because there are Charles Bukowski posters on the wall and enough memories of him to fill anyone's room. Even in death, he's somehow as strong and present today as he was back then, when he was drinking, brawling and whoring his way up and down L.A.'s seedier streets.

FrancEyE, whose last name is Smith, lived with Buk, as he called himself, for almost three years and bore his child, Marina. They separated, she says, because "two crazy people just can't live together." At 80, she doesn't seem crazy, sitting in a rocking chair and peering out through oversized glasses, as pert and snappy as an early spring. Well, yes, there are those fairly long chin hairs she's let grow, but that's just her stamp of individuality, a declaration of self. She's a poet, after all, and you know how they are.

I came across her name in a Bukowski biography by Howard Sounes. There aren't too many FrancEyEs in the world, and when you see the name, it just kind of jumps out at you. I realized that someone named FrancEyE had been sending me poetry over the years. I discovered it was her, Buk's woman, which is why I went to see her.

I'm a Bukowski fan and was even before he died of leukemia in 1994. When I read of his death, I felt like throwing myself from a high window. Not in grief, because he drank enough to have died long before he did, but because

7

I had always wanted to meet the man and just never got around to it. My life is composed of things I've intended to do but haven't, and people I've wanted to meet but haven't. Damn me.

Bukowski was a poet of the street and of the people who still inhabit that world. He wrote poems so powerful, one admirer said, that they constituted "the spoken voice nailed to paper." Some poets whisper, but he roared and growled his verse, daring anyone who read it not to remember its potency. It was filled with black-and-white imagery and visions of sadness that seemed to regard the world not with scorn but with the frustration of a man whose questions were never answered.

FrancEyE remembers him as a guy who could be, as she puts it, "a decent citizen who dressed up to go to work at the post office every day" when he was sober but became a confrontational drunk on weekends when he'd hit the booze. Then, she says, he got stupid and verbally abusive, insulting even those he liked or admired and sometimes getting into bar fights. "He used to say that he needed me to explain things to him, about how to get along in life."

She met Bukowski through an exchange of letters and began living with him in 1963 in a place on Mariposa Street that someone said smelled like cabbage and rats. "He wrote every day after dinner and before going to work at night at the post office," she says. "He always wrote one poem. He had a huge head. I'd look at him and wonder what it would be like to have so much in my head."

FrancEyE was drawn to Bukowski by his poetry. Her real name was Frances, but she changed it when a friend said that Frances sounded plural. She was writing her own verse but didn't know whether she was really a poet. "I didn't have a role model for my work," she says. "Then I read Buk and he just put it out there." They stayed together until their differences split them apart. "He wanted a happy woman singing in the kitchen," she says. "That wasn't me." And yet … and yet….

Afterward she wrote: "… and all I want to do is kiss you and stay with you forever. / Forget I have tiny pig eyes and like to go to workshops / and never sweep the floor. / Forget you called me a whore, / puked in the bushes, / always passed out and had to be dragged to bed."

Bukowski used to say that his poetry came easy. "The wine does most of my writing," he told an interviewer. "I just open a bottle and turn on the radio, and it comes pouring out." But it's the place it comes pouring from, words and imagery on fire, that makes the difference. It's that place in the soul where life and talent merge that produces greatness.

Well, there. I never got to meet Bukowski or drink with him or share stories and lies with him. But I got to meet someone who knew him and loved him and could never really figure him out, even though she slept with him and had his baby. I got around to meeting FrancEyE, anyhow. That's something.

December 6, 2002

❖

LOOKIN' GOOD, FEELIN' FINE

HERE COMES GIUSEPPE ROSELLI, SILK SHIRT UNBUTTONED halfway to his navel, a miniature gold boxing glove dangling from a chain around his neck, trim and self-assured, lookin' good.

He stands in the ornate lobby of the Hollywood Roosevelt, scans the room through oversized, tinted glasses, makes contact and saunters over, graying ponytail bobbing slightly.

His walk is slow and deliberate, but even so there's a kind of rhythm to it, as though at any moment he can be up on the balls of his feet, jabbing and feinting, shoulders hunched, eyes fixed.

He was a boxer once, a lightweight contender in fact, but at 78 he's past all that. He gave up boxing 35 years ago and became a manager. But he got into the ring one more time to teach one of his boxers a lesson that the kid, knocked out cold, never forgot.

L.A. knows Giuseppe Roselli as Joey Barnum, the name he fought under back then and the name he'll take into the World Boxing Hall of Fame next month.

He's a bail bondsman now, "Mr. Bail" on the license of his black Caddy, as much a fixture in Southern California as Wolfgang Puck or Heidi Fleiss, though on a decidedly different level.

A friend of the famous and the infamous, the kid from Chicago's Little Italy is famous in his own way too and soon to become more so. Not only as an inductee into boxing's hall of fame, but also as a star of "America's Dumbest Criminals" on television in early November.

You haven't lived until you see this onetime contender in a push-up bra, a bouffant wig and a sleek red dress.

It is one of his most celebrated stories, a 15-year-old tale told to me over dinner at the venerable old Roosevelt. Joey only picks at his food, a reason why, at 150 pounds, he is only five pounds heavier than his fighting weight.

"I'm at the office," he says, "when I get a call from a guy who says a bail jumper is at a nearby bar, but I'd better be careful because he's packing a gun. I'm thinking, what'll I do to nail this guy?"

Then Joey, who is never without ideas, gets a brainstorm. At Halloween a few weeks earlier. he had dressed in drag, so he hauls out the outfit, complete with a red wig, dresses up as a woman he calls Eloise and heads for the door.

"Where you going?" his wife, Esther, asks. Joey gives his behind a little wiggle and says, "Out."

At the bar, the bail jumper doesn't recognize Joey, which is the whole point of the dress. The guy only sees Eloise. So he buys her a drink and gives her leg a little rub. Then suddenly Esther, who is checking on Joey, comes in and Joey decides he'd better act fast. He dumps his drink on the bail jumper's lap, and as the guy is distracted, Joey hits him with a left hook. The jumper goes down like a punctured balloon.

As Joey cuffs the man and is dragging him out the door, the bartender, who has been observing all this, says with awe and respect, "Man, can that broad hit!"

What you won't see on "America's Dumbest Criminals" is a moment that occurs outside the bar in Whittier where a re-creation of the incident is about to be filmed.

Joey is standing in full drag waiting to be called when two cops see him and, figuring maybe he's a hooker or a nut, want to know what's going on.

Only when they check with the TV crew do they believe what Joey is telling them.

"They should've known," he says later. "I'm too ugly to be a hooker."

By entering the World Boxing Hall of Fame, Joey will join a company of champions that includes Sugar Ray Robinson, Joe Louis and Muhammad Ali. "It's a special place," says hall of fame coordinator Alex Campanovo. "You had to have status."

Over the 20 years of its existence, only 120 nominees have made it into the hall. Among those who recommended Joey is a onetime amateur boxer he beat in Burbank's old Jeffries Barn a long time ago. The guy was so distressed he gave up boxing forever. His name is Kirk Kerkorian. He owns MGM.

All of this sudden attention leaves Joey a little hyper, but there's a steadying quality to his life too, a sadness that keeps him in touch with himself. His beloved Esther, the woman he's adored for 53 years, came down with Alzheimer's disease 20 years ago and has been in a nursing home since 1992. Joey misses her every day of his life.

"She doesn't recognize me anymore," he says, his voice choking. "She can't communicate or take care of herself. But when I talk to her and massage her shoulders, sometimes a tear runs down her cheek. Sometimes I think she knows."

He pauses, shakes his head and moves on.

I see him heading toward the door, this Giuseppe Roselli, tipping the maitre d', telling stories, laughing at himself, soon to be more famous than linguine and clams, stepping out into a misty L.A. night, feeling right, lookin' good.

September 29, 1999

THE ETERNAL COCKTAIL WAITRESS

IT IS COMFORTING TO REALIZE IN THESE TROUBLED TIMES THAT there is always Alice.

She sails through the boozy confines of the Red Dog Saloon like a schooner before the wind, all trim and determined, straying neither this way nor that.

Call her name aloud in the course of her mission and she will most likely ignore you, but, fear not, your sound will register and your drink will be forth-coming.

And she will know what you're drinking, even if you have only come to the storied bar on 2nd Street once or twice, for Alice, Sweet Alice, is the best at what she does.

Her full name is Alice Broude. For 49 years she has been a waitress at the restaurant-bar once named the Redwood, now the Redwood 2nd Street Saloon, but known to generations of habitués as the Red Dog.

This is a port of choice for those who toil for the L.A. by God Times, a place beyond deadlines, demanding editors, foolish policies and often self-imposed anxieties.

The Red Dog, in fact, once occupied a corner of what had been Times Mirror Square and is now just a half-block away or, as a hard drinker once put it, "just a stagger past Broadway."

Where other waitresses have come and gone, Alice has endured, never wavering from a style of service that characterizes her not so much as aloof but efficient. When a man wants a drink, he wants it in a straight line directly from the bar to the table without side trips by the server on whose tray it rests.

Alice sees to it. She is, without doubt, the undisputed queen of newspaper bars.

The 17th of 20 children, the girl from Coon Rapids, Iowa, tired of small towns and hard winters, came to L.A. in 1945, lured west by the weather.

"I left in a blizzard, and it was 84 degrees here when I arrived," she says, sitting at a kitchen table in her small Echo Park home. "It was January and flowers were blooming. How could I not like it?"

She lives not 20 minutes from the Red Dog in a wood frame house that reflects her own tidy nature. Nothing is out of place. The windows shine. Dust would not dare cling to her carpet.

At 82, she limits her workweek to three days but is not likely to retire any time soon. Her mother lived until she was 109, and Alice will probably do the same, hauling drinks and food to their destinations in a calm and orderly manner as the years fold one into the other.

"The worst thing you can do," she says pragmatically, "is to do nothing."

A secret of her endurance rests in the precise and functional style of her service. She remains tranquil by ignoring those who holler for attention, getting to them in her own good time. And when she does reach the table, she spares her customers wasteful chitchat in a room full of thirsty patrons. You name it, she gets it.

One reporter recalls just how efficient she was. Years ago, he worked in an office just above the bar. At night, ready to leave, he'd stomp three times on the floor. When he walked into the place a few moments later, Alice would have his drink ready.

Those who have frequented the Red Dog over the years range from crooks to cognoscenti. Mickey Cohen drank there, tipping everyone in sight, and so did Benjamin (Never Call Him Bugsy) Siegel. Writers, actors, judges, lawyers, politicians, boxing promoters and racetrack touts have all called the place their home away from home. And Alice has always been there.

I stopped hanging out at the Red Dog when I began writing a column about 18 years ago. I just didn't have time for long lunch hours or after-work pick-me-ups anymore.

"You used to drink Beefeater martinis, straight up, olive on the side," Alice said as we reminisced about the days when bulldozing Bill Eaton owned the place. She was right. I'd walk in and a martini would be waiting at my booth like a happy puppy, without a word being said.

Eaton was a tough kid from Jersey with the temperament of a piranha. He'd toss you out with the same enthusiasm that he'd welcome you in. Give him a bad time about anything at all and you were in and out quicker than the bartender could sweeten your lemonade. The fight promoter Don King, with his bulk and his wild hair, was Eaton's good friend, and so was the racetrack tout Sideways Sidney, who held secret conversations on a phone at the end of the bar.

Walter Winchell used to come by when he was in town. Burt Reynolds kissed Alice's hand one late afternoon, "and I haven't washed it since." I interviewed the great LAPD detective John St. John in a corner booth night after night for the book "Jigsaw John." One-eyed and stoic, he was later immortalized in a television series starring Jack Warden. I think Alice, a widow, was in love with him, but she never said. She never says much of anything.

Times change. They still drink martinis at the Red Dog, Alice says, but mostly they're fruit-flavored. Hardly any reporter gets falling-down drunk anymore. There aren't too many fights, and Bill Eaton isn't there to throw anyone out. Only Alice remains a link to an era long gone. As I said, I don't go by much anymore. But I know when I do, she'll bring me a Beefeater martini, straight up, olive on the side. I won't have to say a word.

October 22, 2001

❖

THE LIBERATOR MOVES ON

CLEARLY, MORRIS KIGHT WAS IN A HURRY.

He wanted to get through the ritual, even though it was a day when honors were being heaped upon him as a retiring member of the L.A. County Human Relations Commission.

He fidgeted, made mumbled references to moving on and rose to lean on his walker midway through a laudatory talk by Supervisor Zev Yaroslavsky to indicate that Yaroslavsky should wind it up.

It was, in some ways, characteristic of the man who has been in the forefront of the gay liberation movement for almost half a century. Speak out. Get it done. Hit the streets. Move on.

But no one was listening to Kight this time. Those who had gathered on the eighth floor of the county administration building were not to be denied. Kight was retiring after 22 years, and by God, they were going to honor him whether he liked it or not.

Later, a tree would be planted in his honor in a small park in West Hollywood, a city in which so much of Kight's work had been done. But for now, members of the commission, friends, supporters and co-activists in the gay community wanted to thank him for standing tall when it was neither popular nor safe to do so.

They wanted everyone to know that Kight, almost 83, was a hero of the gay rights movement in L.A., and Kight wanted everyone to know it too. No stranger to publicity, he had telephoned me to be there, and I hesitated not a moment.

Why not celebrate a man who through deed and effort had demanded a place in the sun for a group of people defiled and murdered by religions and governments throughout human history? Why not be there?

"Kight," as someone at the meeting pointed out, "was always there."

Felled by a series of strokes, he is frail and must use a walker to get around these days. And yet, there remains a patrician authority in his voice, a crisp, articulate degree of command that will not be silenced. He was, as someone has said, "the liberator," and in some ways, he still is.

Texas-born, Kight knew almost from the beginning that he was "different." His father, a blue-collar worker at many jobs, knew it too. "He brought me a present once when I was 4," Kight recalls. "It was an embroidery set. Then he kissed me and said he knew something about me. He just sensed it, and he wanted to make it easier for me."

His mother was less forgiving. She maintained a silence throughout her life but left behind notes that burned with hatred toward homosexuals. Kight read them only after her death and destroyed them.

"She'd have been happier," he said to me in a voice oddly muted, "if she had loved me."

It was Rosa Parks' refusal to move to the back of a bus in Montgomery, Ala., in 1955 that radicalized Kight. He came to L.A. because, inspired by

Parks' courage, he felt the time was right for a nonviolent movement on behalf of gays, and this was the place where it should begin.

"I never denied or concealed my gayness," he said, peering out from large, horn-rimmed glasses. His thinning hair is white and his skin pale. "I just eased out of the closet door in stages. But I never pretended to be anything I wasn't."

Once here, he says, he founded the Gay and Lesbian Resistance in 1957, one of the first organizations of its kind in the country. For nine years, he conducted training classes every Sunday afternoon that taught gays how to react in the face of insults and brutality. Twelve years later, he was instrumental in establishing the Gay Liberation Front in L.A., only the third such organization in the nation.

For all those years, Kight has offered leadership to the uncertain, pride to the demeaned and comfort to the dying. In 1970, he and others marched through Hollywood to honor the first anniversary of the so-called Stonewall Uprising in New York. It was the start of the Gay and Lesbian Pride celebration and parade here.

And it galvanized a population that for too long had been almost invisible.

Critics have called Kight theatrical and egotistical, but leaders must always possess those traits. Theatrics are necessary to gather a crowd and self-assurance is required to convince others to follow a path of resistance they might otherwise avoid, or liberation will never be achieved.

"Morris comes from an era where, to be openly gay, you were putting your physical safety on the line," Yaroslavsky once told an interviewer, adding: "When the history of civil liberties is written, he'll be there."

"It has been exciting," Kight says as we talk in a corner of the room where the Human Relations Commission is about to begin its first meeting without him in more than two decades. There is a prevailing sadness to the event, a sense that an important era is ending.

Kight is made an honorary commissioner, and then he's halfway out the door by the time the commission is called to order to begin its formal meeting without him. Walker or no walker, he moves away from the meeting room as quickly as he can. It's time to step out, to get going, to move on.

"That was the past," he says, in a tone meant to categorize his honored yesterdays. "There are still things to do in the future."

And the liberator moves determinedly down the hall toward the elevator.

July 22, 2002

❖

JERRY BROWN ON PLANET OAKLAND

WHEN I ASKED JERRY BROWN WHY HE'D WORKED SO HARD TO become the mayor of Oakland, he replied it's because Oakland is the Archimedean lever that will shift America's interest back to the cities.

I said, "What?"

He said, "Maybe I shouldn't have said that."

Maybe he's right, because guys like me are going to say hoo-boy, there he goes humming and zooming to the outer planets again and taking a whole city with him this time. Archimedean lever indeed.

One of the reasons I've always liked Oakland is that it pretended to be nothing more than a beer and burger kind of town, and now it is going to be saddled with having to find out just who in the hell Archimedes is.

I asked my sister Emily, who still lives there, if she knew, and she thought he might have had a Greek restaurant once on East 14th Street. When I explained that he was an ancient mathematician, she said testily, "Big deal."

I knew Archimedes was a mathematician because in one of the very few math classes I can remember, I had to write a paper on him. I remember Jerry Brown for a similar reason, because I had to write news stories about him.

For your information, the Archimedean Law of the Lever says, to quote Britannica, "Magnitudes balance at distances from the fulcrum in inverse ratio to their weights."

What that means is that Jerry Brown is on the loose again, this time on the Planet Oakland.

I have a proprietary interest in the Brown family. Before Jerry, I wrote about Pat, and after Jerry, sort of, I wrote about Kathleen, and now here comes Jerry again, riding his Archimedean pony into prominence.

I don't know what his landslide election as the mayor of my hometown means to the world, but I have always believed that if anything bad is ever going to happen to humanity on a grand scale, it will probably start in Oakland.

The Last Deadly Bacterial Epidemic that will wipe out the human race will fester in a bottle of Bud in a bar in Jack London Square, and the comet that will devastate our species will plunge into Lake Merritt.

Atomic annihilation is also a serious concern. In Washington, they worry not about nuclear proliferation in the Mideast, but what would happen if, shudder, Jerry Brown ever got the bomb. Probably the same thing that happened when Oakland got the Raiders. Nothing.

I asked Brown during a telephone conversation if his election as mayor meant he would be encouraged to once more seek the presidency. His answer was: (-------------). Right. Silence. I'm not sure what that means, but if he thinks I'm going to cross the country with him again in that damned VW bus with the psychedelic paint job, he's out of his mind.

A native San Franciscan who adopted L.A. as his new hometown, Brown moved to Oakland because, he said, the rent was cheaper. It was only later that he began to see the town as the city of the future.

"Oakland is small enough for the people to take control but big enough to make a difference," he said. "On my mind is putting cities back on the national agenda."

He intends to do that, Brown explained, by turning Oakland upside-down, which probably won't make a lot of difference to a place that has always been slightly askew. Then he mentioned the Archimedean lever as a way of accomplishing his aim. It has to do with theoretical mechanics and the equilibrium of rectilinear planes.

"He has dreams," says Tom Quinn, who was the state's smog czar under Brown. "He always has had. In '76 he talked about the state launching its own satellite and everyone laughed. Now all the big companies want to do just that.

He was 20 years ahead of his time."

I remember Brown during a campaign appearance before a large group of wealthy Democrats in Maryland. Great words were anticipated that would ignite his bid for the White House. Instead, he began talking about how his administration in Sacramento had lowered the amount of water required to flush a toilet.

A stunned silence followed, and then a matron standing next to me turned and said, "Is that young man serious?" I said, "Yes, ma'am, that young man is very serious."

He still is. There's just no Archimedean theory to explain him.

June 12, 1998

❖

THE BOY WITH NO FACE

THE LIGHT IN MARK BASHAM'S APARTMENT WAS DIM, THE FLAT-tened rays of an afternoon sun filtered through louvered shades. Even so, it was not difficult to see the scars left on his face from a fire that almost killed him a dozen years ago, or the fingerless hands he tried unconsciously to keep out of sight.

Neither the pale light nor the skin grafts of a hundred operations could conceal the terrible things flames had done to him as a child in the small Kentucky town where he was born.

"Being burned," he said in hushed, almost whispery tones, "is like suddenly losing your identity. One moment your face is there, the next moment it's gone."

Photographs of the face that no longer exists, the Mark Basham that disappeared in a flash of heat, hung on two nearby walls, to remind him in duplicate of the features that had once been his. The photographs stamped the room with a dreadful reality.

Mark sat tucked in a corner of the couch that was one of the few pieces of furniture in the apartment, as though by sitting in shadow he was seeking even deeper anonymity in an already lightless environment.

We talked about the face that the fire had left him.

"The doctor wouldn't let me look in a mirror when they took the bandages off," he said. "But I saw myself reflected in the plastic above my bed, and I cried. It didn't seem real."

He was 12 when it happened. Mark's stepfather was using gasoline to remove glue from the floor of a house they had just rented. The glue had been used to hold carpeting down. The stepfather left the room to light a cigarette. There was an explosion....

"I remember trying to climb out a window over a clothes dryer. The dryer was hot and I fell off. It was like I was moving in slow motion. When I finally got out, everything speeded up. I was burned black. There was no pain then. Just heat, then chills. The pain came later."

Mark was burned over most of his body. His mother and brother died in the fire. His stepfather disappeared. He hasn't seen him since.

Today, Mark is a tall, slim 24. His face scars are muted but apparent. Only thumbs remain on each hand.

He telephoned me first not to talk specifically about the fire, but to tell me about an RTD driver who had ordered him off a bus because he didn't want to look at Mark.

We discussed briefly what he called "my disfigurement" and the pain the disfigurement was causing him in a society that places high priority on appearance.

"The bus driver wanted me where he couldn't see me," Mark told me at the time. "He wanted me out of the way. He said when he saw me at a bus stop, he wasn't going to stop."

I offered to go to Mark's home and talk with him about it. He declined. He wanted a telephone interview. He didn't want me to see him. I asked him to think about it, and he said he would.

That was a year ago. I didn't hear from him again until last week. This time a doughnut shop had fired him "because of the way I look." He invited me to his apartment.

"I don't go around with a chip on my shoulder," he said, when I suggested that might be his problem. "People don't like to look at me. That's a fact and it hurts.

"Sometimes teenagers will drive by and holler, 'Hey, Freddy!' He was the monster in the movie 'Nightmare on Elm Street.' Another bus driver thought I had AIDS and didn't want me to breathe on him. People will sometimes just stop and stare."

He has difficulty finding work because of the way he looks. He lives on Social Security checks. His housing is subsidized. Sometimes during the day he visits a nearby center for homeless people with mental problems. He feels comfortable with them.

Mark vacillates between hope for the future and utter despair. He denies nightmares, then discusses them. He claims not to recall much of the fire, then describes it in vivid detail.

"I haven't had a fair shake in life. I want to be around others to let them know that people like me exist. I want a job that will take me out in the open."

But then he thinks about the 100 skin grafts and the 20 sessions of reconstructive surgery he has undergone and all the surgery that lies ahead.

"Looking back, I would have rather died than to go through all that. I don't want to go through it again. Just recently I asked a doctor to put me to sleep. I can't take the pain anymore."

We talked into the early evening, until the light inside the apartment had grown even dimmer and the photographs of the other Mark merged into the shadows. I asked what I could do for him, and he said, "Help me find work." I promised to try.

As he walked me to the door, we stopped to look closely at one of his pre-fire pictures. Mark stared at it for a long time and finally said there was one thing about the fire that he could be grateful for. It had left him only stubs for ears.

He looked at me straight-on for the first time and said, "I never did like my ears."

I didn't know whether to laugh or cry.

July 9, 1987

21

THE GREATEST GIFT

GENEROSITY IS A WORD USED SO OFTEN IT TENDS TO LOSE THE glow of its high moral definition. To me, it means someone who gives without any thought of recognition, and no one exemplifies that better than a man called Max.

In a town filled with attention-seekers, the existence of someone like Max, a onetime homeless guy, is an anomaly. He donated a kidney to the benefactor who got him off the street and still asks nothing in return. He doesn't even want to be identified.

I heard about him from the organ recipient, a retired aerospace worker named Loyal Harris, a tall, robust man of 80 who can't keep the tears from his eyes when he talks about his gratitude toward Max.

"Let me tell you," he said to me one day over coffee, his voice choking, "there's nothing closer than two people who share the same kidney. It's hard, very hard, to even explain. He gave me back my life."

Harris was a merchant seaman during the Second World War and it shows in his bearing. His white hair is the foam of the ocean and his brilliant blue eyes the color of the sea. He has a sailor's look if there ever was one.

Harris met Max 20 years ago at a Winchell's donut shop in the Valley. Homeless and hungry, Max was a skinny kid in his 20s who swept up the place for the doughnut ends they'd give him to eat.

Watching him over a period of days, Harris decided no one ought to live like that and offered Max his hand.

No one needed a friend more than the kid who lived off crumbs and slept in an abandoned car. Harris asked Max over to his table, fed him, listened to his story and invited him to live in a motor home on his property.

"I was a little worried about it," Harris says, "but I could tell he was in bad need, so I took a chance. I could see goodness in him."

Harris got Max some new clothes, gave him starter money and took him around the Valley until he got him a job. There were never a lot of thank-yous from the homeless man Harris had befriended, but gratitude was obviously growing.

During their years of friendship, Harris heard a story of survival from Max that was as raw as any he could remember. The old sailor himself is no stranger to surviving. Duty on an oil tanker in three major theaters of war brought him about as close to death as anyone ought to be.

Max's survival was different. He told Harris a story of childhood abandonment by a prostitute mother, of running away from a foster father who beat him, of living like an animal in the Northwest woods, and of finally wandering the country in constant need.

But now, through Harris' magnanimity, he had a chance to live like a human being and was proving himself an able and intelligent worker.

If the thought of paying Harris back ever entered his head, Max said nothing. But the opportunity came four years ago.

In his youth, Harris had worked around cyanide in the gold mines of Wyoming. Unknown to him, the poison had invaded his body, and his kidneys had been irreparably damaged. A routine test showed they were failing fast.

Harris was put on dialysis for a year, but it wasn't working. "I was falling apart in a hurry," he says, recalling the agony. "I wouldn't have lived."

By now, Max was working steadily and had his own apartment. Such was his intelligence, Harris says, that given simple instructions, he had learned how to build his own computer.

Unaware of Harris' predicament at first, Max heard about it from his friend's sister. Told his benefactor needed a kidney transplant to live, Max hesitated not a moment. "I'll give him one of mine," he said.

After months of tests, it was determined that the donation was possible. Surgery was performed four years ago at St. Vincent Medical Center by Dr. Robert Mendez.

"His kidney is right here," Harris said to me that day over coffee, tapping his lower right abdomen. "I didn't ask him for it. I wouldn't have. It was all his idea. I owe him everything."

When I tried talking to Max about it, he refused. His was the ultimate gesture of giving. In a world that feeds on notoriety, he asked for nothing.

Both men, each in his own way, gave the other a gift of life that is beyond nobility, and while I honor Max's desire for anonymity — Max isn't his real name — I would be remiss in letting the story die untold.

It was the ultimate generosity. I use the term without hesitation.

October 16, 1998

❖

A BURNED SPOT ON THE ROAD

I KNOW THAT EVENTUALLY THE SUN WILL BLEACH OUT THE scorched place on the narrow highway. I know that eventually thousands of tires that pass over it will erase its existence and wind will scatter its dusty particles.

But meanwhile, the dark image, spread like a handprint on Topanga Canyon Boulevard, keeps reminding me how fragile life is, fluttering like a butterfly on the edge of time, never far from eternity.

The dark place of which I speak is where Bud and Christina Emerson, two people very much in love, lost their lives four months ago when their motor home overturned and burst into flames.

Fire scorched the surface of the pavement a half-mile from the beach and darkened the earth on either side, leaving the motor home a burned-out shell and ending the lives of the Emersons on a day in spring that should have been too glorious for death.

I had read about the accident, but in L.A.'s canyons, where so many perish through speed or miscalculation, death is no stranger. Small, white crosses on the sides of the highways too often memorialize those who died there.

But I had never encountered the kind of symbol the scorched pavement came to represent. I had passed over it many times after the accident and one day suddenly realized its origin. It began to seem sacrilege to cross it so casually, as though I were violating a burial place.

Two human beings died there with scant notice of either their lives or their deaths, and the big city was rolling over them without a backward glance. I couldn't let that happen.

I came to know them over the following days.

Bud Emerson was 82, Christina, 88. They had been married for 56 years and were seldom apart. They owned a small cleaners in Pacific Palisades and traveled the world together from Latin America to the Orient. Their lives were rich and full.

He was a tall, good-humored Texan who loved to ride horses, and she was a small, fragile lady who took no guff from her towering husband. "She'd tell him how things should be," Ruby Hicks says, "and he'd say, 'OK, OK, OK' and laugh."

Hicks is Bud's sister-in-law. She wonders if he'd suffered a heart attack as their 23-foot motor home began its uphill climb toward the crest of Topanga Canyon on May 3. He had undergone bypass surgery a few years earlier.

The California Highway Patrol doesn't know exactly what happened. There were no witnesses. Bud was at the wheel when the big vehicle went out of control. Its butane stove may have exploded on impact. The Emersons were trapped inside.

"Their new house had just been completed," Hicks says, wondering at the cruelty of a fate that gives and takes so easily. "Their home in Malibu had been destroyed in '93. They were just beginning again."

Fire was their enemy back then, too.

The Emersons lost everything in the flames that swept through the Santa Monica Mountains from the San Fernando Valley to the ocean in a firestorm that ignited the very air and set palm trees burning like tiki torches in the wind.

But they vowed to build again, and Bud told a reporter that next time they'd make it through. "All we need," he said, "is luck."

The lives of the Emersons unfolded before me like a blossoming rose. I could feel their closeness. I could hear Christina's gentle scolding of her big, noisy man. I could hear Bud shouting, "We came to ride, let's ride!"

"He used to say that all the time," Bruce Bailey says. "It was his favorite expression." He repeats it softly now. "We came to ride."

Bailey was Bud's best friend. They were both members of the Santa

Monica Mountains Mounted Police and had known each other for 40 years.

On the day the Emersons died, that day of sunlight and promise, they had been on their way to the Peter Pitchess Honor Rancho in Castaic to join in a fund-raising ride against drugs.

"Someone was bringing Bud's horse and we were going to ride in the hills around the county jail," Bailey says. "We waited and waited but Bud never came."

Nature has a way of dealing with evidence of calamity. Flood waters recede, wildflowers bloom in scorched earth, winds drive storm clouds away. And so it will be with that dark imprint on the pavement where Bud and Christina Emerson died.

This column too will fold into the openings that time allows and be gone with the days that erase the burned place in the road. But it satisfies me at least to have given some substance to their dying and to have shaped the memory of two good people who drove into fate's way on a sunny morning in spring.

August 23, 1996

❖

THE KING OF SKID ROW

NO ONE SPENDS 25 YEARS ON SKID ROW. BOOZE OR DRUGS OR A knife in the back kills them long before that, or they simply disappear like dirty water down a storm drain. Some who leave make it, some don't. The ledger of the Don'ts is fatter than the Bible. The book of the Do's is a pamphlet.

Then there's Clancy Imislund. He's observing a quarter of a century this month in the forlorn cluster of humanity that exists in L.A. as a City of Despair. A tough, caring ex-drunk, Clancy is king of that city, tending to those whose basic needs spin down to food and a place to sleep.

He's managing director of the Midnight Mission, a solid, no-nonsense haven that's as much a part of the row as a drunk in a doorway. Founded in 1922 by a welfare worker known as Brother Tom, the mission has served as a kind of entryway to a new world for those willing to step across its threshold.

Clancy is one of them.

He was once a successful advertising executive, but booze cost him his family, his career and damned near his life until he gave up the bottle 40 years ago.

Fed up with his drinking, his wife had taken their four children and left him to wander the country in a drunken haze. In 1958, he woke up in an alley on skid row, took a hard look at himself and decided that wasn't what he wanted. An alcoholics' rehabilitation center was his next stop.

Only then did his world begin to change.

I met Clancy in the 1970s, interviewing for a story on the killer we were calling the Skid Row Slasher, who was going around cutting throats on the south side of downtown. We ended up talking about victims of a different kind.

Clancy understood, as few men do, the nature of despair, the dissolution of pride and the abandonment of hope. He understood fear and violence and hunger because he had experienced them all.

I heard him once explain skid row to a young, well-intentioned dreamer who thought God and free doughnuts were the ultimate answers to need. Clancy got the look in his eyes of an eagle circling a hare and began in the kind of tone that doesn't tempt debate: "Let me tell you about skid row, Peter...."

He drew a word picture of human calamity that had the kid stunned and fascinated at the same time. Then he said, "Every day I see deaths on the row, but you know the one kind of death I never see?" The kid shook his head. "Suicide," Clancy said. "Suicides are caused by emotional conflict. There is no emotional conflict here, Peter. The people have just given up."

No one knows the row like Clancy. But even as he perceives its misery, he also understands the redemptive qualities of his Midnight Mission. Last year, in addition to serving 654,730 meals and providing 50,335 nights of lodging, the mission also came up with 868 jobs.

"Work," they used to say in the blue-collar bars, "is the curse of the drinking class." Clancy believes it's the hope of the drinking class.

"If the people here don't learn to work, they don't learn to live," he said as we drove around the row in his 21-year-old silver Cadillac. His hair is thinner and his face craggier than when we first met, but the strength in his voice and manner remains.

He's proud of the fact that there's a state employment office in the mission — the only such office not located in an official building. He quotes the old saw "If I give a hungry man a fish, I can ease his hunger for a day. But if I teach him to fish, I can ease his hunger for the rest of his life." He believes that.

Skid row has changed during Clancy's 25 years. Many of the old bars and pawnshops have given way to brightly painted toy factories and small businesses, looking a little like balloons in a graveyard. Families have moved in, adding a tone of stability to the City of Despair.

"You don't see as many old drunks as you used to," he said, driving down 5th Street near San Pedro. "Now they're mostly young crack addicts. They're harder to straighten out, but we keep trying."

Clancy has his family back now. His wife returned after five years, and they're about ready to celebrate their golden wedding anniversary. At 71, he says he doesn't have the drive he once had, but he'd still like to stay on the job. I hope he does. What would skid row be without its king?

September 25, 1998

❖

VOICES FROM THE SHADOWS

SHE SITS HUNCHED FORWARD MOST OF THE TIME AND STARES AT the floor, speaking in a monotone from a far corner of her mind, muted by the limitations life has imposed on her.

Only when she discusses her dream does she look up and smile. She wants to become a restaurant hostess. It's a dream of modest proportions, one that wouldn't make a ripple in the face of the economy, but for her it's an awesome ambition.

I sing today of LaDonna Galbreath, who edges her way hesitantly back into the world from a place of shadows and devils, and who pursues her dream like a child crawling toward a toy.

Both schizophrenic and diabetic, she's a hulking woman of 32 with the mental capacity of a 12-year-old, three times damned by her own birth to an existence on the outer edges of society.

I met her in a small room at Goodwill Industries, where a program has been instituted to help those like LaDonna who tote heavy loads of both physical and mental incapacities.

It's the only such program in California and one of very few in the nation that undertakes to assist those struggling against multiple hardships, the slow dancers in a world of fast music.

Thirty people at a time are led through sessions to help them deal with their own problems and learn to exist in a society that won't slow down for them. LaDonna is one of them.

She's learning to support herself and to deal, through counseling and medication, with the demons that schizophrenia creates. As she told me one quiet spring afternoon, "I don't hear voices anymore that tell me to kill."

We all hear voices. They come from sunlit places and are the subconscious whispers of motivation that tell us to love and care and achieve. They damp our rages and control our excesses.

LaDonna's voices come from the shadows of hallucination. She can't remember when they began, but she's sure it had something to do with an acid trip she took when she was 14 that plunged her into a state of distortion from which she has never fully emerged.

The voices were the voices of the devil in all his multiple levels of evil. They told LaDonna she was bad. They told her to kill her son.

Abandoned by her father and orphaned by her mother, she was raised by a grandmother who did her best to give her charge a decent life. But "slow" by her own definition, LaDonna couldn't handle the demands of school and dropped out in the 10th grade.

Vulnerable and desperate for someone to care about her, she turned to men for comfort and became pregnant shortly thereafter. The men beat her and took what subsistence money she got from the state.

29

LaDonna attempted in her own way to shake the voices that by now roared through her mind like cyclonic winds. She thought her oldest son the devil and gave him to an aunt in an effort to still the roar.

It didn't work. The voices persisted. She struggled with their commands to smother her youngest child; sometimes she could feel the presence of evil in her darkened bedroom.

"I just shut the voices out," she said the other day. "I just listened and went on about my business. I wasn't going to kill my boy. He was just a baby and I loved him."

State-sponsored psychiatric treatment got LaDonna started on medication that began dealing with her hallucinations.

Meanwhile, Goodwill Industries' Special Projects Program had come into being. An evaluation by the California Department of Rehabilitation called it "the finest program of its kind we have ever seen."

LaDonna Galbreath entered the program almost a year ago, withdrawn and confused. A psychologist, a therapist and counselors began working with her.

Slowly, she began to improve. The voices became less frequent and finally disappeared. The commands to kill receded into the shadows and have never been heard again.

Simultaneously, LaDonna began taking classes as part of the program. She's learning custodial work and good parenting, and earns $4.60 an hour working for Goodwill. A "care provider" lives with her and tends her son while LaDonna works, attends classes and undergoes therapy.

Life is different for her now, and the future clear enough to allow for the entrance of modest ambitions.

I'm not sure that anyone so burdened will ever achieve the goals they set for themselves, but at least one person in a city of millions is taking a few tentative steps away from her own terrible night of the soul.

That the wonder of a simple dream will cause LaDonna Galbreath to look up and smile reminds us that the world exists for the slow dancers too. Welcome them into it.

April 12, 1999

A CROSS IN THE SKY

HE WAS LIKE A CRUCIFIX HANGING IN THE SKY, ARMS OUT-stretched on each side as he clung to the doorway of a helicopter, feet planted on its skids, looking off to the distance.

I can see him now against the pale blue of a late afternoon, just over the tops of oak trees that grow in clusters down the hill from my home.

Though the helicopter hovered for perhaps only 30 seconds, the image is difficult to forget amid the circumstances that surround it. I've been trying to shake it for a month.

The aircraft belonged to the L.A. County Fire Department on a rescue mission. The man in the doorway whose posture appeared so cross-like was Jeff Langley, a paramedic.

A few moments after I saw him, he was dead.

The incident occurred on a quiet Tuesday in the Santa Monica Mountains, a few miles from where I live.

A young man, out of breath from running, asked me to call 911. A climber had fallen off a steep cliff in Topanga State Park. Almost simultaneously, we heard the roar of a helicopter.

The aircraft appeared from the west, hovered momentarily and was gone. It was during that brief view of the chopper that I saw the man in the doorway.

As it turned out, the climber they had airlifted from the base of a 150-foot cliff had died in the fall.

The helicopter had returned to recover equipment left at the scene. Exactly what happened next may never be known. One moment Langley stood in the doorway of the chopper as it hovered over a canyon, and the next moment he was gone. They found his body in underbrush not far from where the climber had fallen.

News of his death left an unsettling memory of the scene. Paramedics aren't supposed to die. They're life-givers, savers, last resorts in moments of pain, fire and tangled debris.

We see them hurtling down the freeways and across the canyons of L.A., or overhead in helicopters, chasing the seconds that will bring them to the place where life forces flicker.

They are not supposed to appear Christ-like in the sky and then plunge to their deaths moments later in the awkward performance of a routine mission.

Paramedics, quite simply, are not supposed to die.

I say that from the standpoint of one who admires them. They work 56-hour weeks under circumstances that would easily tax the resolve of those not similarly committed to saving lives.

Wherever disaster strikes, you can count on a paramedic being there, pressing the limits of safety and endurance to stem the flow of blood or restart a silent heart, to deliver a baby or to breathe life back into a strangled child.

Their environment, unlike the sterile workrooms of most medical technicians, is the street. They crawl into tangled metal about to explode into flame, enter buildings about to collapse and rush to riots where bullets fly with deadly caprice.

They work amid the blood and wreckage of situations that occur suddenly and without warning at a rate of stress unknown in any other job.

And sometimes they plunge through the sky like wounded birds and die in the very place where, moments before, they were trying to restore life.

Who chooses this kind of career in preference to less taxing and dangerous work? Jeff Langley, who died at age 28, is one example.

Like a lot of kids, he declared early that when he grew up he wanted to be a fireman. Unlike most kids, he never changed his mind.

"He was born caring about others," his mother, Karen Langley, says.

"He never stopped caring," his partner, Alan Taylor, adds.

The son of divorced parents, Langley didn't know his dad. It hurt him and might have accounted for his own efforts to be everyone's father.

His short life was filled from teenage on with helping young people.

He taught blind children to ski, volunteered as a lifeguard at the YMCA, visited burn units to comfort the afflicted, counseled kids against drugs and, at 16, studied to become an emergency medical technician.

"He was the designated adult in our family," Karen Langley says. "He just wanted to help everybody."

"I don't know why Jeff cared so much," his partner says. "I don't know why I care so much. There's a lot of little boy in all of us."

Langley carried a newspaper clipping with him. It contained an anonymous poem on success that included the closing phrase:

To know even one life has breathed easier because you lived
This is to have succeeded.

Success comes in many forms. Paramedics achieve it in life. Jeff Langley symbolizes it in death. I think about that when I remember him hovering like a crucifix against the pristine sky of a quiet Tuesday afternoon.

April 30, 1993

❖

TEARS ON THE UNICORN

HARDLY A DAY GOES BY THAT TAMMY DAVIES DOESN'T THINK OF suicide. It floats on the edge of her mind like a bad dream, drawing her toward a light she sees in the distance.

It's been pretty much this way since she was a child, which is when she began using drugs. Sometimes she closes her eyes and screams, "God, get me out of this!" and thinks how serene death would be.

The way she sees it, there's only one salvation and that's in the pictures she draws, the strangely delicate and beautiful faces of women, their expressions a compelling blend of wonder and grief.

Art is often born in dark places of the soul, and this is no exception. Davies' baggage contains equal portions of talent and despair, which she must haul with cautious steps along the edge of the abyss.

She lives in a world few would willingly inhabit. At 34, she's used drugs since she was 10, has been on her own since she was 12 and has spent more time in prison than she can remember.

She's sold her body to support a $300-a-day heroin habit and, in the course of prostitution, has been beaten, raped and robbed in spasms of pain and humiliation that even the strongest would find difficult to bear.

But through it all, she has continued to paint and draw in soft pastels, projecting her own anguish onto the models of her imagination.

A figure that emerges when she isn't drawing the faces of women is the head of a unicorn, with a single tear on its face. It's a fantasy projection of her own distorted life, where even creatures of mythology cry.

I met Davies a few days after she had been released from Sybil Brand Institute for Women. She served two months for driving with a suspended license.

It was an accumulation of many brushes with the law. Her license had been lifted in 1981 for felony drunk driving, involving an automobile accident. She did a year for that.

"I'm clean now," she told me the other day, smoking cigarettes and sipping from a soft drink can. She's a thin, edgy woman with stringy brown hair. "I've been clean for 70 days. God, I never thought I could do this for even a month."

She had telephoned me on behalf of another woman in Sybil Brand who was complaining about her inability to receive adequate medical treatment.

But it was Davies who intrigued me most. She had the manner of a wounded bird, wanting desperately but never able to achieve normal flight. Her body covered with tattoos, she seemed a metaphor for the type of woman who, used and abandoned, had lived exactly her kind of life.

She spoke freely of wanting to die as she paced the room of a small duplex in Temple City where she was staying with a friend. Her heavily scented perfume filled the humid air.

"I've been suicidal since I was 12," she said. "A boyfriend tried to strangle me once." She laughed nervously. "I should have let him. Another time, I OD'd and traveled the tunnel. The one with the light at the end?" She paused. A funereal silence lay over the room. Then she said, "I just don't want to be in this world anymore."

She showed me a poem she wrote. It began, "I was born for this? / Was there something I missed?"

It was only when she brought out her drawings that Davies concentrated.

Page after page of a scrapbook revealed her damaged talent. There were faces, butterflies, a rose … and the unicorn, each drawn with a draftsman's precision and an artist's emotion.

She did most of the tattoos on her body herself and once had a job in a tattoo parlor, "but dope wouldn't let me work from 9 to 5." She shook her head in remorseful self-appraisal. "I was a garbage can."

But things are different now, she says. She's ready to try again, and maybe … just maybe … it will work.

What she wants is her own tattoo parlor. She sold an old car to buy the equipment and now needs $3,500 to open a shop that will bear her name. It's a modest goal, but in a life that has had no aim, any goal is a mountain.

Davies still talks about suicide as a peaceful alternative to failure. She's slashed her wrists a dozen times and bears the scars to prove it. The pain of existence seems almost always too difficult to bear.

I'm not sure she won't try it again. I'm not sure she isn't somehow predestined to fail. She's been failing for 24 years. But I think she deserves a chance, and I'm hoping she gets it.

We shed rivers of tears in today's world for beached whales and fallen condors. Will only a unicorn cry for Tammy Davies?

August 10, 1993

❖

STANDING IN SILENCE

AMID THE HOLLYWOODIAN BABBLE THAT ACCOMPANIED THE Oscar-night Lifetime Achievement Award to a onetime film director and Commie named Elia Kazan, I kept thinking of Eason Monroe.

If you know him at all, you know him as the name on an ACLU award given to those who display courage and honor in the conduct of their lives by standing up for what they believe.

Kazan, as you know, stood in a different way. He rose before the career-wrecking House Un-American Activities Committee during the McCarthy era and pointed his finger at those in the industry he once knew to be Communists, because he was once one himself.

While the gesture in hindsight seems almost comedic, it wasn't then. Good people saw their lives ruined in the frantic, surreal effort of the nation's Red hunters to root out subversives. The Cold War threw a chill over freedom that continues to ice our memories today.

Protesters have demanded that Kazan apologize for what he did, but watching that frail and bewildered old man on television the other night, I'm not even sure he remembers what he did, or why.

Courage is defined by the time and manner in which it is displayed, and the 1950s were, indeed, strange times. It took a special quality to stand amid the anti-Communist clamor and refuse to be terrorized into submission.

Eason Monroe was one who stood, and it cost him.

Because he wasn't in show biz, with its noisy recognition of heroes and villains, the man is barely remembered for what he did, but I haven't forgotten.

He was my English teacher at San Francisco State in the 1950s, a cultured, soft-spoken man who guided me through early years of writing and urged me to find my literary voice and use it.

He taught control even as he encouraged style, offering the kind of guidance that never intruded on individual goals. His love for teaching was obvious. His respect for learning was immense. But neither mattered in the autumn of 1950.

The mass hysteria generated by the Cold War, with its deep suspicions, resulted in the passage of a state law that required public employees to swear that they did not advocate the overthrow of the government.

The loyalty oath was poison to anyone who believed in personal freedom, but only a few refused to sign. Monroe was one. And at the ascendancy of his career, San Francisco State fired him.

"How can you swear to uphold the Constitution and thereafter sign away your rights under the Constitution?" he asked. No one answered.

A PhD from Stanford, he had come to State from his first university teaching job in Pennsylvania three years earlier to head the college's language arts division. Recognition of his academic talents was spreading. School districts sought his expertise. UCLA wanted to hire him. Then his world fell apart.

"One day everything," he would say, "the next day nothing."

His hurt was profound, but Monroe never backed away from his commitment to individual freedom. Two years later, he was named executive director of Southern California's ACLU. That's where I met him again.

I came to L.A. in 1972 and learned of his presence here when California's loyalty oath was struck down and San Francisco State was ordered to rehire him. After two decades of "exile," he had been vindicated.

But that wasn't enough. I took it as a personal mission to make clear to all what this man had done at a time of peril to his career. I wrote about him in one of my first major stories for The Times.

In his moment of triumph, he seemed subdued. "Sometimes," he said in a soft baritone, "risk involves regret." The regret was that his stand for principle had cost him the work he loved. But: "Careers must sometimes be risked for things of value."

Monroe resigned from the ACLU and returned to teaching in 1972. He died three years later at age 65, his work undone. In his honor, the Eason Monroe Courageous Advocate Award was created.

"He risked all for principle," Ramona Ripston said the other day. She's the ACLU's current executive director. "He was the true patriot...."

I thought about Monroe as Kazan accepted his award. I thought about honor and about courage. Kazan saved himself at a cost to others. Monroe sacrificed himself for the sake of others. History will honor this quiet man who simply stood and said no.

March 24, 1999

THE BIRTH OF A RACIAL ICON

UNDER A SKY CLEANSED BY RAIN, ON A MORNING THAT GLEAMED with almost blinding iridescence, the writer Alex Haley rose from racial historian Friday to racial icon.

A crowd of 1,500 visitors from across the United States stood in anticipation as a 13-foot-tall bronze statue of the author, the largest in the nation of any African American, was unveiled to hushed silence in Knoxville, Tenn.

It was only after a gold-tinted drape was pulled from the monument by L.A. sculptress Tina Allen that the racially mixed crowd broke into wild cheering. The ceremony way accompanied by a harmony of oration fit for a king.

Haley, a shy, unassuming kind of guy, would have been amazed.

The author of "Roots," who died in 1992, had in death achieved a position in history beyond his wildest dreams, that of a bronze giant in a seated, Lincolnesque pose with a gaze fixed on eternity.

Ex-Gov. Lamar Alexander and award-winning actor Lou Gossett Jr., who starred in the "Roots" television miniseries, joined an army of local celebrities to fix Haley's place in history as a man of all people whose family odyssey from Africa to America elevated heritage to a grand new plane.

"He doesn't just belong to us anymore," former wife Nannie Haley said, staring up at the towering edifice. "He belongs to everyone now."

Even though he would have been stunned by the outpouring, Haley, who made L.A. his home for many years, would have understood its significance. He was, after all, an agent of cultural detente whose book, 12 years in the making, not only dramatized the anguish of a race, but also celebrated the importance of family.

This was never clearer than in Knoxville, a beautiful little city of 165,000 people where Haley lived, taught and wrote for 14 years. Blacks and whites, the public and the private sector, corporations and individuals, joined in raising almost $400,000 to make the statue possible.

The money included the building of Heritage Square on land where the eternal Haley now sits: book in hand, the classic griot, or storyteller, his gaze fixed on the park, the lawn, the Great Smoky Mountains in the distance and on a new brotherhood of races he, in a sense, helped create.

"We're going into the 21st century as a family," Tina Allen said, encapsulating the season of atonement that seemed to prevail, a season for which Haley was at least partially responsible.

"Roots" caused conversation and debate, and though at times the debate grew acrimonious, when people talk, they learn, and learning is what detente is all about. Haley knew that.

"In the end," said Mayor Victor Ashe, "Alex taught us we were more alike than different and that we should celebrate our common connections."

And celebrate they did for two days, and talk they did for two days, visitors from L.A. and New York and Washington and Chicago and Miami and Seattle and from Haley's nearby hometown of Henning, where as a boy he listened to the storytellers in his family until he became one himself.

I was here because I'd known Haley since his Coast Guard days and because we'd written together on many occasions. I knew him as a generous, complex, sensitive man whose vision of racial harmony was as large and imposing as the statue that now celebrates his life.

That isn't to say, however, that Haley spent that life marching noisily for equality. His vision was an internal one that emerged in his work, not in a belligerence of attitude. Even after he had written "Roots," he was unsure why it had become the doctrine of a race.

"I was just trying to write a book," he said to me once, "not a bible." Then he turned to his lifelong friend and assistant, George Sims. "You never know when you start something just where it's going to end."

But while millions around the world were cheering Haley, a handful of critics were savaging him. "That hurt him," Sims said as we sat together under Haley's statue. "He said to me after that, 'You know, George, I don't think I'll ever write again.' And he never really did."

I came to Knoxville as a friend but also as a reporter to acknowledge that in an age bereft of heroes, Alex Haley had rightly become one not just for a single race, but for all races for a long time to come.

The critics should see him now.   *April 28, 1998*

AL MARTINEZ

YEAR OF THE WOLF

EVERY ONCE IN A WHILE, WHEN THE MOON IS FULL, THERE'S AN eerie howling outside my bedroom window, and a chill goes through me.

It's out there again, I say to myself ... the creature ... the animal on two feet ... the beast that prowls the night....

I can see it now outlined in the pale moonlight ... wearing a dark suit and a red tie ... a big cigar in its mouth ... closer it comes ... and closer ... and OH MY GOD IT'S SAM ARKOFF HUSTLING A NEW MOVIE! Screeeaammm....

Hi.

I knew it was him. Sam, you see, is the guy who made "I Was a Teenage Werewolf" 35 years ago, before teens really became werewolves, and now he's doing a sequel.

By that, I do not mean to imply he is doing a movie about a retired werewolf with a recreational vehicle, only that he is doing an updated version about a teenwolf.

Toward that end, he has interviewed about 300 young people in New York and L.A. to play the part of the person who becomes half-human and half-animal.

They showed up with hair glued to their faces in order to convince him that they were the ones to play the boy-beast, or possibly the girl-beast. Some howled, some growled, all dreamed.

"The movie's about vulnerable kids," Sam explained the other day.

He's a cross between George Burns and the Maytag Man, a puckish movie mogul at momentary ease.

"Our werewolf 35 years ago was a classic American misfit who couldn't get along with anyone," Sam said. "But instead of getting into trouble, he became a werewolf. Today, he adds with almost grandfatherly pride, "they are the parents of werewolves."

You remember "Teenage Werewolf." Michael Landon played a kind of a sweet James Dean who fell under the evil influence of a mad scientist. The scientist, using chemistry and hypnosis, took Landon back to his primeval animal state in order to learn how to do the same with all humanity in order to make us better.

Not a bad idea, but it goes wrong and Landon becomes a werewolf. Well, mistakes happen.

"Fifty million people saw the movie," Sam said the other day in his Burbank office. He blew cigar smoke across the room and added, "Those who say they didn't see it are lying through their ... teeth."

In the room with us was a prospective werewolf, Kristina Lolatte, a bodacious babe with dyed blonde hair, blue eyes and bright red lipstick.

I was there because I have always been a werewolf fan, going back to a bleary-eyed Lon Chaney Jr. in "The Wolf Man."

I even tried once to sell a werewolf movie. It was about a kennel owner who stumbled across a werewolf and trained him to fetch and heel. I called it "The Strange Summer of Wolfy Allen," not to be confused with Woody Allen, who is having a pretty strange summer of his own.

I showed it to Danny Arnold, who was producing "Barney Miller." He said, "Sorry, kid, I've already got a werewolf script." I followed that with an idea for a comedy based on a mortuary. I took it to a man at CBS. He said, "Sorry, kid, we already have a mortuary comedy."

"Will the movie live forever?" I asked Arkoff.

He thought about the question as he relit his cigar. "I don't make movies for eternity," he said. "They end up in museums and colleges."

Kristina nodded her head. Kristina nodded at almost everything Sam said and laughed at every joke. That's understandable. She wants to be the next teenage werewolf. I laughed and nodded when I was young.

She admitted to never having seen Sam's first werewolf movie, but likes the idea.

"When I heard about it," she said, "I thought oh, cool, it's not a bimbo role."

"A werewolf role is better?" I asked.

"It's a role you can sink your teeth into," Sam said.

Kristina laughed and nodded.

"She could have the vulnerable quality we need," Sam said.

"The person should definitely be vulnerable," Kristina said, appearing suddenly vulnerable.

I had the feeling that if Sam had said the werewolf ought to be able to sing and dance, she'd have agreed to that too.

Sam has been married happily for 46 years, a rarity anywhere. "I told Hilda when we got married I would never wash dishes and I would always smoke cigars."

"My father smoked cigars," Kristina said cheerfully. "I actually love cigars." She nodded automatically.

"One final question," I said. "Is the business any different today than in 1957?"

"It's still a carnival," Sam said. "I don't take it seriously. But, hell, how can the man who made 'I Was a Teenage Werewolf' take anything seriously?"

Kristina laughed and nodded.

August 20, 1992

CHAPTER TWO

ANYTHING FOR A LAUGH

"Humor is emotional chaos remembered in tranquility"

—JAMES THURBER

IN SEARCH OF HIP

I'VE DECIDED THAT AN ELEMENT OF MY CULTURAL EDUCATION that is severely lacking is being able to determine what's in and what's out. Listening to friends who are masters of hip, I began to feel a woeful lack of insight into those places in L.A. preferred by the young and the restless, as it were.

Since so many conversations revolve around restaurants, I chose this as a starting point. To hear my friends talk, food and sex are the primary concerns of the Today Generation, and I felt I ought to have a little more expertise in one or the other.

When I mentioned this to my wife, she said, "It had better be food," and so it is.

I'm not including nightclubs that may or may not be in because I know nothing about the places where you pop happy pills and dance your panties off to unbearable noises they call music.

When I came to town 30 years ago, restaurants were as scarce as IQs over 100. There were Chasen's, Scandia, Perino's, Big Boy and the Tick Tock Cafe. Now there are restaurants around every corner, some out and some in and some in and out, and books by the hundreds that list and rate them.

I don't actually know what kind of food is in, but was told it's steak and sushi. I realize that's a strange combination of health and death, but there's no explaining it. Well, maybe there is, up to a point. An in place must be reasonably new, have decent food, a young chef, beautiful customers and remain in business for at least three weeks.

And, oh yes, it must be noisier than a hog farm.

On a recent night, for instance, I was pleased to dine at one of the newer in restaurants, called Katana. It's an upstairs sushi place on Sunset Boulevard that embraces all of the qualities required of being in.

If you are older than 26 and weigh more than Calista Flockhart, however, forget about Katana. You don't belong there if you're too fat to expose your navel. I am over 26, weigh about two Flockharts and won't show my navel under any circumstance, but it's not good business to toss a newspaper columnist into the street, so I got in.

I realized instantly that this was an in place because (1) it was jammed with the aforementioned young, skinny, beautiful hip people and (2) the noise approached the sound level of a departing 747.

Adding to it as we entered the dining area was the sudden burst of shouting by a number of attendants at the sushi bar.

It is meant as a form of greeting but could well be mistaken for the sudden appearance of Britney Spears at a stag party. Each time someone entered, they shouted and I jumped. It was, as you can imagine, a nervous evening for me.

Loud noises are a condition of our culture. They simultaneously define fun and blast away the haunting unpleasantries that might otherwise fill our minds. Women don't laugh, they scream. Men don't talk, they bellow. Conversation is barely possible under these conditions. I have only a vague notion of what was said. The food was fine, but at 110 decibels, I couldn't hear myself eat.

Mastro's is the steakhouse we visited. The same beautiful, skinny people who ate sushi at Katana eat red meat at Mastro's, but they're older and not nearly as noisy, decibel-wise: not a departing jet or artillery fire at close range, but the first balcony at the L.A. Philharmonic. I can take that.

Mastro's has a small, downstairs "convenience" bar for those who stumble in off the hard, lonely streets of Beverly Hills and need an instant martini. Seated at the bar in plain sight of the front doorway as we entered were two women who were doubles for all of the other beautiful women who inhabit the in places. There's got to be a factory somewhere that clones the type and sells or rents them to the in places for the few weeks that they remain in.

There's a downstairs dining area for people with noise aversions and an upstairs bar-dining room for those conditioned to conversing in smiles and gestures. The women here are grown-up versions of the Katana babes who now either run major corporations or are with rich, old men who run corporations. No flashing navels here, just a kind of sexy dignity that goes along with being able to afford a $39 steak.

Over a period of weeks I found myself at restaurants called Jar, Nic's, Lucques, Alex, JiRaffe and some others I no longer recall. They were in at one time or another, but may no longer be regarded as such. As far as I know, the restaurants I like have never been in, but that's just as well. Le Sanglier, Mirabelle and the Grill on the Alley tend to attract people with taste who are not necessarily skinny or beautiful, just tired of the ins and outs of the in restaurants.

But you've heard all this from a guy who loves hot dogs and meatloaf, so don't take my word for it. I've been known to frequent places that advertise "Eats," and even Spam appeals to me under certain conditions. Sautéed, of course.

July 1, 2002

❖

NOTES ON A TOFU TURKEY

I HAVE A FRIEND IN TOPANGA NAMED ARLO WHO IS AN UNEMPLOYED actor and an animal activist and who each Thanksgiving lobbies me to preach mercy for the unfortunate turkey.

"Arlo," I said to him the other day, "don't bug me about brutality to turkeys. I have a cold and a sore throat and am not in the mood to be merciful to anyone. Ask my wife."

"If you're feeling lousy today," Arlo replied testily, "imagine how the bird feels."

We've had this argument before. He says turkeys spend their lives in plots of land so small they can hardly move, and I say so do the Japanese and it sure as hell hasn't hurt them any.

Then he says, "Yes, but the Japanese aren't eaten at Thanksgiving" and I say, "Leave me alone, Arlo."

It is not that I am without compassion. God knows, I would not want to be a turkey myself. It's just that I suspect Arlo is more interested in furthering his own acting career than he is in prolonging the life of the turkey.

That is why I will not use his real name. I do not want to be a party to a man climbing to the top over the bodies of dead turkeys. There are no free lunches, Arlo.

However, he is not the only one who has lobbied me to encourage a new attitude toward turkeys. A growing number of others have begun to suggest that the bird has suffered enough, which leads me to believe that saving the turkey has all the earmarks of a national campaign.

While I can empathize with the cause, I am reluctant to support anything likely to cost me one of the few animals I am allowed to eat.

Due to years of excess I am supposed to watch my cholesterol, and several well-fed physicians have suggested I watch it by limiting my ingestion of red meat and eating more turkey.

In other words, it's either me or the turkey, and I wouldn't bet on the bird in this case if I were you.

"Why the poor turkey?" Arlo moaned over a beer at Bruno's Dead Dog Saloon as we discussed the ramifications of Thanksgiving.

"Because," I said, "the Indians did not sit down with the white man and feast on dolphin."

"You think that's funny?" he demanded.

"I think it's somewhat amusing," I said. "Imagine all the dressing you could stuff into a dolphin."

Arlo leaned across the table toward me and said in a gravelly voice, "Any man willing to wipe out an entire species to fatten his own behind ought to be taken out and shot."

I thought for a moment and then said, "George C. Scott!"

Arlo smiled and said, "I'm getting that one down pretty good."

I was kidding about the dolphin. I don't eat animals threatened with extinction.

Had I been around in the era the dinosaurs were dying, I would not have sat down to a meal of tyrannosaurus, though tyrannosaurus, lacking my compassion, might have sat down to a meal of me.

Translating that principle into current epiphanies, I similarly will not dine on white rhinos, humpback whales, bald eagles or the beautiful Komodo dragon.

"I'll tell you something else," I said to Arlo. "I will never eat anything live."

"You couldn't eat a live turkey anyhow."

I'm not talking about turkeys. In Rome one summer, a friend named Giorgio took us to dinner and ordered clams. He suggested I squeeze lemon on them. When I did, they cringed.

"My God," I said, "they're alive."

"Right," Giorgio said proudly.

When he left the table for a moment, my wife said, "Eat them or you'll hurt his feelings."

"I'm not eating anything that cringes," I said, thereby establishing a principle from which I have never varied. I put the clams in my pocket and said they were delicious.

"That doesn't exactly make you a humanitarian," Arlo said. "Did you return the clams to their natural habitat?"

"Sort of. I dumped them into the Fontana di Trevi. Hence the song, 'Three clams in a fountain....' "

Arlo groaned.

"Tell you what," I said. "I'm a man who loves all living things."

"Sautéed with mushrooms and onions."

"No, I mean it. So I've come up with a substitute for eating live animals during the Thanksgiving season. Arlo, go forth and create the tofu turkey."

The last I saw of him, he was heading out the door saying, "You know, that might work," in a voice that sounded suspiciously like Humphrey Bogart in "The Maltese Falcon."

Maybe he'll come up with something. Meanwhile, enjoy your turkey. Try to forget that it was raised under circumstances more crowded than Tokyo, though if it makes a takeover bid on the cranberry industry, you'll know it hasn't suffered a bit.

November 24, 1988

❖

THE OBSESSION OF CAPTAIN KAZOO

ALBERT BRODER WAS IN A HIGH STATE OF ANNOYANCE. THE CUSTOMER who had just walked into his Fairfax Avenue office had committed the unpardonable sin of putting the wrong end of a kazoo in her mouth.

"My God," Broder was saying, "haven't you ever played a kazoo before?"

He is a large, balding man with an aggressive manner and a voice as flat and dry as a Texas desert.

His customer, on the other hand, was a small, whispery woman in her mid-30s who was obviously not accustomed to verbal assaults by kazoo salesmen.

"Only as a child," she replied in a teeny-tiny voice.

"Where you from?" Broder demanded.

"West Covina."

"What do you do?"

"What?"

"What kind of work?"

She said she was an actress and a part-time chandelier salesman.

Broder shook his head, the implication being that he has had trouble before with West Covina actresses who sold chandeliers.

"You do it this way." He put a white kazoo with a Coca-Cola logo in his mouth. Then he played something that sounded like "Stars and Stripes Forever."

"Try it," Broder said to the poor woman.

That was when she made her second mistake, or perhaps her third, if you count walking into the store in the first place as a mistake. She blew into the kazoo.

"You don't blow into the kazoo, for God's sake!" Broder said, grimacing. "You hum!"

He demonstrated a second time, gave the woman a bag full of free kazoos and sent her on her way. She hurried out, never knowing that Broder in reality is a kind and generous man. He is just very passionate about kazoos.

"Educating the public is my No. 1 job," he explained with a sigh. "I even had an instruction booklet made up."

He handed me a booklet: "The Kazoo. A Fun Music-Maker for All Ages. Operating instructions: (1) Place larger end in mouth. (2) Keep fingers and thumb clear of turret and small opening. (3) Hum (don't blow). Note: If instrument fails to activate, loudly say the word 'doo' into the larger end."

The instructions are accompanied by the silhouette of a man playing the kazoo properly. One can almost sense the presence of Broder just outside of the picture, watching.

Broder has been selling the instruments for three years. Before that, he drove a taxi in Detroit. He considers himself Mr. Kazoo.

You can't miss his small, kazoo-cluttered office across from the Farmers Market. In front, there is an animated gorilla with a clown on its shoulders and a kazoo in its mouth. The gorilla's head moves from side to side.

I visit Mr. Kazoo occasionally to see what he's up to. He is not the only promoter I have ever known, but he is the only promoter I have ever known who is trying to be to the kazoo what Colonel Sanders was to fried chicken.

His latest kazoo-oriented undertaking involves wrestling.

"I'm looking for a wrestler I will call Captain Kazoo," Broder said. "He'll wear a Captain Kazoo outfit and hand out 5,000 kazoos with his picture on it every time he wrestles. You like wrestling? I'll get you tickets."

I said I didn't want any wrestling tickets.

"I'll get you tickets to 'Cats' then. You know the guy who wrote 'Mairzy Doats'? Al Trace. He's doing a special song for Captain Kazoo. All I need is the right wrestler. When do you wanna go?"

"I don't want tickets to 'Cats,' " I said.

Broder played "Mairzy Doats" on the kazoo. It also sounded like "Stars and Stripes Forever."

"You ever hear of the Kaminsky International Kazoo Quartet?" he demanded.

I said I had not.

"They're famous, for God's sake!"

"I still haven't heard of them."

Broder scowled. "The Kaminsky International Kazoo Quartet plays all over the country," he said. "They're coming here to some colleges. They'll be using my kazoos. I'm trying to set them up to play half-time at a Lakers play-off game. You like basketball? I'll get you some playoff tickets."

"I don't want playoff tickets."

"They used my kazoos once, but they always wait until the last minute. I can't wait that long. Take a look at this."

Broder handed me a piece of flared plastic, allowed me to examine it, then took it back. He affixed it to the outer end of a kazoo so that it looked a little like a miniature plastic trumpet.

"I invented that," he said. "It's so you can tell one end of the kazoo from the other. It'll be ready in 30 days. Write that down."

"Hey, you can't ..."

"Write it down, for God's sake."

What the hell. I wrote it down.

"It makes a different sound," Broder said. He played a tune. "You know what that was?"

" 'Stars and Stripes Forever'?"

He didn't say whether I was right or wrong. He just said, "What kind of cigars you smoke?"

"Broder," I said very slowly, "I don't want to see 'Cats,' I don't want to be at a Lakers playoff game, I can't stand wrestling, I've quit cigars and to hell with the kazoo."

"Hey," he called as I stomped out past the animated gorilla, "will I see you again?"

Of course.

April 24, 1986

❖

HONEY DON'T EAT NO FLESH

WE WERE IN A RESTAURANT THE OTHER DAY WITH A COUPLE WE had just met, and the waiter was extolling the virtues of their finest entree, chicken cacciatore.

He was a drama student who had just completed a course in foreign accents at UCLA and was speaking in his best ersatz Italian, saying that the chicken was so fresh and tender he had eaten it him-a-self that very night.

We all said OK, we'd give it a shot, except for the woman whose name was, so help me God, Honey. She said stiffly, "I don't partake of flesh."

I thought she was kidding at first and replied, "We aren't advocating cannibalism here," but she said, "I don't partake of any animal flesh."

I should have known that anyone who used the biblical partake had no capacity for humor and was therefore serious as hell in every phrase she uttered.

"Honey is a vegetarian," her husband, Mac, explained uneasily, clinging to his Scotch and water so hard I thought the glass would break.

"I would prefer that no one partook of flesh at this table," Honey said with great finality.

My wife, Cinelli, is an accommodating person who tries to avoid trouble whenever possible and ordered rigatoni with a non-meat sauce.

I, on the other hand, offer no compromises to the damned and told the waiter that I would partake of chicken flesh, adding, "Could you kill it at the table?"

Honey got the message and jerked Mac up off his chair like he was a dog on the couch and off they went.

The waiter, who had been silent during the ordeal, finally found voice and said, "I'm-a sorry, sir, we don't-a kill chickens at the table."

I mention the incident only to illustrate a rising level of intolerance to personal annoyances.

It began with a drive against cigarette smoking led by tense, skinny people who carry bottles of Evian water with them wherever they go, the better to damp the fires of their all-consuming zeal. They drove smokers out of many public and private places into small clusters on street corners, then began looking around for who to get next.

I'm for the campaign against cigarette smoking, but opposed to the climate it has created for attacking those with habits or lifestyles of which we do not happen to approve.

Honey is a good example. I don't care whether she eats broccoli and tofu the rest of her miserable life, but it's none of her damned business what I eat unless I drop under the table and start gnawing on her leg.

We have become a people obsessed with annoyances.

One neighbor complained about my old dog Hoover barking because he's a television writer and needs his quiet. Not Hoover, the neighbor.

I suggested a compromise, that Hoover would give up barking if he would give up writing, but it was no deal. He moved. The writer, not Hoover.

Hoover, by the way, is about 102 dog years old and his bark is no louder than a baby's burp, but I guess anything can be jarring when you're writing for such sensitive shows as "Roseanne" and "America's Funniest People."

The evening of the Honey-don't-eat-no-meat incident, we came home to newscasts that featured a restaurant owner railing against chewing gum, and residents of an upscale retirement village suing a church over its bells.

The restaurateur was annoyed because somehow all of Newport Beach had taken to leaving its chewed gum on the sidewalk in front of his establishment. He was therefore demanding that everyone stop selling gum.

The retirement villagers were angry old people in Florida whose lives revolved around golf and Bloody Marys, and whose degree of civic participation was limited to hating the Sunday-morning bell chimes at a church across the way.

The simultaneous attacks on God and Wrigley's Spearmint got me to thinking about all of the complaints I had heard or read about lately. A lawyer in Calabasas hates airplanes flying overhead. A woman in Westwood is liable to assault anyone wearing animal skin for clothing. An activist in Woodland Hills wants a world free of skateboards. A purist in Topanga will punch out anyone who uses the word "ambience."

We have no tolerance for minor aggravations.

For instance, I annoy Cinelli because I hum and meander when I walk. "You are like a giant bumblebee," she said to me once, "wandering in space."

But she allows me my humming and meandering with wry forbearance, which is a lesson we might all learn, to bear small annoyances with equanimity.

Unfortunately, most people won't learn the lesson, and the world will end not with a bang, but a petty complaint.

I don't know about you, but I hate the very idea.

November 24, 1992

❖

THE DAY THE RUSSIANS CAME

IT WAS THE DAY THE TEMPERATURE REACHED 112 IN DOWNTOWN L.A.
I was wearing the lightest suit I own, which is one of those rumpled, off-white things favored by British black marketeers in Kuala Lumpur.

I was also wearing a Hawaiian shirt I bought at Penneys. It was drenched with sweat and stuck to my body like flypaper. I looked like hell.

That was particularly obvious because I was in one of the toniest stores in Beverly Hills, interviewing the mayor of Moscow near shirts that cost $300 each and a cashmere sports coat worth more than everything in my closet.

Even a leather chewing-gum case sold for $145. I don't think I paid that much for my suit.

The place was Hermes, an establishment that is to Penneys what Paris is to Burbank.

There were actually four Russians in the party, and they were visiting at the invitation of the L.A. Fashion Institute of Design and Merchandising.

They straggled in about an hour late, looking more like survivors from the battle of Stalingrad than messengers of a New Russia. That's what heat and smog can do to a man.

The mayor of Moscow, Yuri Louzshkov, was not the most important Russian among them. Pavel Bounitch was. He is an economist, a member of the Supreme Soviet and the architect of perestroika.

This was whispered to me by several people in the entourage, both American and Russian, who hovered over me like bees at a honey farm.

Well, I was all they had.

No other media people showed up. It was just the Russians, two translators, two public relations people, some Hermes sales personnel and me, in my Kuala Lumpur suit.

I am thinking, at last, an opportunity to write an Important Column, which is what my leaders are constantly urging me to do. Never mind your dog-and-pony essays, they say. We want substance!

I will call it simply A Very Important Column, discuss perestroika and glasnost in concise and vivid terms, and be invited to join the International Fellowship of Pundits. My dog and my pony will prance with joy.

But things went wrong.

Assistant store manager Elisabeth D'Chartoy presented each of the four Russians with a $95 silk tie. While they were thanking her, she made the mistake of offering to let them exchange their ties for other designs and/or colors if they wished.

The mayor of Moscow, who looked a little like Charles Durning playing Nikita Khrushchev, said OK, or the Russian equivalent thereof, and chose another one. I've never seen a mayor make a decision that quickly.

It was a ridiculous black-and-white speckled number, but, hey, these are people raised on borscht and boiled potatoes. They've got a long way to go before they attain even my level of *haute couture*.

Two of the others also made up their minds quickly, but Bounitch, the architect of Russian perestroika, lingered … and lingered … and lingered.

I saw my Bird of Significance flutter out the window and die in the crushing heat.

Someone suggested I ought to start interviewing the mayor, since time was fleeting and Bounitch was drifting somewhere between Ivy League diagonals and paisley prints.

If the theory of perestroika were neckties, he'd still be working on it. Every once in a while he said, "Goot," meaning not bad, but then went on to something else.

Our translator was Sophia Lansky, who did a very nice job, but there was more than a language barrier here.

Louzshkov, being a mayor, was fluent in the dialect of diversion and managed to avoid adding anything noteworthy to the current dialogue between us and what used to be known as the Evil Empire.

He did say that the capitalistic elegance characterized by Hermes seemed to be unnecessary, but since the store had customers, it was OK. I'm paraphrasing, of course.

He was basically saying, if it sells, sell it.

What Russia needs, he added, was more of the kind of peasant clothes I was wearing: good, I mean goot, basic stuff. "Our market is thin," he said, "and so deep in its emptiness."

I tried to get a little into what appears to be an end to the Cold War and possibly to Godless Communism (do we still call it that?), but platitudes prevailed.

He is glad we are friends, he is having a fine time in Beverly Hills, and he is delighted that the Soviet Union is concentrating on the production of clothes instead of tanks. Food will come next.

Just about then, Bounitch chose a tie of golden zebras grazing in the pale blue Masai Mara and everyone marched out the door, taking my chance at significance with them.

So much for the Russian Bear. Wanna hear about my dog and pony?

June 28, 1990

❖

LENNY'S MAMA

THIS IS THE YEAR OF CELEBRITY MOTHERHOOD IN L.A.

First, Sylvester Stallone's mom hit the media circuit, cheerfully discussing everything from her son's sex life to the intellectual fallout of female mud wrestling.

Then along came Cher's mama, whose contribution to vacuity was an announcement, apropos of nothing, that she had been celibate for six years.

And now, God help us all, we are witnessing the reemergence of Sally Marr, the mother of — you ready for this? — Lenny Bruce.

You remember Lenny. He was the stand-up comic who was either the dirtiest or the most courageous man on the American stage, elevating scatology to a level of public discussion it had not previously enjoyed.

Lenny died of a drug overdose in 1966, beating by days, it is said, plans by militant Christians to burn him at the stake. There have been sporadic efforts ever since to canonize him as the patron saint of saloon humor's First Amendment.

Lenny, his advocates will tell you, won the right of free speech in nightclubs and taught us that violence, not sex, is dirty.

His detractors, on the other hand, still regard him as the most foulmouthed man ever to stand behind a microphone, and hold him personally responsible for the proliferation of moral filth in the 1980s.

All of which ought to make for one hell of a time when Lenny's fans try to put his star on the Hollywood Walk of Fame.

Such an effort is actually underway. I learned of it the other day from spry, bawdy Sally Marr, who at 83 can still lift her foot above her head, an ability she was pleased to demonstrate in the middle of a trendy Westside restaurant called Ciro's Pomodoro.

"Pep is all in the mind," she told me, doing a little dance next to her table while other diners watched curiously. She wore a white running suit with red and blue sequined lightning bolts across the front. "Age has nothing to do with pep, sweetie."

"Sweetie," by the way, was not the strongest term Sally used, but for all the trails her son may have blazed, he blazed none for those of us in the mainstream media. We still hide behind dashes when obscenity rears its head.

For instance, a not untypical comment by Lenny's mom about her son's infancy: "I'd talk to him about how full of s— people were, but he was too little to understand."

Sally's own roots are in show biz. She was a stand-up comic in New York during the 1940s when women didn't do those kinds of things, and later taught strippers how to take it off at the old Pink Pussycat in L.A.

"I never used dirty words on stage," she said, "but I was pretty controversial. I'd do jokes about Eleanor Roosevelt running all over the country with a lesbian. You had to add to the public intellect."

At 50, she married a writer 31 years her junior who, under Sally's tutelage, became a hairstylist. The marriage ended, she said, when the kid became too possessive.

Now her efforts are geared toward getting Lenny a star. If Billy Graham got one, she asks, why not Lenny Bruce?

Lenny and Billy, side by side on the streets of Hollywood. Is that a great irony or what?

Sally's crusade was prompted by the owner of Ciro's Pomodoro, Ciro Orsini himself, an international restaurateur who wears more jewelry than Liz Taylor and thinks Lenny Bruce the greatest contribution to American culture since linguine and clams.

Ciro (pronounced Cheero) saw the movie "Lenny" some years ago in his native Italy and became an instant fan.

"When he came to this country," Sally said, "he wondered why the hell he couldn't find Lenny on a horse somewhere. The guy expected a statue in the park."

He did the next best thing by creating a Lenny Bruce shrine in one corner of the Pomodoro. It consists of photographs and covers of the comic's record albums, including "The Sick Humor of Lenny Bruce." The cover depicts Lenny picnicking in a cemetery.

"He was ahead of his time," Ciro said, standing reverentially before a picture of Lenny. "All the others followed."

Ciro came up with the idea for a star, enlisted Sally's aid and hired press agent Bob Abrams, who shot a letter off to the Hollywood Walk of Fame Committee just a few days ago.

The committee, possibly still in shock, has yet to respond.

Sally, meanwhile, is keeping busy. She has plans for developing new, young comics to follow in Lenny's footsteps, and a movie on her life may be in the offing.

But her most significant accomplishment is an exercise video for people over 70. It begins with Sally cursing the old people.

Lenny would have loved it.

October 24, 1989

❖

BEAUTIES AND THE BEAST

THERE IS SOMETHING ABOUT 71 BEAUTY CONTESTANTS IN ONE place that has a numbing effect on the brain. They tend to blur into a single entity after a while, with one brilliant smile, one dazzling hairdo, one cute behind and one proud bust line.

Watching them, an observer is inclined to fantasize that they are, indeed, one person, sharing the same age, the same goals, the same interests and the same desires.

They are 19, measure 34-24-35, plan on a career in modeling and/or neurosurgery, are serious students of facial aerobics, and number Mikhail

Gorbachev, Bon Jovi, Mother Teresa and Brooke Shields among those they most admire.

Put them all in a jar, add water, shake vigorously and, *voilà*, Miss Universe 1990. Applause, hugs, brave smiles, tears, cash awards, fade out.

So.

As you might suspect, I stopped by the Century Plaza Hotel the other day to observe a preliminary activity for the Miss Universe contest, which will be televised Sunday on CBS.

Those who rely solely on the fast-format, easy-readin' L.A. Times for their information may not be aware the pageant is even taking place. We have not covered it with what is known in the trade as a real reporter.

They sent me instead.

I happened by on Swimsuit Day, during which all the "delegates," as they are known, paraded in their bikinis before at least an equal number of photographers and then settled into a single cluster for additional picture-taking.

I was, of course, appalled by the sexist nature of the event in this era of gender neutrality and left immediately after the last pert tush had vanished behind closed doors.

While I was there, however, I was impressed by the clockwork efficiency of the colloquium, which, by the way, concluded with the selection of Miss Photogenic. I don't know who won, but does it matter?

Statistics for the composite beauty contestant mentioned earlier were furnished by the pageant's public relations team, although I admit to embellishing them for, as we say, satirical purposes.

Truth is not a serious factor when you're covering a beauty pageant. Let the good times roll.

I was even supplied with a list of questions I might like to ask, including, but not limited to, "Can delegates be married?," "Are delegates allowed to have cosmetic surgery?" and "Are delegates required to have a coach?"

Thank God, the answers also were furnished (no, yes, no), thus sparing me the necessity of doing anything but evaluating the relentlessly smiling delegates, some of whom had obviously challenged the limits of their abilities by also learning to cock their heads.

Simultaneously smiling and cocking one's head is no small accomplishment among those who aspire to beauty-hood, requiring as it does an almost instinctive ability to gauge angle and tilt factor with rigid coordination.

It should not be tried at home by amateurs.

The delegate from Argentina, a green-eyed beauty named Paola Torre, led the alphabetically arranged parade of nations past photographers who had come to L.A. from as far away as Turkey specifically to emulsify this event.

There is something about a photographer, no matter where he's from, that brands him by trade, much as a pentagram in the palm identifies a werewolf.

I was especially impressed with the universal nature of a cameraman's ability to communicate complex requests in simple terms. One, for instance, shouted "Hey, Korea!" to indicate he wanted Miss Korea to pose for him.

Over the years, I have also heard them shout "Hey, Pope!" meaning the holy pontiff, and "Hey, Queen!" meaning her majesty Queen Elizabeth II.

In heaven, should one ever get there, I have no doubt he would shout, "Hey, God!"

The only moment of distress in the morning's proceedings came when Miss England, a beauty therapist (whatever that is) from Nottingham, appeared to have fainted.

For a moment, I thought she had simply over-cocked her head and fallen off the bench.

It was explained later, however, that Carla Barrow, who lists "eating out" among her hobbies, had failed to eat breakfast that day, a mistake somehow leading to her momentary swoon.

Even the keeling-over of Miss England, however, was handled with discreet good taste by pageant officials, who are no doubt trained for just such an emergency. Miss E. reappeared later, her equanimity intact.

I was, in fact, impressed generally with the ability of the girls, I mean delegates, to strut their saucy stuff under such trying circumstances.

It can't be easy maintaining your composure when everyone is staring at your erogenous zones.

April 12, 1990

A MAN, HIS DOG AND HIS WOMAN

IF THERE WERE THREE THINGS SIDNEY ALTMAN LOVED MORE than anything, it was his bathroom, his dog and his woman. Apparently in that order.

This has caused something of a problem.

Until his death two years ago, Altman made millions selling bathroom fixtures in West Hollywood, which explains his first love.

His second love was Samantha, a cocker spaniel, and his third love was his blond girlfriend, Marie Dana.

That sequence of affection is revealed by the fact that when Altman passed on to the Great Bathroom in the Clouds, he left Samantha $350,000 and his house in Beverly Hills. He left Dana an annual stipend of $60,000, but only if she cares for the dog until it dies. After that, she's on her own.

This has naturally made her a little nervous since Samantha is 75 in dog years and not likely to live forever.

Well, yes, Dana was left another $50,000 to redecorate the house and to go on a shopping spree, but that, by her measure, wasn't good enough.

She is suing for half of Altman's $6-million estate, claiming to have been his lifelong companion, a term that in today's lexicon could mean anything from his lover to his golf partner.

Altman described her in his will as "my good friend," a status one level below man's best friend, traditionally his dog.

I mention this today to emphasize the height of passion to which we have risen in our love of animals. I am especially sensitive to the existing climate of animal love because I am under attack by iguana people.

By that, I do not mean creatures in a 1952 science-fiction movie, but those who, for peculiar reasons of their own, keep iguanas as pets.

I have earned their antipathy due to a recent column in which I addressed the question of what to do with a surfeit of iguanas in America. I suggested we eat them.

This is not a new idea. Iguana stew, for instance, goes back 400 years, earlier than either Rice-a-Roni or Hamburger Helper, two Valley favorites, but iguana lovers were still offended by my suggestion.

One even asked over the Internet, "We also have an excess of elderly people in nursing homes. Should we eat them too?"

The column was published in a magazine called Serpents, to which, alas, I do not subscribe. My comments triggered a response by those who own computers and who, when not busy petting their lizards, spend their time replying to anti-iguana tirades.

I wasn't suggesting in the article that one eat his personal iguana any more than I would suggest eating one's personal chicken if Chickie were your child's favorite friend. But we do eat non-personal chickens, cows, pigs, ducks, frogs, eels and sheep, so why not an iguana?

Roasted slowly over a low fire.

An iguana is not like a dog. You don't snuggle with an iguana if you're a whole human being, and you don't take your iguana for a walk. Also, to the best of my knowledge, no one has ever left his estate to an iguana, but stories of dogs inheriting money pop up everywhere.

For instance, in Rockville, New Mexico., Master Teddy, a white spitz, was left $102,000 and a house. In Anchorage, Alaska, an English bulldog named Butch was left $98,500 to keep him on his regular diet of fried chicken, scrambled eggs, cottage cheese and ice water until his death.

Then there's Samantha, who has a house and probably the finest bathroom fixtures in L.A. Her deceased owner, Sidney Altman, was famous for having put a waterfall in one bathroom. And although Samantha may be a very nice doggie, I doubt that she deserves all that much more than Marie. Think about it.

I have a dog named Barkley whom I love dearly but I would not leave him the house. I would leave him dog food, dog treats and the old leather chair he considers his. He sits on it and looks around, wondering where he is.

Barkley is not the smartest dog in the world. We even have to teach him to bark. He makes a kind of a faint yowling-yipping sound that makes us suspicious of his capabilities as a guard dog. In an effort to educate him, wife is trying to teach him. She sits on the floor and barks for him. He yowl-yips in return.

"Perhaps," she says, despairing of his inabilities, "we should give him my side of the bed and I'll roam the yard at night."

That's a right generous offer. When I die, I'll leave her the house and both bathrooms. But Barkley gets the chair.

October 30, 1998

❖

WHEN LADIES OF THE NIGHT UNITE

IN AN AGE OF MIXED MORALITY, THE MEMORIES OF A WHORE seem quaintly innocuous.

They become, by nature of our cultural collapse, no more outrageous than those National Geographic documentaries of lions coupling on the Masai Mara.

We are in an eternal rutting season in America since the Bill and Monica Show legitimized sexual dalliance and since Kenneth Starr turned their groping and puffing into a national bestseller.

Encouraged by the notoriety, the nation's wily new merchants of salacity have filled cyberspace with enough pornography to stop an old man's heart. And while I have no firsthand knowledge of the subject, I am told that even phone sex is making a comeback.

Which leads me, however circuitously, to Norma Jean Almodovar, the cop-turned-hooker who is attempting to become to erotica what Karl Marx was to communism. She's calling upon the sex workers of the world to arise. So to speak.

You remember Norma Jean. She quit the LAPD in 1982 to pursue a more lucrative career as a prostitute and wrote a book about it. She still calls herself a whore in symbolic unity with women on the street but won't say whether she is still active.

67

I doubt that she has the time. Her International Sex Worker Foundation for Art, Culture and Education keeps her running. Just opening a museum for whores sounds like a lot of work.

Norma Jean has gone big-time. This became clear the other day when I met with her and her publicist, Max Green, in a Panorama City apartment that has become a kind of temple to whoredom.

In an effort to humanize the plight of sex workers since the days of Mary Magdalene, her organization has placed a $5,000 down payment on a building in Butte, Montana, that is believed to be the nation's oldest brothel. They want to turn it into a sex museum.

Art and artifacts of the world's most vilified profession will be on display, including work created by today's hookers and trinkets left behind by yesterday's darlings. A kind of whore's journey through time.

For $100, you can adopt a brick in the 108-year-old building, and for a $3,500 donation, they'll put up a plaque with your name on it where the ladies once turned tricks. Not exactly a star on the Walk of Fame but close.

"We want to challenge the perception people have of us," Norma Jean said, curled up shoeless on a couch but, I hasten to add, otherwise fully clothed. "We're not from another planet. We have husbands and kids. We have lives."

The term "sex workers," she explained, is intended to embrace not just prostitutes, but also those who work the phones, take pictures and even merchandise aphrodisiacs on the Internet.

"It's sort of like everyone who covers the news is a journalist," she added, "but you break it down into reporters, photographers and you."

Much of the memorabilia that will fill the old whorehouse in Butte was found in the building: the bones of a canary owned by one of the girls, a World War II food ration book someone traded for sex, a black silk stocking, whips, spats, lingerie and even wind chimes for the truly perverted.

Norma Jean brought them out one by one with the loving care of an archeologist at a dinosaur dig, accompanying the display with a running commentary intended to place harlotry in the context of history.

Upstairs in an office cluttered beyond clutter, she displayed her own work, doll-sized clay sculptures that will be part of a planned traveling exhibition titled "Commercial Sex: The Way We Work."

Among the pieces are the depiction of comedian Eddie Murphy in a red convertible picking up a prostitute, and a housewife at home ironing clothes and raising kids while working at phone sex.

The purpose of it all, Norma Jean says, is to educate the world. "You can scream all you want to get the message out, but if no one listens it goes nowhere. So we're using art and a museum to get attention."

I've never been certain whether Norma Jean's reinvention of herself as the Queen of Whores is altruism or self-promotion, but for whatever reason she's putting a lot of energy into uniting the sex workers of the world.

It gives one pause to wonder what might happen if they formed their own labor organization. It could be more powerful than the Teamsters and noisier than the Writers Guild, and send the cost of sex skyrocketing. Makes a man think.

October 6, 1998

❖

NICK THE WOODMAN

NICK HALABY WAS STANDING IN A CLOUD OF LACQUER FUMES when I first met him. The fumes were being accidentally blown into the front office of his furniture-restoration shop through an air-conditioning vent that originated in a rear workroom.

It felt like I was breathing through a used paintbrush.

"Let's get on with it," he was saying, "because I've got to meet Sammy the Syrian. We're going to Vegas together and Sammy is the kind of guy you don't keep waiting."

"How can you work in this?" I ask, trying not to inhale the lacquered air.

"How can I work in what?" Nick says, lighting a Camel cigarette.

"The fumes."

"They ain't bad," he says, looking up toward the ceiling. "In fact, they might even be good for you."

I am at Nick's place because a friend told me Nick was the best in the business and I have a chair that needs repairing.

When I telephone to ask if he can fix my chair, Nick replies that there isn't anything in wood he can't fix.

"Are you expensive?" I ask.

"I'm nicely priced," he says.

That was good enough to get me to his shop, which is in one of those strip-zoned Chatsworth mini-malls, next to a cleaners that boasts same-day service and a few doors down from Christy's Better Brands for Less.

"You know whose bathroom that was in?" Nick demands when I step in the front door.

He is a wiry little man with the piercing gaze of a chicken hawk, and gives the impression that if the question is not answered correctly, he will swoop down from the lacquered clouds with talons fully extended.

"Do I know whose bathroom what was in?" I ask uneasily.

"That," he says, pointing toward an antique screen leaning against a wall. But, before I can answer, he says, "John Barrymore!"

"Well," I say, and "well, well, well."

Then he utters a sentence so filled with expletives that I cannot even begin to quote it here. If I took out the obscenities, only "but" and "if" and maybe "they" would remain.

"I do work for some of the biggest names around," Nick says, gesturing to indicate that they walk into his shop almost every day.

"Marc!" he shouts suddenly toward a back room, "who's the famous broad we do work for? The one who dates Kurt Russell!"

A voice from the back room says, "What broad?"

"The one in Malibu!"

"Goldie Hawn!" a different voice from the back room replies.

"That's the one," Nick says. "What a sweet broad."

Then he mentions Barbra Streisand and Kenny Rogers and someone whose name he cannot remember who used to be president of a steel company, or maybe it was a car company.

"Who the hell knows?" he says, shrugging.

Nick is a second-generation furniture restorer. He learned the business in his father's shop on Brooklyn's Atlantic Avenue and loves the work.

The two voices from the back room belong to Nick's sons, Marc and Jorge, who also do not believe that lacquer fumes are bad for you, although neither of them will go so far as to say they are good for you.

There is a third son, Charles, who is a professor of sociology at the University of Wisconsin and who, Nick confides, thinks Daddy "not quite normal."

"He don't understand me," Nick adds somewhat wistfully.

Nick, by the way, is 66 but could easily pass for 65. He was born and raised in the Red Hook area of Brooklyn, which, he explains in no uncertain terms, is the toughest place in America.

"I was raised with people like Sammy the Syrian and Jimmy the Arab," Nick says. "I have three sisters, all widowed."

I don't ask how his sisters got widowed because I am not sure I want to know. There are certain questions you don't ask a guy who has friends with names like Sammy the Syrian and Jimmy the Arab.

Nick came to the San Fernando Valley from Brooklyn 30 years ago, not because of the Valley's sunshine and beauty, but because one of his widowed sisters bought him a one-way plane ticket out of Red Hook.

"Everyone was looking for me in Brooklyn," Nick says. "I was a gambler. I did horses during the day and floating crap games at night. I was at rock bottom, so she hijacked me."

Nick figures he lost everything he ever earned up through age 35 by playing horses and shooting dice. He quit for 15 years and then went back to it, but quit again. He hasn't gambled for 11 years.

"It's stupid," he says. "I was a sick man."

He is going to Vegas with Sammy the Syrian, Nick explains, only because Sammy is an old friend. He will take in some shows and go to some restaurants, but he will not bet chip one.

As I am preparing to leave, two women come in. Nick turns to talk to them while I inspect an antique desk in a corner of the office.

Nick sees me looking at the desk.

"A piece of garbage!" he hollers across the room. "A Mexican imitation!"

"That's the desk you tried to sell me," one of the women says.

Nick nods solemnly, remembering.

"A work of art," he says.

Then he is off to Vegas with Sammy the Syrian.

May 28, 1987

❖

BUY TWO, THEY'RE CHEAP

MY WIFE CAME HOME FROM SHOPPING ONE DAY AND ASKED HOW I wanted to go.

I said, "Go where?"

She said, "You know, to the Great Beyond."

I said, "New York?"

"What do you want done with your remains?" she asked, becoming annoyed at the vague direction the conversation was taking.

"I'm not through with my remains yet."

"Can't you answer a simple question?" she demanded, raising her voice. "WHAT IN THE HELL DO YOU WANT DONE WITH YOUR BODY WHEN YOU'RE DEAD?!"

"I don't know," I said. "Surprise me."

The subject made me uncomfortable. During much of my growing-up years, death was a word my mother wouldn't let me use.

"If you say it," she warned, "it will happen."

It wasn't until the sixth grade that I discovered it was going to happen whether I said it or not, but I still don't like talking about it.

"I heard on the car radio that now is a good time to die," my wife said.

"You can buy caskets dirt-cheap, so to speak. Buy one, get one at half-price."

It was a commercial for a place called Direct Casket in Van Nuys. The idea simultaneously amused and intrigued her.

Together we are compulsive spenders, feeding each other's inclination to buy at first sight. Had we both gone to Direct Casket, we'd have probably come home with four of them, the price was so good: one for the dog to sleep in, one as a planter box and two to save for later use. So I went alone.

The business of selling coffins directly to the public began in 1994 when the Federal Trade Commission ruled that funeral homes could no longer charge extra fees to those buying their caskets elsewhere.

The FTC decision was a wake-up call (sort of) in the $10-billion death industry. It led to companies popping up everywhere to take advantage of the ruling, offering cut-rate bargains in their showrooms, over the phone and on the Internet.

Among them was Direct Casket. Its president is a happy, chubby, energetic young man who knows a good thing when he sees one. That would be Ray Silvas. I spent an afternoon with him.

"Here's the best deal in the house," he said enthusiastically as we meandered through a room full of coffins, their lids half open. "We call it the Harrison. It's 16-gauge steel with a heavy velvet interior, champagne-toned inside and out. At $1,795, a bargain. You know what you'd pay at a funeral home?"

"Not a clue," I said. It was my first time pricing caskets.

Silvas leaned in close. "Thirty-eight hundred." He nodded in satisfaction. I almost expected him to hand me a set of keys and say, "Give 'er a spin." Side air bags and anti-lock brakes not included.

A casket called Going Home was also a sweet little number. "We bought it for my mother's cousin when he died," Silvas confided.

"The funeral home charged us $2,900. Here it's $1,195."

He showed me a casket named Traditional, another named Moses. There were also really cheap ones ($275 and $445) made of particleboard and cardboard named, oddly, Congressional and Pentagon.

"They're mostly for those who want to be cremated," Silvas said, clearly not interested in singing their praises. Like cars with dents and bad paint jobs, they didn't represent the best of the industry.

The business of selling death isn't an easy one, but Silvas, 31, is good at it. Listening to him, I could almost see the advantage of a nice brush-lacquered metal coffin with a crank-adjusted pillow and swing-bar handles. I am less certain about the casket that offers interior backlighting to better display its owner. I don't think I want to be displayed.

Unlike the traditional concept of a coffin merchant, he is also a man with a sense of humor about what he does. "I could offer to sell you a 100-year warranty against rust," he said, referring not to the body but to the coffin, "but who's going to check?"

Silvas was born in East L.A., a fourth-generation Angeleno, and has been an entrepreneur since he was 16, when he founded his own cleaning service. He joined Direct Casket last July as head of the company's West Coast operation.

"You can buy everything else in a store," he said, as we sat in an office over the showroom, "why not a casket?"

He was politicized, Silvas says, when he discovered that the $6,500 coffin his family bought for his grandmother in 1994 could be purchased directly from a company for $2,200.

"Caskets are marked up 300 to 500% by funeral homes," he said, obviously indignant. "Our markup is only 30 to 70%."

Direct Casket will ship the box of your choice to a funeral home, or you can store it in your garage until the appropriate time. Credit can be arranged, or, with 50% down, one can opt for a layaway plan. Really.

"Customers are grateful to us," Silvas said, handing me a press packet that included a cheerful yellow fan and a refrigerator magnet bearing an open casket. "We often get calls from them thanking us."

"You get calls?" I couldn't conceal my amazement. Cell phones in the Moses?

"From their loved ones," he added. Oh.

The logic behind the current sale — buy one, get one at half-price — is to encourage couples to plan in advance, Silvas explained, thus sparing their survivors the cost of buying coffins later.

He smiled the benevolent smile of a saint. "It's a great gift to the kids," he said.

Maybe so, but I think I'll stick to perfume and neckties this year.

October 3, 1997

❖

SNIFF THE WORLD GOODBYE

A WOMAN WE HAVE KNOWN FOR YEARS REFUSED AN INVITATION to a dinner party at our house recently on the grounds that it could make her environmentally ill.

When I asked what she meant, she said she'd noticed that at our last party, some of the women wore perfume and the men cologne.

"It wasn't a fragrance-free party," she said.

"That's right," I replied. "Some of them also drank alcohol, ate chicken and, one presumes, wore nylon underwear. It was therefore not an alcohol-free, chicken-free or underwear-free party. What's your point?"

"It's not a laughing matter," she said in a tone reserved for incorrigible children or demented uncles. "I've discovered that I am chemically sensitive."

She let that sink in for a moment and then added: "It's the wave of the future."

Oh my God.

She was serious. The woman, whose name is Edna, adopts every new cause that comes down the Hollywood Freeway and this is her latest: the creation of a hypoallergenic world.

I'm not surprised. She's a born crusader. The only environmental group she has ever knowingly avoided was an organization convinced that cow flatulence was damaging the ozone layer.

She agreed that it probably was but didn't know what to do about it.

75

The allergic condition of which Edna spoke is called Multiple Chemical Sensitivity, or MCS for the culturally hip. By one estimate, 40,000 Americans suffer from MCS. By another, about 100 million. Take your pick.

It has gained such popular recognition that some churches and governmental agencies have declared themselves fragrance-free, banning aromatic accessories while in the presence of God or the bureaucracies.

San Francisco adopted a fragrance-free plan once, but, like the war on cow flatulence, it was deemed impossible to implement and went unenforced.

In wealthy Marin County, hot tub capital of the world, our tax money helped build a $4.5-million prototype "Ecology House" apartment complex for those who claimed to suffer from chemical allergies.

Not only couldn't you wear perfume to live there, but also a "sniff team" was employed to smell the raw building materials in order to detect potentially irritating chemicals.

Those who ultimately moved in got sick anyhow, and the whole thing was declared a disaster not unlike the ballyhooed creation of hypoallergenic dog kibbles that caused the animals to vomit and pass out.

News of the fiasco, however, has failed to damp the hot evangelistic zeal of those who have convinced themselves that perfume, like cigarette smoke and cheap wine, is hazardous to one's health.

A particularly vocal proselyte has promised that 10 years from now it will be politically incorrect to wear fragrances in public, whether you're dabbing yourself with Giorgio or splashing Old Spice on your weathered face.

I say it's a campaign I'm not about to join.

I no longer feel able to keep up with the sensitive, '90s kind of crusades that are threatening to drown us in political correctitude. I lack the ability of Sally Struthers to cry for the world at a moment's notice.

Oh, I've joined some crusades over the years. I raised my voice in defense of the California condor, as stupid as the beast seems, and was one of the first signers of the historic Manatee Rights Declaration.

I only eat tuna that is dolphin-safe, I don't play with war toys, I won't wear ermine, I don't use aerosol sprays, and when Willy was imprisoned in Mexico, I prayed for his freedom.

You have probably seen me at candlelight ceremonies against acid rain and found me next to you swaying gently to the music at concerts held to raise money for snail-darter safety zones.

I even fought the disposable diaper industry for mucking up our city dumps, although I will admit I was a little confused in the war against fruit flies whether I ought to protest the chemicals falling on our heads or the brutality committed against one of God's little flying friends.

Despite my liberal cant, however, I will not join the crusade to ban perfume, though it was pointed out to me that even moths have abandoned enticing odors as a means of attracting a mate. Now they click instead.

I personally would not like to hear women clicking up and down the street, but, despite its audiological hazards, I wouldn't protest. There's enough in the world that's wrong and dangerous to worry about perfume and a little clickety-clacking among the singles.

I wish, however, that Edna would do something about those damned cows.

February 13, 1996

❖

THE SANDWICH AND THE ACTIVIST

ON THE SAME DAY PEACE ACTIVIST JERRY RUBIN BEGAN A HUNGER strike against war, a woman telephoned demanding to know why we hadn't covered the National Sandwich Contest. For some reason, the call came to me.

"I don't know about the sandwich contest," I said. "Call the sandwich editor."

"You didn't know about the final judging of the Dream Sandwich? It was right here in L.A."

"That's wonderful," I said. "Now if you'll excuse me, Jerry Rubin is out there about to starve for peace and I have to …"

"Who is Jerry Rubin?"

"A guy who goes on hunger strikes occasionally in order to lose weight and end war. In this case, he's trying to lose weight and avert war."

"I have no interest in Jerry Rubin."

"Well," I said, "Jerry Rubin probably has no interest in Dream Sandwiches. But come back about two weeks into his fast and I'm sure his attitude will have changed."

I told her about the time I interviewed Rubin during an earlier hunger strike. I ate lunch in front of him to test his antiwar commitment.

He watched every bite I took, from plate to mouth, his eyes burning with hunger even as we discussed his yearning for peace. But despite the abundance of food, he never once demanded even a taste.

"Because of that," I said to the lady on the phone, "the world remained at peace through the entire lunch hour."

When I finished the story, she said, "What about the sandwich contest?"

I mention this to explain the diversity of interests that exist in L.A., and why, no matter what we cover, it is never enough.

Another example of this was contained in an article that appeared recently in a sprightly regional publication that specializes in liberal causes.

The writer, Bruce Mirken, pointed out that activists working on behalf of a variety of causes were complaining that The Times routinely ignored their protest demonstrations.

A chart that accompanied the story drew the following contrasts:

On July 26, 100 people picketed the office of U.S. Sen. Pete Wilson to protest his stand on the questioning of Supreme Court nominee David Souter.

The Times printed nothing on the protest but did carry a story 19 column inches long on how guppies are helping prove the theory of evolution.

On August 31, there was an anti-Mideast-involvement rally at the Unocal Building.

The Times carried nothing on the rally but did print a 12-inch story on a new nursery for tortoises at Cal State Dominguez Hills.

The intent of Mirken's combined 36-inch story and chart was, of course, to expose our biases. What they overlooked, however, is that there is a protest in L.A. every third day of the year. We can't cover them all.

Even as I write, for instance, Gloria Allred is leading victims of sexual crimes through town to protest the anti-abortion record of Dan Lungren, a candidate for state attorney general.

Maybe we should cover it, but there has recently been a change in reporters assigned to Allred protest parades. The last one suffered feminist burnout and has been reassigned to animal rights.

I think that's how the guppy and turtle stories made it so big.

We face an additional problem in L.A. that most cities don't have to contend with: the Celebrity Factor.

On Thursday, for instance, I was about to check out Ed Begley's appearance on behalf of transit improvements when I realized that if I did I would miss the Leonard Nimoy appearance on behalf of the environment.

Also, although I didn't know it at the time (the lady on the phone mentioned it), even the sandwich contest had a celebrity. Dom DeLuise was a judge.

I didn't go to any of them, opting instead for the Martin Sheen presentation of the Mitch Snyder Humanitarian Award later in the evening.

When I mentioned this to a friend, however, he said how could I possibly go to a Martin Sheen event and not attend a dinner at the same time for Bob Hope, who was receiving the Hal Roach Entertainment Award?

We face these kinds of decisions every day: The Dream Sandwich or the Jerry Rubin fast? A pro-abortion protest or a guppy press conference? An anti-war rally or a ribbon-cutting for a tortoise nursery?

Sheen or Hope, Begley or Nimoy, Allred or nothing.

There's a lot going on in this town all the time, and no matter what one chooses to cover, someone is going to be unhappy.

I just hope to God Julia Roberts doesn't appear in a thong bikini on behalf of organic radishes at the very same time a press conference is being held to announce we have learned to communicate with earthworms.

I'd have one hell of a time choosing between them.

November 3, 1990

CHAPTER THREE

CAUSES, CONCERNS AND CALAMITIES

"The ultimate measure of a man is not where he stands in moments of comfort and convenience, but where he stands at times of challenge and controversy."

—MARTIN LUTHER KING JR.

AT THE END OF THE ROAD

AN IMAGE OF THE MAN LYING IN THE MIDDLE OF THE ROAD implants itself on the mind like the memory of a stormy day, all dark clouds and gloom.

I am both transfixed and horrified as I watch a dog emerge from out of the camera's range to nudge the man's body, then pull at it, a toy to be tested for life.

The drama ends as the camera widens to reveal a small group of policemen moving in slowly. The scene dissolves as they hover over him, and the world moves on.

Real violence as public theater has once more drawn a crowd on television.

The incident occurred almost two weeks ago, but I can't get it out of my head. Michael Alan Thayer's life drained away on a San Diego freeway and was offered up as it happened, live and in color. We could almost hear his last heartbeat.

Thayer's death ended a three-hour chase by police that began in San Bernardino County when a sheriff's deputy spotted expired registration tags on his car.

A parade of patrol cars pursued him through four counties. He stopped only when a spike strip laid down by the Highway Patrol punctured one of his tires on Interstate 805.

As cameras from five television news helicopters tightened in on him, Thayer emerged unsteadily from his car, displayed what appeared to be a gun and was brought down in a volley of more than 40 bullets. Seventeen hit him. He didn't have a chance.

And then we moved on to other news.

Once more television, pandering to our blood lust, has brought us a dark moment to ponder. Like ancient crowds at the Roman Colosseum, we gathered to watch death in a public arena and were mesmerized by it.

The line between fiction and reality has become blurred in the fading days of the 20th century. The death of Michael Thayer, a 49-year-old ex-con, could have occurred in any number of movies or TV series, after which he would have risen, wiped away the false blood and went on to another role.

But this was real, the way the Gulf War was real, the way those smart bombs were real, the way the killings in Kosovo were real, however remote they seem on the face of the tube.

Long after the news programs had switched to other matters, I sat staring at the screen. Few moments have affected me more than the last seconds of Michael Thayer's life.

He imprints himself on memory not because of who he was or what he may have been attempting by brandishing a starter's pistol in the face of real guns. Drugs or so-called suicide by cop may have motivated him, but that's not the point.

The entire incident speaks to our fascination with car chases, or at least what television believes to be our fascination.

"What occurs on our freeways affects us all," says KTLA co-anchor Terry Anzur, an assistant professor of journalism at USC who generally defends television's coverage of car chases. "People watch and are grateful that what's happening out there isn't happening to them."

She and others cite similar coverage given the Kathy Fiscus case 50 years ago. She was a 3-year-old who fell down an abandoned well in San Marino.

We heard her faint cries on live television and watched as rescuers worked for 50 hours in a courageous but futile effort to save her. Television watched and listened with us.

Today, her grave marker identifies Fiscus as "a little girl who brought us together." Those who defend the coverage of Michael Thayer's death use the same phrase: It brings us together in moments of high drama.

They're not the same. The effort to save a little girl in no way compares to the bloody end of a car chase. One was the celebration of the human spirit, a prayer offered up to preserve a small life. The other, as someone put it, was electronic voyeurism, violence without involvement.

If we are as fascinated by car chases as television thinks we are, it's because there are so damned many of them, about 800 a year in L.A. alone.

The last one I saw was a few days ago. Channel 7 followed a stolen sport utility vehicle pursued by a line of patrol cars down Crenshaw Boulevard. As it flashed by an intersection, a man dressed as Santa Claus waved happily. It was an L.A. moment.

"We watch car chases for the same reason we watch the Super Bowl," Anzur says. "To see the outcome. I wish it were different, but it's not."

So Michael Thayer lies in the street, shot down by cops, tugged at by a dog, and the ratings kick a notch higher in the theater of the dead.

December 8, 1999

❖

THE JANE FONDA SYNDROME

IN EXPERIMENTS WITH CONDITIONED REFLEX, IVAN PAVLOV taught a hungry dog to salivate at the sound of a bell. That was about 100 years ago. In contemporary usage, the same conditioning apparently prevails among veterans of the Vietnam War. They salivate at the mention of Jane Fonda.

It doesn't even have to be Fonda herself. Last week, I included the name of her ex-husband, Tom Hayden, in a column and there was instant salivation by association.

Oddly, the vitriol that followed was directed at Fonda, not at Hayden, although both went to Hanoi during the Vietnam War and both are considered traitors by those veterans who, emotionally at least, have never shed their uniforms.

One e-mailer was especially outraged because, he said, Fonda was being honored as woman of the century. The only reference I could find was that in April 1999, Barbara Walters included her in an ABC special that featured "100 years of great women."

Those veterans and their followers whose salivating had lessened found reason to drool anew, causing the American Legion to issue a statement saying that including Fonda in the century list "is a disservice to all the others who have done so much for America."

Glory hallelujah, how the venom flowed thereafter. "Traitor" became one of the milder epithets hurled at her, among many I can't even mention. She's the antichrist, no doubt about it, and maybe worse.

I began wondering why, after all these years, there was still so much hatred of Jane Fonda. We've forgiven the Germans, the Japanese, the Russians, the North Vietnamese, the Chinese and maybe the North Koreans.

Hell, we've even softened toward England, Spain, Mexico and the Confederate Army.

Then why can't we forgive a woman who, in a climate of protest, went to Hanoi seeking peace, the way Henry Kissinger sought peace later to great applause?

The answers I've received range from the arrogance of her presence in a man's domain to the idea that she's a symbol to all those in uniform who were targeted as criminals by antiwar activists during the turbulent 1960s.

Often mentioned is a radio address Fonda made in Hanoi in 1972 in which she praised the Vietnamese and damned Nixon, and a photograph of her at a Communist gun emplacement, wearing an enemy helmet and smiling prettily.

"She became a symbol with that photograph," Al Lance said in a telephone interview. He's national commander of the American Legion. "Anyone who was ever spit upon or called baby-killer associates that with Jane Fonda, no matter who actually did the spitting."

Much said about Fonda by Vietnam-era veterans is untrue, Lance said in a surprisingly moderate tone. He paused and then added: "If I sound conciliatory, it's because she recanted."

His reference was to Fonda's 1988 televised apology "to men who were in Vietnam, who I hurt, or whose pain I caused to deepen because of things that I said or did."

Did we forgive and forget? Not everyone:

"Jane Fonda was a traitor, naive or not. She should have been shot and will never be forgiven."

"They [Fonda and Hayden] danced while we died and that will never be forgotten or forgiven."

Marita Sturken suggests that unlike veterans of World War II, Vietnam War veterans are locked in a time warp. "They still hold 24-hour vigils at the Vietnam War memorial," she says. "They still wear their camouflage uniforms and they keep the MIA issue alive when there's no reason to. Some veterans have never managed to move past all that."

Sturken is an associate professor at USC's Annenberg School for Communication and author of "Tangled Memories," a book partly about the war in Vietnam.

Jane Fonda is "easy to hate," Sturken says, because she's a celebrity, she's privileged and "she's not pathetic." It was Sturken who speculated that another reason for the vitriol is that she's a woman who violated a man's world.

Fonda has reinvented herself many times, from actress to activist to fitness queen to dutiful housewife and, most recently, to born-again Christian. Contrary to Sturken's comment, she is in many ways pathetic. But she's never been important enough or evil enough to be a national enemy.

While no one who has ever been in combat should forget either war's pain or war's victims, there comes a time to hang up the uniform and get on about our business. I had to, and you should too. Stop salivating, boys. The war's over. Move on

July 30, 2000

SHADOWS IN THE RAIN

SEEING THEM FOR THE FIRST TIME, ONE MIGHT ASSUME THEY ARE store clerks or office workers taking an early lunch. There is nothing unusual about their appearance, either in clothing or gesture, that would connect them with San Quentin's death row. One expects, perhaps unfairly so, the mothers of condemned men to somehow reflect the brutality of the crimes their sons have been convicted of committing.

But neither Melanie Bostic nor Doris Harris bears any physical traits that would associate them with murder. Bostic is a handsome woman of 58 who glows with vitality. Harris, 65, is a soft-spoken, almost whispery woman with cultured good manners.

But there are shadows on their lives.

Bostic is the mother of Robert Bloom Jr., convicted of the 1982 Sun Valley murders of his father, stepmother and 8-year-old stepsister.

Harris is the mother of Lanell Craig Harris, sentenced to die six years ago for killing a Van Nuys father of six while attempting to rob a group of men playing cards.

Both women bear in different ways the anguish of knowing that their sons have dates with death. And they are similarly burdened by the beliefs of others, both spoken and unspoken, that they are somehow responsible.

I was brought together with them by a militant, anti-death sentence activist who has good reason to be so. Janice Gay, a grandmother of 11 children, is married to death row inmate Kenneth Gay, one of two men convicted of killing a Los Angeles police officer in 1983.

I met with the three women in the cafeteria of the Van Nuys courthouse on a day dark with rain. We weren't there to debate the guilt or innocence of the men they believe with all their hearts should not be on death row. We were there to talk about feelings.

Gay, a 56-year-old home care worker, contacted me because I have written of my opposition to capital punishment. Talking to reporters is a part of the reaching out she does as founder and head of an organization called Wives,

Families & Friends, bringing comfort to those with loved ones on death row and fighting to end capital punishment in California.

I was drawn to Bostic and Harris, not because of militancy, but because I was trying to imagine what it would be like to have a son on death row.

"I can describe it in one word," Bostic says, staring at me through eyes that narrow with intensity. "Pain."

"Every night at 10, my son kneels in his prison cell and prays," says Harris, a hospital office worker. "And every night at 10 I close my eyes where ever I am and pray with him that he will not die in San Quentin."

In a society reluctant to forgive, we condemn the mothers along with their sons. The sins of the young are borne, however unfairly, by their progenitors. Few stop to consider parental feelings and many, in fact, are quick to heap invective on them.

"We feel hated," Gay says, isolating their single most overriding emotion.

The hatred stems as much from their cause as from their relationship with condemned killers. They are visibly and militantly in the forefront of opposition to capital punishment. Sometimes it costs them.

On a march protesting the death penalty, Bostic was approached by a man who grabbed at the Star of David around her neck and snarled, "How did Hitler miss you?" It was during the time San Quentin was still using gas to execute its condemned prisoners. The horror of the comment was not lost on Bostic. "But," she says, "I'll keep right on marching."

She empties a plastic bag of badges on the table. They say, "Light the Torch of Conscience" and "Why do we kill people who kill people to show that killing people is wrong?"

"My son is mentally ill," she says. "I found him holding his breath one day after he was convicted. He said it was because he was practicing to die."

Harris' son was a normal child, raised in a family of eight children. "We made them all do their homework before they could play," she says. "Lanell was on the football team. At Thanksgiving he'd help me cook and take food to the homeless people in the park."

He rode his bike as a child and played with other kids. He laughed a lot. But when does laughter stop and a murderous attitude begin? Who draws the line between insanity and irresponsibility?

Bostic, Harris and Gay write, march and speak on behalf of ending capital punishment. Their cause is political. But the ache in their heart is real.

January 14, 2001

❖

THE UNEXPECTED FACE OF HUNGER

JUST OUTSIDE THE STORE, NEAR THE MAIN ENTRANCE, THERE ARE bins stacked with gleaming rows of oranges, green apples, persimmons, pears, mangoes and papayas.

Inside, the store opens to a panorama of abundance, fruits and vegetables of every description laid out like an artist's dream in alluring patterns and colors.

Past them are counters of meat and fish and poultry, then aisle after aisle stacked high on either side with ... well ... everything.

All of it constitutes the face of opulence, full and rich and satisfying.

The store is the Whole Foods Market in Woodland Hills, but it could have been Gelson's or Ralphs or Vons.

The point of my being there on this day was to realize and understand abundance. Not just to pass it by, but to absorb it, to assess it, to know how much we have in this country, to stand in this place of plenty ... and then to visualize hunger.

This is the time of year when, in different ways, we celebrate excess, and food is the center of the jubilation. The fat get fatter and, in ways we can hardly understand, the hungry get hungrier.

Earlier, I had visited the Los Angeles Regional Foodbank, a 100,000-square-foot warehouse sprawled over a side street in an industrial section of East L.A. I had been drawn to it by a report that 1.4 million people in this county are "food insecure." An additional 584,000 "experience hunger."

These are sanitized descriptions of a need so deep and profound that only one who has been hungry can understand exactly what they mean. I was one of them once, and the humiliation of hunger is a memory that never fades.

At the food bank, I talked to Michael Flood, its executive director, one of many trying to serve the needs of the dispossessed.

He walked me through the warehouse, past stacks of boxes and cans and bags of donated food destined for a thousand charity organizations that deal with hunger. He wanted me to know that hunger wasn't just a problem for the homeless, but reaches into neighborhoods and communities where one wouldn't suspect it existed.

"Hunger is families with kids," Flood was saying amid the roar of trucks backing up to load. "Hunger is seniors. Hunger is the family next door. It could be anyone. Hunger doesn't discriminate."

There are 2 million pounds of food in the warehouse at any given time. Thirty-eight million pounds will be distributed this year.

"It isn't enough," Flood said. He's a dark-haired man of 39 who decided in college that serving the needs of the people would be his life's work. He has headed L.A.'s food bank, the second largest in the nation, for a year and a half.

"We've got to triple or quadruple our output, but to do so we have to obtain more food and more funding. The need is outstripping the supply." He paused, thinking. "But you've go to be positive. There is a cure for hunger. We'll work at it this year, and next year we'll do more. What we're trying to do is win the day."

The face of hunger is gaunt and troubled.

Years ago, I came across a man going through food in a garbage can at the rear of a supermarket. He was carefully inspecting what he came across and placing what was edible in a paper bag.

He didn't hear me approach, and I stood there for a few moments, watching. When at last he detected my presence, he looked up quickly. Our gazes met and held for a fraction of a second that burned itself into my memory.

His expression reflected many emotions. There was humiliation, guilt, anger and desperation. There was a sadness so deep it was almost palpable. We didn't say anything. After a few moments, I walked away. But I'll never forget the man's face. It was to me then, and always will be, the face of hunger.

I can relate to that grim quest for food. It's an uneasy shadow from my childhood that helped shape the habits of the person I am today. Hunger haunted our house with terrible intensity and darkened the lives of just about everyone I knew.

The time was the Depression, when the need to survive made scavengers of us all. I, too, searched for salvageable food in garbage cans behind markets. I stole food from stores and ate it crouched in the bushes of a vacant lot not far away. Even raw potatoes are a feast when the stomach growls. Meat was a luxury.

Today when I shop, I fill my cart with enough food to feed a family of 15. Unconsciously, I continue to live with the fear that there won't be enough, that I'll be reduced once more to the indignity of stealing to eat or eating what others have rejected.

Hunger is more than a physical pain. It creates empty places in the soul that are impossible to fill. I live today with needs I don't understand and with a craving that abundance can't satisfy.

That's why I stopped by Whole Foods Market after visiting the food bank. It's why I write this column today, Thanksgiving Day, to remind myself at this time of abundance, how many there are who have nothing. And to come to grips with a face of hunger that is simultaneously the man at the garbage can, and me.

November 22, 2001

PIECES OF A FAMILY

I HAVE PINNED ON THE WALL NEXT TO ME A LINED PIECE OF NOTE-book paper on which is printed, "I love you mom."

It is written in black crayon in the careful hand of a child who might be 7 or 8 years old.

On the back, in the same black crayon, is a picture of a house in rough outline with doors and windows. It stands almost bleakly alone, without life, without warmth, without surroundings.

The piece of paper is special to me.

I found it one day at the northern end of the Long Beach Freeway, in a lot once occupied by a group of homeless people.

It was lying amid the debris of what had been their encampment. Only pieces of their existence remained: a barbecue grill, a paper cup, a few cans, a ragged shirt ... and that note.

A woman who works at Modern Maturity magazine told me about them. She wasn't sure how long they had been there, and didn't know if they were actually a family or simply people thrown together by necessity.

She just knew she saw them all the time living among some trees where the freeway ends at Valley Boulevard in Alhambra. I went searching.

I'm not sure what compelled me to look. L.A.'s Shelter Partnership estimates there are up to 80,000 homeless people in the county.

Like everyone else, I've gotten used to seeing them around. As long as they aren't intruding on your life, you tend to ignore them. They're like passing traffic, or leaves carried on a stray wind.

When I got to the place where the freeway family had been, no one was there. I searched both sides and then concentrated on the open area off Highbury Avenue, where the encampment had existed.

A few of the neighbors remembered seeing homeless people around the concrete-sided L.A. River, but couldn't tell me anything about them. Students from Cal State L.A. living at the Phi Sigma Kappa fraternity house let me scan the area from their backyard, but I found nothing.

The day was hot and smoggy, and I wasn't about to spend a lot of time chasing shadows. But then, as I was walking toward the car, a homeless man emerged from a group of eucalyptus trees.

I swear I'd searched the area and hadn't seen anyone, but there he was, a guy in his late 40s, dirty, bearded and wearing clothes as old as rainfall.

He was probably mentally retarded and was vague about almost everything, but he did point out the exact spot where the family had been. He'd been there a couple of nights too, until they'd all been told to move on, he didn't know by whom. They were always being told to move. Who told them wasn't important.

The last I saw him, he was walking south along the 710, going nowhere.

The hand-printed note — "I love you mom" — was in plain sight near the barbecue grill. I'm pretty sure of the age of the person who wrote it and who drew the picture of a house on the back. I have grandchildren who are 7 and 8, and it looks like something one of them might have done.

I stood there for a long time just looking at the note, drawn slowly into it, increasingly unaware of the heat and smog. The din of freeway traffic muted to a distant hum, like flies at a picnic table.

I could picture a little girl sitting in the terrible loneliness of the vacant lot, carefully printing the words, and just as meticulously drawing the picture of a home that may have existed in a corner of her memory.

Was there actually a mother she was writing the note to, or was the mother just the phantom figure of a child's longing? Had there once been a home, or had all of her young life been spent wandering and dreaming?

The house she drew was a house without her in it, a place beyond the horizons of her reach, cold and distant and empty. It was like one of the homes that surrounded the vacant lot, viewed through despair.

This is not a good time for the homeless. A growing hostility toward their existence is forcing them out of sight. It's because, I think, we see the homelessness in ourselves, the utter, devastating failure of spirit to soar with the rest, and we can't bear the introspection.

I live now with the vision of the child who wrote the note. I always will. There are 5,600 homeless families in L.A. County. Eleven thousand of those family members are children.

One of them may be a little girl whose warmth and loneliness claw at the heart. If so, I hope she's loved as she loves, because sometimes — in the emptiness of a world filled with sadness — love is all we have left.

August 27, 1994

❖

A MEMORY OF DISTANT GUNFIRE

HE HEARD THE SHOTS THROUGH THE BLURRED PERSPECTIVE OF memory, as though they had come from the past and had nothing to do with the present.

They were sharp, popping sounds, and for a moment James Moore sat at the kitchen table, staring and trying to figure out if they were real.

It was late afternoon, and a pale sunlight washed the room with faint shadows. Food cooked on the stove of the tidy west Compton home. Traffic hummed on nearby Redondo Beach Boulevard.

The time required for Moore to separate reality from memory was the blink of an eye, but it seemed forever. When the separation occurred, it was a thunderclap.

Moore bolted out the back door, down the stairs and toward the fence, his brain reprocessing the echo of three gunshots, gauging their direction, placing his son in the vicinity, screaming not again!

When he reached the fence he shouted, "Gregory!" and almost instantaneously saw his son and two companions on the ground ... then rising and running toward him, unhurt.

Another drive-by shooting, his brain said.

Moore closed his eyes. It was then, he says, that it all came rushing back....

Three years ago, he and his wife, Ceola, were at the same kitchen table, having a last cup of coffee. It was 4 a.m. A night of family card playing had ended. The children were in bed.

"We were just sitting here talking," Moore said. "All of a sudden, bam, bam! I turned to her and said, 'Ceola, you hear that?' "

Moore's wife of 20 years didn't answer. One of two bullets fired at random toward their corner house had pierced her skull. She was brain-dead by the time she slumped forward. She stopped breathing several hours later.

A drive-by shooting with no specific victim in mind, a bullet fired toward a light in a window, had claimed the wife Moore loved beyond measure.

"I was just getting over it," he said the other day as we sat at the same kitchen table, "when the other shooting happened."

He is a 50-year-old black man who could pass for 40. For the last 20 years he has worked as a lab technician at the B.F. Goodrich Chemical Co. Ceola had been a nursery school teacher and an active church member.

"All the emotions I felt when she was killed came back to me," Moore said. "I felt grief and fear and anger. Now I'm just plain angry. This is no kind of life! What the hell is going on?"

It was the same question Moore asked when he called us, and the same question I asked as I drove through his neighborhood of neat homes and mowed lawns, of trimmed hedges and fresh paint.

Pride had gone into this neighborhood. Care had gone into it. A young man worked on his car. Children played under shade trees. Neighbors stopped to talk to each other. Stanford Street deserved better than gunfire.

"What kind of existence is it sitting here every day waiting for something to happen?" Moore said, nervously lighting a cigarette. "Everybody is sick of it. It's getting like the Wild West.

"The kids are scared to death and beginning to carry guns for defense. But one thing leads to another. Where does defense end and offense begin? I wake up every night, listening...."

Three of Moore's children were living at home when he wife was killed. Dennis, 22, has since moved away. Gregory, 19, and Rhonda, 14, are still there.

Five gang members were arrested after the shooting two weeks ago. No one has ever been arrested in Ceola's murder.

To the best of Moore's knowledge, the shooting that took her life was the first in the neighborhood, but since then there have been at least three others, one of which wounded a young boy.

Gang graffiti proliferates on the edges of Stanford Street. Drug dealers clog Visalia Avenue.

"I've gone down there and watched them deal," Moore said. "They're blond and blue-eyed people, obviously not from around here. I'd take down license numbers and be more a vigilante, but suppose they track me down and go after my kids?"

Moore is trying to unite the neighborhood to somehow solve the problem. He's asking for more random patrols by sheriff's deputies, but he's not sure they're that interested in helping.

"The night my wife was killed," he said, "I heard one of the detectives say, 'Just another day in the ghetto.' Does that sound like they care?"

James Moore won't run. The house he has lived in for 10 years is the house his wife chose, and her memory is still bright. But the question he asks is the question we all ought to ponder.

Will it ever be safe again?

September 12, 1989

❖

THE ANIMAL IN US

NOT SINCE THE DAYS OF THE OLD JOHN BIRCH SOCIETY HAVE I been so overwhelmed with written comments on a single true-believing subject.

With the Birchers, it was their love of God and America and their hatred of Communists that fired their passions.

With today's animal activists, it's their love of dogs and cats and rhinos and manatees that stirs their deepest emotions.

I used to receive mail on cue when I discussed the excessive nature of Bircher patriotism. They were handwritten letters, usually anonymous, and they called me every name their limited vocabularies could manage.

Now I receive e-mail on cue from "animal guardians" who, proving how united they are, use almost the same phrasing and logic suggested to them by the Webmasters who manage online animal networks. It's a chorus sung fortissimo.

In their zeal to respond to a column last week, some of the activists refer to my comments on pit bulls and Rottweilers as "racist" and say I am calling for an animal "holocaust." Usually, nothing I receive from rabid activists surprises me, but applying these terms to dogs does, I must admit, cause concern.

When passion exceeds common sense, it impedes an ability to think. That's when activism becomes extremism with a tilt toward mindless devotion, limiting the view of other needs.

If, for instance, we had spent as much time bleeding over humans as we do over dogs, the world might be a better place today for both species.

The column that set animal lovers afire compared the river of tears shed for the dog tossed into traffic near San Jose with the lack of tears shed for the victims of killer dogs. In it, I made reference to weepy animal guardians and wailing animal advocates.

They fired back by calling me stupid, a fool, ignorant, dangerous and snide, in addition to the previously mentioned terms that hinted at racism and genocide. Others suggested that it was perhaps my "ethnicity" that clouded my mind, calling into question deeper feelings among animal lovers toward us "minor" members of the human race.

Most of the e-mailers understood my point. Some mentioned that I was wrong in hinting that a love for animals and a love for humans were mutually exclusive. I know they aren't. It's just the cant of a culture suddenly gone mad over animals that calls attention to the subject.

Many told me horror stories of attacks by pit bulls and Rottweilers, others about the loving nature of both breeds. One writer said that even television's "Crocodile Hunter," Steve Irwin, owns a pit bull. Although that may not be the ideal endorsement, it's something. I guess.

A semi-famous, and very funny, comedian, Elayne Boosler, tells me more or less I'm full of it. An animal issues activist, Phyllis Daugherty, tells me I'm right on.

Émile Zola is quoted and so is Albert Schweitzer. I could help out by quoting W.C. Fields, who loved dogs more than children, and John Steinbeck, who elevated Charley to international prominence, but I won't.

So.

I'm delighted that so many out there expend as much time, effort and money on behalf of humans as they do for animals. But I don't think that's generally true.

The world is full of followers, of those who pursue safe paths of protest to ease their consciences. They wave banners opposing cruelty to animals because no one is going to wave banners advocating cruelty to animals.

Brutality does exist on both personal and commercial levels and should be protested. So should cruelty to children and seniors and whole groups of people being tortured and murdered for who they are or what they believe in.

One of the reasons we turn to the clamorous protection of animals is that everything else seems so far out of reach. We feel powerless to intervene in the ethnic cleansings of Eastern Europe, the AIDS epidemics of Africa or the religious wars of the Middle East.

So we weep for a little white *bichon frisé* while mayhem rules the planet.

Regarding dangerous dogs, e-mailers who opposed my point of view suggest that it's the owners' fault when dogs attack. So do we naughty-naughty the owners while the dogs rip up kids and old ladies? I don't think so. We get the dogs off the street, then go for the root causes.

I'm sure I haven't pleased anyone, but that's OK. I see my job as raising questions, not providing answers. Personally, I tolerate just about all animals. Dogs scatter my garbage, raccoons trash my utility room, coyotes eat my cats, cougars prowl my mountains, and rattlesnakes share the trails I walk.

I have two dogs, two cats and 12 fish. At times, I've owned goats, horses, guinea pigs, gerbils and rats. And while I don't exactly pal around with them, I do take exceptional care of whatever animal I possess. But they don't take precedence over my wife, my children, my grandchildren, my friends or my neighbors.

They're animals. I feed them, water them, walk them and fight their fleas, but I do not discuss my columns with them or ask for their preference on what TV shows to watch. Weep and wail all you want. A dog is a dog. Period. I'm outta here. Goodbye.

July 9, 2001

❖

THE SMELL OF MURDER

HOMICIDE DETECTIVE JOHN ST. JOHN USED TO SAY THAT MURDER has a smell that lingers long after the bodies have been removed and the crime scene cleaned.

He wasn't speaking of a specific odor, but of the heavy aroma of grief that seems to permeate the very air of the place where a killing has occurred.

I sensed that the other day on Baldwin Park's Stewart Avenue, standing before the modest wood-frame house where two young girls and two men died so violently on the preceding Sunday.

Dark skies lay over the neighborhood like a funeral shroud, and a cluster of candles in front of the house flickered in the melancholy morning.

Flowers were placed against a low metal fence that surrounded the home, adding splashes of oddly inappropriate color to the prevailing gloom.

"Stewart Avenue makes me shiver," said a young mother who had stopped to pay her respects. Diana Torres has lived on the street all of her 29 years. "I was never afraid until now."

Fear is an element of murder's unsettling fragrance, and those whose perceptions allowed them to recognize it left the scene quickly.

Others simply stared, by their concentration seeking answers to the riddles of human violence that leaves so much pain in its wake.

I was there to wonder along with them, the perceptive and the stunned, and to once more absorb the tears of the ghosts that haunt us.

The murder victims were Evelyn and Massiel Torres, 8 and 12, their uncle, Roberto Diaz, 34, and a gardener, Jose Rojas, 33. Three others were wounded.

Police said they were shot and stabbed by David Alvarez, 28, who was looking for his estranged wife. He remains at large.

What brought me to Stewart Avenue was not just this slaughter of innocents, as devastating as it is, but also the terror that late summer and autumn have again visited upon the places where we live.

I wrote once in a column I called "The Guns of August" about the multiplicity of homicides in one month four years ago, and now it has come again, this time in September, as the days shorten and the weather cools:

A man kills his neighbor in Fullerton. A postal worker is murdered at an ATM in the Crenshaw District. Four are killed in a Canyon Country murder-suicide. A woman checking her car alarm is shot to death in South-Central. A young man is killed near a high school in Placentia. A 19-year-old is murdered in an Arleta drive-by. A Duarte man is shot in a traffic argument in Alhambra. A man is stabbed to death in Canoga Park. A woman is killed in L.A. in a home-invasion robbery. A man murders his wife and two daughters in Pico-Union....

And on and on and on.

I'm not going to speculate on why the season seems so violent. It is complex enough to ponder the rage that drives a man to murder children. To attempt to unravel the mysteries of cosmic influences on our sanity would be impossible.

I'm just trying to communicate the horror that murder brings to places like Stewart Avenue.

"You never get used to it," Joe Holmes was saying. He's the homicide detective investigating the crime for the Sheriff's Department. Holmes has been a cop for 23 years.

He was talking about the scene of horror inside the small house where four people died. He was talking about the children, about their head wounds and about the massive amounts of blood spilled onto the floor.

"You have to maintain your composure even through the disgust that fills you, but your emotions are always behind the composure. They don't disappear. You keep thinking about your own children, about your grandchildren...."

The Stewart Avenue killing was his fifth multiple-murder case this year. "I hate doing this," he said, "but it's my job. Every time I enter an autopsy room I think, 'Suppose it's someone I know?'"

It's my job, too. Not to investigate, but to weave woes and wonders into the tapestry that will one day be viewed as representative of our time.

Murder was once a rare occurrence, a headline shouted on the streets, and now it is commonplace enough to be barely noticed in the pulse of events that comprise the rhythms of daily living.

Sebastian Torres, who has lived on Stewart Avenue all of his 31 years, remembers when it was a quiet street no one cared much about. "Now," he says, "it's a tourist attraction."

Then let it be just that. And let it be a metaphor for all that is sad and odious about this fading century. Go by Stewart Avenue. Smell the aromas of murder, and then bow your head and mourn for us all.

October 4, 1996

❖

FEAR AND AN UNSEEN ENEMY

ODD HOW THE MUNDANE PLAYS AGAINST CALAMITY IN THE presence of war.

In the heart of darkness, death and destruction rule over a charred earth. Panic and urgency blacken the very skies.

But beyond the perimeters, doctors' appointments are kept, markets remain open and gas stations continue to function.

Life seems to go on as usual. But the faces of the people tell a different story.

As I drive and walk through L.A., I see expressions of horror and disbelief. I see tears. I see anger.

Wherever I go, either television or radio is reporting the breathless news: New York, beautiful, dynamic New York, is afire. In Washington, D.C., portions of the Pentagon are in ruins. In Pennsylvania, a jetliner is down.

Manhattan is a symbol of the destruction. Landmark buildings have fall-en, altering one of the most beguiling skylines in the world. Many have died.

In Los Angeles, airports shut down, streets close and federal buildings are under guard. No explosions rock us, but the city crouches on high alert. What next? Where?

And yet, stricken as we are by what has happened a continent away, we carry on. We keep our doctor's appointments. We fill our gas tanks. We shop.

Telephones ring and worried relatives ask, "Are you all right?" as though the terrorists that brought fire and death to New York, Washington and Pennsylvania have also come to L.A.

Yes. We're all right. That is, our personal safety is not immediately threat-ened. But something deep and abiding has happened to us inside. Our souls are in pain.

Terrorism is less about horror than about fear, though they walk hand in hand across the smoking ruins. Terrorism strikes at the psyche of a people, shattering the internal functions that keep us normal. Terrorism disrupts, con-fuses and paralyzes.

I hear from friends who swear they'll never fly again or they'll never enter a federal building again or they'll never stay in the upper floors of a hotel again.

Parents keep their children home from schools. Others worry about the safety of loved ones in hospitals. Will the sick and dying be targets too? Is there no mercy in this strange and awful war?

As I write, I hear of candlelight ceremonies tonight at churches and parks, then a voice from the radio asks, "But who's going to risk going out?"

Our enemies are shadows, figures that move furtively in and out of reali-ty. We shout while they whisper. We lumber while they sneak. How do we fight them? There are no front lines to hold, no obvious bastions to attack.

Armies amass in vain, bombers fly without targets. Who's to blame? Who murdered our people and destroyed our buildings? Who dared intrude on the serenity of the mightiest nation on Earth?

Who are you? Shadows. Where are you? Silence.

People want to talk about it, as though communication will somehow lead to clarification. Strangers approach me on the street. "God, what a day," one says. "Can you believe this?" another says. We cluster. We discuss.

My son awakened me with a phone call the morning of that terrible day. "Watch the news," he said. It's surreal: The silhouette of a commercial jet approaches one of the twin towers of the World Trade Center. A "spark" strikes the tower, then bursts into yellow flame and billows of smoke. The flicker of the spark has concealed disaster. It's a jetliner striking the building.

We see it over and over again in video taken by professionals and amateurs. We are both repelled and transfixed by the hellish scenes. Smoke blows past the cameras, people run through the streets, screams and sirens intermingle, confused voices overlap each other on CNN. It all seems strangely manufactured, special effects and miniaturization combined to present trailers for a disaster movie.

Can it be real? Can this be happening?

Pearl Harbor is mentioned often. I think of London and Berlin a lifetime ago. I think of firebombs. I think of Hiroshima and Nagasaki. And now I think of New York.

One can figure that the Pentagon at least could be classified as a military target. But not the twin towers. Not this gathering of the innocents in their place of work. Not our wives and husbands and children trapped in the cruel confines of a dying jetliner.

Retaliation is inevitable. That's the nature of war in any form. They hit us, we hit them and they hit us again, until the cycle is exhausted. We will all suffer.

I saw New York only a few weeks ago, more radiant than it has ever been, cleaner, nicer, safer. I heard its music and embraced its people. And now this.

Watching the terrible destruction, one can only wish the clock had stopped then, before the fire, before the deaths, before the event that has changed our world. The words of William Shakespeare, written more than 400 years ago, resonate down the years to this mournful moment: "O, call back yesterday, bid time return."

September 13, 2001

THE LADIES LINKED ARMS

I AM SITTING IN A HOT LITTLE UPSTAIRS ROOM IN SANTA MONICA, surrounded by television cameras and listening to an attractive young woman talk about how to guard the doors when the war starts.

"You link arms," Robin Schneider says, "and you line up in three rows in this manner."

She demonstrates to the assembled reporters by placing maybe a dozen trainees near the door to the room and showing them where to stand.

"The reason you face in different directions," she explains, "is if their people try to crawl through, they can't."

Next she uses the trainees to demonstrate an escort strategy, moving someone from here to there safely. Arms are linked again. Words like "combat" and "skirmish" creep into her language.

Strobe lights pop. Television cameras hum. On-camera news personalities nod authoritatively, the way they've been taught to do when they're still trying to figure out what's going on.

Schneider is executive director of the California Abortion Rights Action League, under whose auspices this combined press conference and battle demonstration is being held.

"Any questions?" she asks at the end.

It is the first day of spring. There is a faint aroma of Giorgio in the room. The whole thing is surreal.

Talk of war has got me thinking. "Is there a possibility they have spies here?" I ask.

"That's possible," Schneider says, waiting for my follow-up question. I have none. It was a whim of the moment.

I think about asking if anyone will parachute behind enemy lines, but dismiss the idea.

"Is it possible you have infiltrated them?" I finally ask.

"That's possible," Schneider says.

"Well, well," I say, writing furiously in my mauve notebook and thinking that we never had mauve notebooks in the old days of newspapering.

Welcome to the war.

Today begins three days of confrontation during which those who oppose abortion will try to shut down the abortion clinics in Southern California. They'll crawl through the doors if necessary and sit in.

It is also the beginning of a three-day period during which those who favor abortion will try to stop those who oppose abortion from shutting down the clinics in Southern California. They'll link arms and stand firm.

The anti-abortionists call themselves pro-life advocates. The pro-abortionists call themselves pro-choice advocates.

You are either for life or for choice. If you favor choice, you're a whore and a murderer, which are terms employed by the attackers. If you are pro-life, you are a sexist pig and a religious nut, which are terms employed by the defenders.

During the Korean War, I tried to engage a gunnery sergeant on the relative merits of communist ideology. "It don't matter what their merits are," the gunny replied. "Shoot them."

Wars are like that. We don't expect any shooting during what the anti-abortionists call the Holy Week of Rescue. But there will be a kind of cultural violence unleashed upon us all. Hatreds will explode like missiles. Words will wound like bullets.

I talked to a woman earlier this week who couldn't wait to shut down the abortion clinics. "God will prove us right," she said, her voice rising. "He will crush them and bless us!"

"Shoot them," the gunny had said.

"We are here to prepare ourselves for the skirmish this week and to be troops in the battles ahead," Robin Schneider says into a cluster of microphones at the press conference.

Behind her is a large poster: "Keep Abortion Safe and Legal." Lady Liberty holds her torch high.

"You are heroes in defense of our civil rights," actress Brynn Thayer says. She's a regular on the series "TV 101." No press conference is complete without a celebrity, however scant and temporary fame might be.

"We are not vigilantes," Schneider says to the trainees. "We do not want to do anything to increase the level of conflict in the three days ahead. Do not wear dangly earrings!"

I write that down, but it occurs to me that I don't know why the defenders of the clinics shouldn't wear dangly earrings. "The pro-lifers grab for them," a pro-choicer explains later. "Necklaces too."

The gunny had said to me, "Write your mother while she's still alive and don't worry about the other side."

Ah, war. Ah, spring. How strange.

March 23, 1989

CHAPTER FOUR

A FAMILY OF FRIENDS

*"Most families don't worry about a daughter until
she fails to show up for breakfast.
And then it's too late."*

—FRANK McKINNEY HUBBARD

TWO DAYS BEFORE CHRISTMAS

I HAVE A FRIEND NAMED JEFFREY WHO IS 3 YEARS OLD AND THE smartest boy in the world.

The reason I know that is he was helping me wrap presents the other day by holding his finger at the juncture of two ribbons when he suddenly said, "Did you know there is bread inside of toast?"

It was a startling revelation to me, so I said, "No, I didn't know that!"

"It's true," he said, suddenly releasing the ribbon. I watched it unravel on the table, a twisting combination of reds and greens, as he walked to the kitchen to retrieve a half-eaten piece of toast.

"Look," he said, forcing open the piece of bread to show me the soft insides. "There's toast on the top and bread inside."

"That's amazing," I said.

"But no butter," he said. "I don't like butter. Do you like butter?"

"I can take it or leave it," I said.

"Why?"

Jeffrey loves whys. He picks passing whys out of the air and from the rain-dampened flowers that grow in our garden. He grabs whys from the stars and from the sleepy things he sees at night just before dropping off.

"I don't know," I said, "Sometimes I like butter, sometimes I don't."

"I don't like vegables," he said, frowning at the memory of carrots and broccoli. "Do you like vegables?"

"I love vegables," I said.

"Why?"

I am not a big present wrapper, requiring as it does a skill beyond any I possess. My mother wrapped presents with a facility that was awesome. She wrapped presents and folded towels. Those were her only talents.

When I wrap, the paper is either too large and I have to cut it, or too small and I have to tape two pieces together. Also I can't get the corners to lie smoothly. They bunch up. My mother's corners never bunched.

This year I had help. Everyone else had gone shopping, and Jeffrey and I were home alone, being friends. My job was to wrap a few presents. His job was to play and see that I stayed out of trouble.

Midway through play he began taking an interest in my effort to hold one end of a ribbon in my teeth while attempting to loop the other into a knot.

"I'll help," Jeffrey said, perceiving my difficulty.

He climbed onto my lap, which blocked my view of the job. I was about to say he couldn't sit there, but stopped myself.

Nature sometimes gives us second chances at being good parents and this was one of them. What I was always too busy to do with my son, I can now do with his son, realizing at last that warm glory of being close.

"Would you like to help me tie a knot?" I asked.

"Why?" he said, letting me guide his finger to the juncture where the ribbons crossed on the package.

I don't think he had intended to ask why that time because he didn't appear to expect an answer. He must have seen a why fluttering in the sunlight that streamed through a window and grabbed it before it could get away.

"I just like you helping me," I said.

He told me about the toast with the bread inside and then said, "You know what? I have a trick." He grabbed a ball that was on the table, waved it around in a theatrical manner and tucked it under his shirt. Then he flung his arms out in a grand gesture. "Ta-da! Magic!"

The magic is in the child, the wonder of a little person growing and learning, filling pockets and purses with as many whys as they can hold, pondering the mysteries of barking dogs and falling rain.

"If I never see another magic trick I'll remember that one," I said.

He nodded solemnly as I gathered up the ribbon again that had unraveled on the table. The ball made a small round place under his T-shirt.

We finished wrapping the present and I was about to make out a name card when it struck me. "You know what?" I said. "I forget what's inside the package and who the present's for."

A why darted past him and around back by the fireplace, but Jeffrey let it go. "Maybe it's peanut butter," he said.

I nodded. "Or maybe a hot dog for the cat."

"You don't wrap hot dogs," he said firmly.

"Why?" I said, finding an old whimsical why in my pocket.

Jeffrey thought about that for a moment and then shrugged. "You want to go for a walk?"

We left the presents and ambled hand in hand up a trail behind the house on a day as sweet as a baby's kiss, watching for a hundred whys in a wind that touched our faces and blew winter's leaves in swirls around this grand and wondrous boy.

December 24, 1996

❖

FOR THE LOVE OF SHANA LEE

I KEEP SEEING THE FACE OF THE BOY, A CHILD OF 3, LOOKING OUT at the world through troubled eyes.

His expression is pensive, a look caught in the microsecond of reflection, a thought emulsified on film, trapped and frozen, the fading spirit of a young life ended.

Who killed Joey Phelps?

The question haunts me.

Who caused him pain? Who triggered soft whimpers in the night? Who finally and with savage brutality struck the blow that damped the last tiny ember of his life?

Who is responsible and why did they do it?

A picture appeared in The Times. Joey Phelps was beaten to death in the bedroom of his Sylmar home. His injuries, a coroner's assistant said, were like "being hit by a truck."

Joey's mother and her boyfriend are accused of felony child abuse. As the case moved toward trial, the mother was also charged with manslaughter.

On the night of Joey's death, a neighbor heard heavy thumping that went on for an hour in the moments past midnight.

Then she heard a soft whimper.

And then there was silence.

In that silence, the heart of Joey Phelps stopped beating, an almost imperceptible disruption in the rhythms of life that pulse around us.

In that instant, he became a face in a photo, a snippet of news that will fade with the passing days.

But Joey left a special imprint on my life, and I'll tell you why.

I'm no stranger to death. I have walked through dark shadows for many years as a Marine at war and a journalist at work.

I have heard cries of pain in such awful vibrato that decades later they enribbon my sleep.

But still …

I see Joey's face with all of its bright promise and sad vision, and it troubles me. Given the circumstances of his fate, it would trouble me at any time, but especially it bothers me today, for there is a sudden sweetness in my own life.

I have a new friend.

Her name is Shana Lee and she was born to the world on a gleaming, wind-swept morning into a family that adores her.

She's beautiful and I'm crazy about her.

"I keep doing this," her pixie mother said to me, "just so you'll have something more to write about."

Then she handed me that special little girl and said, "Meet Shana Lee."

I held her in my arms and shared the life burning within her, as elemental as the howling night winds that brushed pastels into the dawn of her birth.

I heard small sounds from new lips and touched the tips of fingers that would one day reach for stars.

"Shana Lee," I said to her mother, "is one hell of a baby."

I held her for a long time, quieting the cries, rocking her gently into sleep, leaving her tucked in soft blankets in a room warm with love.

I returned from the hospital still filled with the wonder of my new friend … and was confronted by the picture of Joey Phelps.

A colleague had left it on my desk because, I'm sure, he felt the same pain I would feel when I looked at the little boy's face and tried to imagine the reach of his anguish in the last terrible seconds of life.

An existence so new, so violently ended.

The picture was left for me to absorb and write about by someone who could never anticipate the dichotomy of emotions it would produce on this special day, or the tones of irony that would shape this column.

I find in the death of Joey a message of brutality that fills me with great sadness, as I find in the birth of Shana Lee a message of love that fills me with elation.

Here was a boy of significant promise brought into a world of troubled circumstances, gone without a chance to ever reach up and out, to touch the stars that Shana Lee will touch.

Who knows what Joey Phelps could have given the world?

Who knows what bright potential gleamed in eyes so suddenly robbed of light?

Life deals us futures laced with chance. Some survive the capricious odds, some don't. One flower lives, another dies. Both share the same sun, the same earth, the same rain.

What genetic acids blend to destroy a Joey Phelps and what wonders combine to give us Shana Lee? What blesses one and condemns the other?

That isn't a new question and there isn't a good answer, but I'll keep asking it and so will you, until someplace down the road we can isolate the factors of savagery that conspire to take a little boy's life on a dark and lonely night.

I hadn't intended this as a requiem for Joey Phelps, because the wonder of Shana Lee is so much with me.

I had only meant to chronicle the sweet, funny, panicky, worrisome moments of birth and greet with trumpets the new friend who will walk with me over trails she has never walked before.

A friend through whose eyes I will view life in tones of color I had not noticed in the past.

Welcome to the world, Shana Lee. Welcome to the world, small beauty.

And, oh yes … goodbye, Joey Phelps.

February 26, 1987

❖

FIFTY YEARS IN ORBIT

IF THERE'S ONE THING I'M GOOD AT IT'S PICKING LINT OFF THE carpet. I'm OK at picture-straightening too, but it's lint-picking that I have refined to the status of art. Bend, reach, snap it up, there goes the lint.

"I will admit you're an expert at it," my wife, Cinelli, said to me last Friday. It was July 30, our 50th wedding anniversary. "Watching you pick lint is like watching Tiger Woods swing his 10 iron."

"I don't think there is a 10 iron."

"Well, whatever. No one picks a better lint. You're the best."

"Are you saying that just because it's our anniversary and you can't think of anything else to say?"

"Not at all," she said. "You do a lot of things pretty well. Let me see, you … er … um…." She thought about it. "You built that towel rack in 1957 at our old house! I'll bet it still stands, not a crack in it." Pause. "I believe that was the last physical work you did? The rack of '57?"

"You've forgotten the fish pond of '82."

"Do we count the fish pond?"

"Why not?"

"Well you dug the hole all right ... but nothing else happened and the hole filled with dirt again."

"Well, to hell with the fish pond then."

"That's what I say, Elmer. To hell with the fish pond."

"Can you believe we've been married 50 years?" I asked.

"Oh, yes," she said, quick as a wink, "I believe it all right, that's for sure, uh-huh, yes-sir, I sure do."

We were in a restaurant overlooking the San Fernando Valley as darkness approached. I could see her reflection in the window facing the view. Lights speckled the night behind her, creating an illusion of stars in her hair.

"You're staring at me," she said.

"I'm studying."

"I feel like a bug under your microscope. What do you see?"

I see a face caressed by time, the way spring deepens into summer. I see a smile that, like a river, changes with the light. I see eyes whose gaze exceeds the horizon. I see roses. I see sunlight.

"How did we manage 50 years of marriage?" I asked.

"By dividing the chores. You write and I do everything else."

There has never been boredom in our marriage. Our points of view crackle with emotion. Our arguments flash and roar like a storm over the ocean.

I can remember a marriage-threatening clash over whose turn it was to feed our old dog Hoover. We broke it down into small elements of time, proving, disproving, maintaining, relating it to other events, demanding, assuring.

The debate lasted 20 minutes. Hoover got tired of waiting. He shuffled into the dining room and ate our dinner right off the table.

I like being with Cinelli. I think that's part of why it's lasted. I mean, we don't wear his-and-her T-shirts or matching jumpsuits, God forbid, but we do like hanging out together. She says I barely make it as a husband but I'm a terrific date. Whatever.

There is no perfect way to sustain a marriage. "Round each curve with caution," a friend once said. It's advice best ignored. We sail the curves at high speed, faces to the gale, laughter to the wind.

Most relationships are Ferris wheels, circling in the same place, seeing the same views. Ours never has been. Think of a Ferris wheel breaking loose and soaring over the Pacific, up past the clouds and into space. Think of a Ferris wheel in orbit.

That's what makes it interesting. We go to Africa. We go to China. We go to the Arctic Ocean. We drive into quiet corners of Europe. We crisscross the United States. The winds of distance call. Adventure beckons. We orbit.

We also understand stability. The importance of family. The maintenance of home. The dedication to work. The need to give back. We understand that life isn't all party. Someone has to pay the bills. Someone has to pick up lint.

An editor said, "What's it like being married 50 years?" It's like renting your first apartment. It's like having your first baby. It's like buying your first house. It's like war and bylines and growing a garden. It's the heat of summer and the cool flow of autumn.

But most of all it's watching the face of someone with stars in her hair and never tiring of it. Time and the seasons pass gently that way.

August 4, 1999

❖

SWEET BYPASS BLUES

I AM LYING IN A BED AT GOOD SAMARITAN HOSPITAL IN ONE OF those gowns that does not cover your behind, when a medical assistant at the foot of my bed says, "OK, let's go." I say, "I've changed my mind."

"Sure you have," he says, loading me onto a gurney. I have already been sedated so I have no strength to rise up and punch him in the mouth, which is my tendency.

"One of these days," I say to my wife, Cinelli, as they wheel me down the hall toward surgery, "I am going to come back and beat the crap out of him."

She is walking beside me holding my hand, as she has always held my hand when times have not been good for me.

"He's pretty big," she whispers. "Maybe you should just plan on writing the crap out of him."

I am sinking deeper into a kind of twilight world, but I do remember thinking as we approach the operating room that there are familiar elements here for something creative, but I can't focus on what that might be.

My surgeon is a preppy young doctor from a famous family; another cardiologist is a cute, perky woman with a Peter Pan haircut. A third is a French-Canadian with Paul Newman eyes, and the anesthesiologist is a hip guy who wears a gold chain around his neck and speaks jive.

Then it hits me. "My God," I say to Cinelli, half-rising from the gurney, "this is a television series and they're wheeling me onto a sound stage."

"I'll call your agent," she says, kissing me gently. Tears shine in her eyes. The door of the operating room opens.

"I wonder if I'll be any taller," I call back, as the world I knew before closes behind me. "They say some people get taller after a bypass...."

I did not come casually to this moment. I hurtled downhill from a place where I smoked cigarettes, drank martinis, ate cows and floated in seas of sauces and whipped cream.

Two of my arteries were clogged and they weren't going to get suddenly unclogged. Miracles don't work for me. That was proved beyond doubt when Cinelli and I spent the night in Lourdes once while driving through France. Where others were being cured at the grotto, I got the flu.

I remember Cinelli saying, "I don't know what somebody's trying to tell you, but I wouldn't ever count on God or Bernadette for quick cures if I were you."

"It's no screaming emergency," the surgeon at Good Sam was saying, "but don't wait until Christmas to have it done."

"All right," I said, "let's do it." I felt like Walter Mitty before the firing squad. To hell with the blindfold.

"Just one thing," I said to the cardiologist. "No country-western music."

I had just seen the film "The Doctor," in which the cardiologist performed surgery to a background of spit-kickin' music. If anything went wrong, I didn't want to die with "Okie From Muskogee" running through my fading subconscious.

"I don't do the procedure to music," he said, peering at me through round, wire-rimmed glasses.

When he left, I turned to Cinelli. "Thank God, it's a procedure, not actual surgery where they have to cut you open."

"You keep bugging them," she said, "it'll be a barbecue."

The surgery, I mean procedure, involved three major risks, the cardiologist with the Peter Pan haircut had said to me earlier. I don't remember the other two, but one of them was death.

"We have to say that," she said, "but I don't think it will be a problem in your case."

She was right. I emerged from the anesthesia cursing the tubes in my nose, my chest and in other areas I do not choose to mention. There is a healing quality to rage. I will not go gentle into that good night.

Also, I did not hallucinate, which was supposed to be a post-procedural problem. At least I don't think I did. Sometimes I'm not sure where reality ends and hallucinations begin. That's why they made me a columnist.

Was I afraid? Everyone's afraid of something. Darkness, pain, memories, the thought of Jerry Brown somehow winning the presidency. My only fear is that I might actually learn to like tofu.

I don't mean to minimize heart bypasses. It's serious business and should not be tried at home on your little friends.

But it's over for me, and I feel like an old alley cat, back prowling the streets again. You helped. You sent cards and left phone messages.

You said, "Come back, old alley cat. Dance under the moon again."

I've been given another chance, one more dance in L.A. It's a kind of renewal, so I'll end this column the way I ended the first I ever wrote, with one variation:

Good morning. My name is Martinez. I write.

Still.

November 7, 1991

WHERE THE WIND SLEEPS

A VERY SMALL AND A VERY WISE LITTLE GIRL TOLD ME ONCE THAT the ocean is where the wind sleeps.

Her name is Nicole. She's 10 now and we went out looking for the wind Saturday on a boat called the Vanguard that sailed to the sea off Ventura.

Well, we weren't actually looking for the wind, I guess, we were looking for whales and we found them pounding through the waves heading toward the Arctic Ocean.

But the wind was out there too, blowing in our face and stinging our skin under a sky as gray as the eyes of a troll, teasing us with a faint remembrance of winter's last shudder.

Whale-watching is something you do this time of the year, because the big mammals follow instincts as old as life, mating and feeding where the lure takes them, responding to rhythms deep in their biological composition.

They've been doing this for more than a million years, migrating back and forth along the coast from the warm lagoons of Baja California to the chilly Arctic seas, and we pay to watch them doing what they'd do for nothing.

There were about 35 human mammals aboard the Vanguard, most of them children, and they loved every plunge of the boat through modest swells toward the open sea.

Nicole and I stood at the bow because, as everybody knows, if you're going to find the wind, that's where you have to be. We were joined by a whole herd of little girls whose laughter trailed like satin ribbons behind us toward the disappearing coastline. Then suddenly someone shouted, "We're there!"

"How do you know you're there if you don't know where you're going?" Winnie the Pooh once asked Christopher Robin, which is a very good question.

I guess the skipper of the Vanguard knew where we were going because pretty soon the big gray whales appeared, cruising along at about 5 miles an hour through the deep green Pacific, 40 tons each of easy determination.

I don't usually go out of my way or pay to watch animals. Mostly I watch the fish in a 30-gallon tank in my writing room, especially the kissing fish.

I don't know what its real name is, but it goes around puckered up looking for something to kiss, like those people in show biz at the Oscars presentation, except that the fish is probably a little more sincere.

The big gray whales didn't kiss or perform much, they just pulsed northward at an even pace, blowing air and spray into the iron gray sky occasionally, diving sometimes to flash their tails to the crowd.

I guess that was performance enough because a lot of the human mammals went crazy with delight, and many of the dedicated animal activists were even elevated to the alpha state by the experience. Some salivated.

Nicole didn't say much, but you could tell she was absorbing the experience and someday it will emerge in a story or a picture because that's what she does. It won't be about just any old whale, however. It will be a magical whale with diamond eyes in a lemonade sea. I know this girl.

Pretty soon the whales went their way and we went ours, and everybody moved to the stern of the boat. Some bought popcorn or hamburgers in the galley, others just sat there trying to stay warm and thinking about the whales.

Nicole and I remained alone at the bow, where the spray floated over us like a bridal veil, and watched the indolent gulls circling overhead, riding the secret currents with effortless curiosity.

This was the best time of the ride for me. The ocean has a way of involving a person, drawing one into its immensity, demanding the complete attention of all human senses. The sea wafts salty perfume on the breeze, pounds the ribs of the boat and dares us to contemplate its horizons.

It's no wonder the wind sleeps here, because only the ocean can provide room enough for its vastness. Sometimes, when the night is still and the dogs aren't barking at the back door, you can hear the soft sigh of the slumbering gale whispering through your dreams.

I explained all of this to Nicole, who nodded in response and kept her face forward, perhaps hearing something no adult could hear, stories told by the wind to children.

The Vanguard slipped into its berth with a dancer's grace, and we all filed off. I saw Nicole look back once and say something, and the air was suddenly still. Perhaps she was telling it good night. I wonder.

March 25, 1997

WATCHING WEDNESDAY'S CHILDREN

THIS IS A SEASON OF PASSAGES, OF JOURNEYS ENDED AND JOURNEYS begun, a time to look back and a time to move on.

Never was this clearer than last Wednesday at Castaic Elementary School, where a friend of mine named Travis Bach said goodbye to the airy pleasures of fifth grade and turned to face the more serious demands of junior high.

He is among 150,000 such students in L.A. County to be moving from the protective embrace of a village atmosphere into a less comforting arena. I wanted all of them to know we understand what they're going through.

Growing up is hard to do.

Travis seemed to sense that as he walked through his schoolyard for the last time. Goodbye to the musty, pale yellow portables, the asphalt with its spidery cracks, the basketball courts, the swings, the rolling brown hills.

Goodbye to little-kid things in a world that demands a quickening maturity, goodbye to innocence in a world that shoves adulthood into children's faces, goodbye to easy safety in a world where peril waits in the shadows.

He said his goodbyes without words, but they were in his eyes and in his expressions. Farewell to all the yesterdays and hello to all the tomorrows in places beyond imagination, in forests of uncompromising newness.

Passages, passages …

Middle school is a difficult time. The instinct to belong, to be accepted, clouds rationality in unformed minds. Swagger was invented in junior high. Gangs form there. Drug dealers haunt the age group.

A door opens at this age to a world that, as poet Robert Nathan wrote, "is changed like the sea in another light, a storm light. A world of raging waves and sudden terror."

I thought about that on Wednesday as 91 fifth-grade students of Castaic Elementary rose to accept their certificates of promotion from Principal Beverly Knutson, each of them saying goodbye in his or her own way.

Among them were Christian Velazquez and Sharonjeet Ghuman and

Chris Tsangarakis and Ryan Neal and Jose Uribe and Ala Hadji and Melissa Holbrook and Jeremy Schwartz … and my friend Travis.

He stood straight and tall before the microphone, and thanked his teachers and his parents for seeing him through the first five grades of his life, then crossed the stage to his chair with the stride of a dragon slayer.

I remember him from smaller steps in days past, when he was 2 and I took his hand in mine and we walked slowly through a misty rain up a trail of the Santa Monica Mountains.

I see him on a hilltop looking toward a far horizon, feeling the wind, then throwing his head back, mouth open, to taste the distance. And I see him years later on his first day of school, glancing back to toys scattered on the lawn, and taking 5-year-old steps toward this today, this here, this now.

Passages, passages …

There was a sense of family in the steamy auditorium of Castaic Elementary. It was just before the heavy rainfall, and the day dripped with humidity. Even a breeze that whispered through the open doors of the building bore the hot, moist traces of a coming storm.

"Each of you has brought something special to our school," Knutson told her fifth-graders. "You come from almost every continent on the planet. You speak nine different languages. You have brought us many pleasures…."

They were words meant for Daniel Esiquio, Jeremy Linebager, Aanont Santisaranyu, Lauren Mazzeo, Allan Jones, Eda Tangco … and Travis Bach.

"Today is the day we can go on with our journey," Knutson said. "We have learned to rely on each other. You will be missed."

There is a kind of melancholy to growing up, and a kind of bravery too. In rituals as old as summer, the young move beyond our protective vision to chart their own way through dark and unmapped woods.

This isn't easy. Not all birds fly swiftly. Not all small animals escape their predators. To continue into the unknown takes courage in the hearts of those to whom courage is new. To choose the right path takes judgment where none existed before. They must be acquired quickly in junior high school.

I tried to tell Travis that as we left the schoolyard, even as I once told his mother, Linda, a long time ago. Be brave. Be swift. Choose carefully.

And take my love with you wherever you go.

Passages, passages ...

June 20, 1995

❖

GIGGLES IN GOTHAM

EVERY TIME I VISIT NEW YORK, I REALIZE HOW MUCH I HATE IT.

I hate the noise, the traffic, the hype, the crowds, the prices and the extravagant size of everything.

And every time I leave New York, I realize how much I miss it. I miss the noise, the traffic, the hype, the crowds, the prices and the extravagant size of everything.

I can understand the longing of those who abandon the high drama of Manhattan to make money in our languishing City of Dreams. There are no masses to jostle them here, no din to addle them, no taxis to terrify them.

There is an emptiness in the heads of displaced New Yorkers where once calamity dwelled. They never stop aching for the place poet Byron Newton described as

> *Vulgar of manner, overfed,*
> *Overdressed and underbred,*
> *Heartless, Godless, hell's delight,*
> *Rude by day and lewd by night.*

One can readily see why it can be an almost spiritual longing.

L.A. is no New York, and the difference is more than just buildings and bustle. It's in the Manhattan attitude: the stride, the swagger, the arched eyebrow, the icy disdain. And it's in their, well, ever-present cockadoodledooing.

Which is why we took our good friends Nicole and Shana there last week.

My wife, the luminescent Cinelli, wanted them to see America's ultimate island before it sinks under the weight of its own ego. The girls are 15 and

125

ready to expand their worlds beyond the limitations that dependency impos-
es.

Soon, in the time it takes for an eye to blink, for a laugh to fade, for a tear
to dry, they will be out there on their own, daring, risking, experiencing. We
wanted to give them a small head start.

In New York, they discovered a new world. And I rediscovered the
teenage girl-giggle.

It is an expression of delight that brings the tinkle of wind chimes to a
moment of silence, a burst of bubbles into the quiet air.

A girl-giggle can pop into existence without warning and without apparent reason. With Nicole and Shana, as it once was with my own daughters, a
giggle is an acknowledgment of secret moments.

Adolescent girls see things we miss, funny things that fly by and tickle
their noses, outrageous things that stick out their tongues and make faces.
Magic flourishes where teenagers walk.

And, yet, there were silences too as we toured Manhattan, moments of
observation that continue to resonate: Nicole, viewing the dot that is Earth in
a mass of galaxies at New York's stunning new Hayden Planetarium: "We're
so tiny." Shana, viewing a photographic wall of diverse faces on Ellis Island:
"We're all immigrants."

Each day was different in the exploration of new places. A stroll through
Central Park became a walk on the moon. A view from the top of the Empire
State Building was a sight from outer space.

At night, there were elegant, dressed-up dinners at Tavern on the Green
and Cafe des Artistes, an introduction to manners they will need when the giggling years have passed.

As I watched them carefully sipping their iced teas and selecting the correct
forks, I realized how sophisticated they can be, how proper and grown-up.

Were these the tiny babies I once carried in my arms? Were theirs the
small hands I held as we walked tree-shrouded pathways and wondered at
things that scurried in the bushes? How swiftly the years pass, how swiftly the
stages of life blur one into the other.

We took them to Broadway shows, to museums and to art galleries. We rode taxis, buses, subways and a horse carriage. And as cool as teenage girls occasionally try to be, the child's wonder in their eyes glowed.

At the end of it, as we left the small and lovely Hotel Salisbury, a final touch of luxury was a stretch limo to the airport. If we expected aloof sophistication here, what we got were two girls, too high for cool, giggling and waving back at the Manhattan skyline, their laughter trailing like silver ribbons toward the lofty horizon, a gift to the Big Apple from the City of Dreams.

Only on the flight home did quiet set in. Two young adults thought their private thoughts and wondered their silent wonders and remembered how it had been, before New York, when they were still children.

August 6, 2001

❖

HISTORY THROUGH A CHILD'S EYES

IT WAS HOT, IT WAS WET, IT WAS SMOGGY AND IT WAS THUNDERY IN Washington, D.C., last week, but by God through it all the flag was still there.

There was even a 45-minute power outage on the western end of Pennsylvania Avenue near the White House, but one could see by the light of a big, yellow moon that the flag was still there.

And when lightning flashed and thunder shook the world, beating like drums against the corridors of power, the flag still whipped bravely against the gray and unsettled skies, its colors flashing defiance to the turmoil.

The observation in all instances was made with some wonder by my good friend Travis, who had accompanied my wife and I to the nation's capital in celebration of his 13th birthday.

It was as though he were seeing the flag for the first time, overwhelmed by its presence in a setting of history and power, and he wanted me to see it that way too.

I'm not taken much with symbols, whether it's a national emblem or the logo on a jar of peanut butter. You won't find me out there campaigning for laws against the desecration of either one.

But witnessing anything through the eyes of a child is always a new experience no matter how many times one has seen what the child sees, and the sight of the flag was that way with me. Its colors glowed with a special radiance.

The trip was not intended to be taken in close proximity to Independence Day or to furnish me with a column on the 221st birthday of the nation, but I'm grateful for the coincidence.

I am also grateful for the equally coincidental thunder and darkness in Washington during our stay, for they are likely to fix what we saw into Travis' memory the way clashing cymbals punctuate a Stravinsky opus.

One is never certain what is absorbed by the young and what is discarded. Pubescence, if it isn't in full animation, often wears a mask. Was he bored? Did he hear? Does he care?

I wondered about it as we stood at the foot of a Thomas Jefferson statue in the rotunda of his memorial, looking up at the image of a man who in real life stood taller than any monument we could ever build.

I'm not good at teaching lessons, so I simply allowed Travis to assimilate in silence what he was seeing. When he finally asked, "Who was he?" all I could think to do was read words from the Declaration of Independence chiseled into a wall of the memorial. "When in the course of human events...."

Travis listened without comment, and then stood back to take pictures of the man whose words and vision had shaped the contours of history's best effort at government by the people.

"He was the principal author of the Declaration," I said as we walked down the stairs. "He articulated freedom."

Travis nodded. "Cool," he said.

Both my wife and I sensed the boy's growing awe with what he was seeing by the way he hung on every word during a debate in the Senate, viewed with hushed silence the rooms of the White House and dismissed with scorn an incident on the steps of the Lincoln Memorial.

"Did you hear what she said?" he asked in a tone of derision, referring to a woman and a young boy. "She said, 'This is where "Forrest Gump" was filmed.' Is that all she thinks this is?"

We sat on the steps for a while and ate red, white and blue Popsicles and watched flags flutter in the sticky air down the sides of the Reflecting Pool where peace marchers once gathered and where Martin Luther King Jr. voiced his dream in words still heard across the land.

There was much we wanted to show Travis, and we wore ourselves out visiting America's repositories of history: the National Archives, the Smithsonian, the Washington Monument, the FDR Monument, the U.S. Holocaust Museum....

We saw memorials to war and talked about the wrenching pain of war's reality and a growing awareness of its futility. I wanted Travis to know that a free society should ultimately grow beyond cruelty. Even as it beats its chest, it clears its mind. We learn. We evolve.

"We haven't always done everything right," I said as we concluded our trip. "But most of the time we do the best we can. We try."

The sky darkened and lightning flashed as we rode to Dulles International Airport. Thunder boomed over the White House and the U.S. Capitol and over the Jefferson Memorial, truly the drums of history and remembering.

In the sense that his observations were metaphorical as well as true, Travis was correct. We have endured many storms during the past 221 years. And the flag is indeed still there.

July 4, 1997

THE FIRST BIG STEPS

I HAVE A FRIEND NAMED NICOLE WHO IS 11 MONTHS OLD AND who took the first unassisted step in her life last week.

She hung tentatively to the tiniest edge of a coffee table, one small finger alternately touching and releasing the corner, and then with a courage we can only imagine, she walked.

It was not a long journey by the standard of miles she must trod down the years of her life, only a few unsteady steps across the golden tile. But oh, what a distance.

When she reached the window box that was her ultimate destination, she turned and flashed a smile as sweet as the first sunrise, holding it with an instinctive pride that wanted this moment in summer never to be forgotten.

I admit to a total lack of neutrality toward this dark-eyed girl who has entered my life with such light and warmth, and regard with special consideration whatever milestone she achieves on her journey from the cradle.

A step has special significance.

First words are less obvious to define, since babies seem to leap from the womb shouting mama and dada, and mothers are always prone to believe that nagobodoodimyma means energy equals mass times the speed of light squared.

In Nicole's case, that's probably true, but since she is no doubt saying it in Latin, I can't be sure.

A first step is a more obvious triumph, a visual motion toward the years ahead, a symbolic leap from the starting blocks, arms pumping, energy burning.

The image of that beautiful child standing proudly at her destination stayed with me throughout the day, and that night I tried to imagine where the first step might ultimately take my sunshiny Nicole.

It was after midnight and everyone was asleep.

I sat at my desk in a quiet house and shuffled through stories I had clipped from newspapers during the week, wondering how I might measure

Nicole's first step against an era fraught with special dangers.

They weren't clippings of major stories, not bloodstains on the Persian Gulf or the death of honor in Washington, but instances of more immediate peril in our own neighborhoods.

A young policeman murdered trying to stop a dope sale. A small boy killed in a drive-by shooting. A pit bull that savaged three innocent people. A prep school closed because its owner could no longer tolerate teenage hostility. A Jewish temple desecrated with Nazi symbols.

Each incident isolated an area of danger Nicole must face as her first few steps grow to a dozen steps and the dozen to millions.

It won't be an easy journey.

Quiet rural neighborhoods have become war zones, and our homes exist on perimeters of self-defense, bristling with dogs and weapons and alarms that scream like banshees in the night.

A disregard for life has become so acute that even drive-by shootings on the freeways of Los Angeles are a numbing reality, introducing random factors into urban assaults that chill the blood.

We face a growing realization, perhaps not yet a fact, that schools aren't safe, parks aren't safe, neighborhoods aren't safe, freeways aren't safe, buses aren't safe, dogs aren't safe and even the kid next door is suspect.

A night walk invites disaster, an open window risks horror.

I'm not a philosopher and I'm not a social psychologist. I have no idea why violence grows and peril rides the winds. I can't remember when cocaine became a status symbol and gunfire a form of street talk.

I only know, as a friend of mine says, that it's a distorted time in history, and ironies abound in a society that seems oddly out of sync.

Neighbors shout because a woman keeps a miniature horse in her yard, but silence greets the death of a small boy in a bloody drive-by.

Two young women are arrested for selling roses without a license in L.A. and Bernhard Goetz goes free after shooting four teenagers in New York.

The homeless are pulled from the gutters of skid row only to complain about the dirt of the earth that surrounds their free tent homes.

Thugs rule our streets and fools run our governments, and the rest of us struggle to survive in a world beyond the looking glass.

Into this, Nicole took her first step, and I worry where the trail might lead.

I walked through the silent house and up the stairs to where she slept in her crib, an angel wrapped in the serenity of warmth and infancy.

How I wish there were ways I could shield her from the calamities of violence and protect her from the hounds of misfortune that bound through the back alleys of night.

But I have no magic to shape her future and no amulets to guard her life, so I kissed her gently on the cheek and climbed into my own bed.

I lay awake for a long time thinking about a little girl stepping tentatively across a sun-splashed floor, and then brooded over a moment in summer that couldn't last forever.

June 29, 1987

❖

MY SISTER EMILY

MY SISTER EMILY CALLED FROM OAKLAND ON SUNDAY NIGHT after the latest verdicts in the Rodney King case.

"Are you all right?" she asked in an anxious voice.

"I'm fine."

"I worried about you during The Trouble."

"There was no trouble," I said. "Everything is normal."

"Are you sure?"

"Of course I'm sure. We couldn't be more normal. There was a car fire on the San Diego this morning, a mattress on the Ventura and a naked fat lady hitchhiking on the Hollywood. Life goes on in post-Verdict L.A."

"I prayed for you."

She has been praying for me for 50 years.

She prayed for me when I discovered sex, when I entered college, when I went to war, when I began drinking martinis and when I moved to L.A.

Since I have managed to survive all those episodes, she gives full credit to her supplications. It's like the guy who hangs garlic on his door to protect him from vampires. Laugh at him and he says, "I've never been bitten by one, have I?"

Emily, like everyone else, doesn't believe the media. She is certain there was trouble in L.A. but it is being covered up.

"Let me assure you," I said, "there was more chaos in our house Saturday than there was in the South-Central section of the city."

Our grandchildren were over for the weekend. Travis, Shana and Nicole. They ran hooting clockwise through the house.

Nicole led the rampage. "Everybody holler and wave their arms!" she said.

"I'm not sure there still won't be trouble," Emily said.

"Don't do this to me. We've come through a long, cold winter of the soul. Let it be."

"But you still have elections coming up," she warned. Dire warnings are as much a part of Emily as drool is to a baby.

"Our elections don't cause riots. They're never that exciting. The most noteworthy moment of this campaign, for instance, was when one candidate almost drowned trying to hold an underwater press conference."

"Oh, my God," Emily said. "I'll pray for him."

"I think it's too late."

"He died?"

"No, but he hasn't got a chance in hell of winning."

I became more emphatic.

"Look," I said, "the crisis is past in L.A. We're OK, really. There are bluebirds over the white cliffs of Dover."

Emily loved the songs of World War II. She still prays for them.

"What about that boogie-woogie concert?"

She meant the rap concert at Six Flags Magic Mountain.

"That was just your normal too-many-people, not-enough-seats rap and civic disturbance concert. Psychologists would explain it by saying those unable to get in suffered flashbacks of infantile rejection and were expressing repressed anger."

"Didn't they break windows at some restaurant?"

"That had to do with self-hatred," I explained. "They were smashing their own reflected images. They'll be on the Phil Donahue show Thursday to explain everything."

"I'll pray for them."

I was delighted to report to Emily how truly boringly calm everything seemed to be that Sunday night.

I had watched the 11 o'clock news just to be sure. There wasn't even an animal atrocity in Sun Valley.

Emily called after the newscast was over. She never sleeps. Good Catholics are always on the alert for evil.

When I was 12, I ran away from home. They found me sinking in quicksand at the Oakland Estuary at 3 o'clock in the morning.

Emily was ready. She prayed for me. "Thank God you're safe," she said when they dragged me out.

"You rotten little scum," a Protestant cop said. "You do this again, I'll break every bone in your mackerel-snapping body."

"Torture him," my sister Mary said. She was less merciful than Emily.

When we got home, Emily gave me the Dutch rub. It consisted of rubbing one's knuckles hard over the victim's head. She was not completely without what Horace called "a transient madness."

"That'll keep him out of the muck," Mary said. "Now smack him."

By the time Emily hung up Sunday night, she was reasonably convinced she had once more conned God into looking out for me.

"But if there's even the hint of trouble," she admonished, "you call me right away."

That goes without saying. There's nothing like prayer, bullets and fear of the old Dutch rub to ward off the evil spirits of L.A.

April 20, 1993

NO RECKONING WITH HOMEWORK

EVERY ONCE IN A WHILE, SOMEONE CALLS UPON ME TO HELP them with their homework, which is usually a mistake.

So when my friend Jeffrey needed assistance with math one day, my wife suggested that perhaps I wasn't the person for the job.

"We're all grateful that you were the first to teach him to recognize the shape of a martini glass," she said, "but I'm not sure math is your strongest point."

"He's in the third grade, for God's sake," I said. "If I can't do third-grade math, we're all in trouble."

"Then you've learned a lot since our own kids were in the third grade," she said with a shrug. "Good luck, Jeffrey."

OK, so I'm a little slow on multiplication, but give me 2 plus 8 or even 16 into 42 and I'm sailing, baby.

"It isn't exactly math," Jeff said, opening his folder. "It's called reasoning."

"Hey," I said, "I did that in school. 'You've got three people on one side of a river and one boat. How do you get them across the river in two trips with only one person in the boat at a time?' Or something like that."

"Did you solve it?"

"No, Jeff, I didn't. They all died of hunger on the same side of the river."

"Oh, Grandpa."

He handed me a paper. "Try this one," he said.

He visits once a week. Sometimes we watch Animal Planet together. Sometimes I tell him stories. Always we snuggle.

"Let me see," I said, reading from the paper: "Marie and Emily will stand side by side. Marie has blue eyes, but Emily does not. Marie will stand in front of someone who does not have brown eyes. Marie and Emily both have red hair. Howard will stand behind a girl. John will not stand behind Howard. Howard has brown eyes, but John does not. John will stand behind a girl with red hair."

My wife walked through the room. "… And Elmer is sitting next to Jeffrey looking perplexed and wondering how he's going to squirm out of this one."

"I'm not a bit perplexed," I said. "I just have to simplify the problem."

She calls me Elmer because I mumble when I answer the phone. Sometimes people think I'm saying my name is Elmer Teenez.

"Admit it," she said. "Your mathematical logic is limited to '99 Bottles of Beer on the Wall,' and I can remember times when you failed that."

"Don't worry, Jeff," I said when she'd left the room, "we'll solve this sucker. First of all, we'll change the names."

"I don't think the names are important," he said.

"Good stories," I explained, "always have intriguing names. Emily and Howard, for instance, are not intriguing names. How about Jorge and Tiffany?"

He laughed. I love hearing kids laugh. "I don't think my teacher wants Jorge and Tiffany," he said.

The object of the problem was to put each person in his or her proper place, eliminating inessential clues. We didn't get stuff that hard until my third year in college. Times have changed.

"You sure Miss What's-Her-Name didn't confuse your paper with something she was using for her master's thesis?" I asked. "It's pretty advanced."

"Her name is Miss Stalcup," Jeffrey said. "Everybody has the same homework."

Teachers never have first names. It was a policy established at the start of the 20th century. They had to drop their first names in order to teach. Also, they had to wear sensible, flat-heeled shoes and be quick to spot anyone chewing gum.

I read from another paper: "Bob ran 5 miles. Rita ran 3 times as many miles as Bob. Jan ran 2 more miles than Bob. Nan ran as far as Bob and Jan together. Pete ran 4 miles less than Nan. Lee ran twice as many miles as Bob."

"It's a junior track meet," Jeffrey explained. "The winners get medals."

"In high school, I ran the 100-yard dash," I said. "Once I did it in 10.3. I was gold-medal material in those days, Jeff. I remember running against Oakland High. There were these hotshot twins. Swedes. Two of the ugliest kids I'd ever seen. Their father used to sit in the top row of the bleachers and spit on the milers as they passed by. One day their mother … "

"What're you doing?" Cinelli demanded, standing in the doorway.

"We're doing a paper on reasoning."

"You sure it's not a paper on disgusting events from your past?"

"I'm trying to add color to an otherwise uninspiring problem."

"I'd better do the helping here," she said. "You'll have little martini glasses running around the field or hookers standing in a circle."

Too bad she took over. We were getting to the easy part. "On Tuesday, David saw 3 squirrels and 8 chipmunks. On Wednesday, he saw 6 chipmunks and 1 squirrel. How many squirrels did David see on both days?"

Stay with me. I'll have it in a minute.

November 5, 2001

❖

TASTING THE DISTANCE

I HAVE A VERY GOOD FRIEND NAMED TRAVIS WHO IS 2 YEARS OLD and who is going through a negative stage. I do not understand many of the stages of growing up and growing old. Midlife, for instance, escapes me completely, and I don't ever remember being a teenager.

I do, however, understand the negative stage since it is one, for God's own whimsical reasons, I have never grown out of. I therefore relate to Travis, and sometimes we wander up a trail in the Santa Monica Mountains together and shake our heads and say no and uh-uh and to hell with it.

Most people I know feel that I probably ought to encourage Travis to be more positive, because he might not grow up to be a newspaper columnist and there are very few other occupations that require or will even tolerate a nature such as mine.

But these people do not understand the essential elements of the kind of negativity Travis and I embody. It is offered by my small friend, for example, with a shrug and a smile and sometimes with a sound of laughter so sweet it is almost like music.

He says no with a twinkle, and while I would rather cut out my tongue than twinkle, I realize that the nature of a no is often shaped by, if not a twinkle, a wry grin.

Travis and I discussed this the other day as we meandered along a trail that begins near my house in the Santa Monicas.

A light rain was falling and occasionally Travis would throw back his head and open his mouth to catch the moisture. I took his hand to guide him while he was thus involved and not watching the ground. It is a small hand, warm and trusting.

"The thing is," I said to him, "those of us who are negative are not easily understood by those who are positive, namely people with 'I Love God' bumper stickers on their modest Honda Civics."

"Nope," Travis replied.

"Being negative involves the ability to say the truth when the truth is not popular," I observed.

He said, "Uh-uh."

"Do you mean," I continued, as he turned around once to see if the rain would turn with him, "that you agree or disagree with me?"

"Hellit," Travis replied.

"We're going to have to work on that one," I said.

Travis is learning to talk quite well, but he seems to be having trouble saying "to hell with it." We practice the phrase once in a while because I feel it is important for a negative person to be able to dismiss criticism with a cluster of words that are simultaneously negative, noncommitive and all-inclusive.

"To hell with it" does not single out any one group or even any one event, but summarizes a good-natured feeling of frustration and impatience with, well, everything.

"Are you really teaching him to say 'to hell with it'?" Travis' mother asked one day, not quite believing that even I could stoop so low. Her name is Linda.

"Someone has to teach him," I said, "and it might as well be me. I am quite good at it actually."

Linda has known me for a very long time, so she just shook her head and smiled.

"Boy," I heard her say to her mother, "you really married a nut."

Meanwhile, back on the trail:

"In terms of negative," I said to Travis, "you must ..."

"Nope," he interrupted.

"You have to wait until I'm finished," I said.

He said nope again and no and hellit and shook his head and added "Mine!," which is his entire repertoire.

Then he laughed, because he understood, that bright little boy, what a good joke he was playing on his old pal.

"Well," I said, "maybe you're right, Trav. Because, I guess, if you're conscious of your own negativism, then you aren't really negative, are you?"

He threw his head back again to catch the rain in his mouth, tasting the place where storms are born. He closed his eyes and spread his arms at the same time. He was pretending he was flying, which shows a depth of wisdom difficult to find in one so young. He understood that the spirit soars when rain falls.

I mention this today only because while searching about for a holiday column, I began to realize that I was awfully grateful to have Travis around. He has defined for me the nature of no in a manner that explains my own sour approach to life.

Travis catches rain in his mouth because rain is real, and he takes my hand because his trust is real. Words are bubbles that pop and disappear. No is a game people play.

"You're a very nice boy, Travis," I said, "and I'm terribly glad to have you around this holiday season. I only wish everyone had someone as perceptive as you."

He laughed a laugh that enribboned the dark day with a light of its own. Then he shook his head no very, very hard, as hard as a boy of 2 can shake it, and he said, "Yes!"

I picked him up and hugged him and walked along the trail with Travis in my arms. His head was thrown back, his eyes were closed and his arms were outspread. We were flying.

December 5, 1985

❖

A STORM FILLED WITH PROMISE

I HAVE A NEW FRIEND.

His name is Joshua. He was born on a day when rain darkened the sky and thunder rolled through the clouds, drumming in the presence of a new baby. When the storm had marched on, a full moon shone down, filling the night with an iridescent glow.

It was a time of high drama over the City of Dreams, as well it should have been for a moment so significant. Joshua is, after all, destined for great things.

He indicated as much as I held him in my arms on the third floor of West Hills Hospital, 7 pounds 14 ounces of life and wisdom. Like Plato, he asked questions, and like Aristotle, he listened.

We communicated in the way that adults employ with their new friends, a link that is instantly established not in spoken words, but in a manner that transcends speech. I can't explain it, but does such a moment really need explaining?

He asked the nature of the world into which he was being born, and I said, "Look around you."

I don't know that babies could ever have a better support system than Joshua. Pride and love glowed in the eyes of his parents, his sister and his brother, and in the eyes of those of other generations to whom new life will always be a wonder.

"Yes," Joshua said. "I see." Then he said, "But what about the rest of the world?"

Oh, Joshua.

It is at once a world of wonder and danger, of thunder and full moons. Humanity remains as unsettled as the air that vibrates in a storm, and as dominating as a moon that rules the night.

In practical terms, that means governments are still killing each other for God and country in battles I'm sure God never intended, over land that ought to belong to everyone. Fools and maniacs call for blood, and the people follow like mindless packs of hungry wolves.

We continue to honor instincts rooted in our predatory past, Joshua, in that dark time before human history. Although the brain has become more complex, the abstractions of compassion and patience still elude us.

We are no closer to a peaceful world than we were in your father's time and in my father's time. Violence chains us to the past. We are prisoners of our history.

Having said that, small boy, I also promise days of laughter and fulfillment as you journey over the hills and into the forest.

To the extent that we're willing, we create individual destinies apart from the world's savageries, and are capable of shaping the misty qualities of our ambition into firm and shining substance.

Resist the urge to ignore. Never look the other way. Involve yourself.

We had a good talk, Joshua and I.

And as we pondered the world, I rocked him gently and watched as his hand reached out, touching the new place in his existence, leaving a handprint on the stormy air.

Then he slept.

There is so much more I can tell him, and as the years pass, I will. I'll describe the heady nature of success and the deep pain of failure, so he'll know the faces of both.

I'll take him on walks up the trails that surround our home and point out the trees and the horizons. I'll walk him in the sun so that he will know warmth, and in the rain so he will know storms.

I'll show him the ocean, where my concept of endlessness began. And I'll tell him how I crossed that ocean to face a war, where my concept of endlessness ended.

Being a boy of keen awareness, Joshua will, of course, learn without me. His parents will teach him, and so will his brother and sister. He will learn in school and learn in life. He will absorb the messages that are transmitted from a thousand different sources and filter from them the essence of knowledge that leads to achievement.

I'll tell him stories and take him to places in the imagination where trolls and poets live, and to corners of the mind where the fairies hide.

But my real job for now is just to hold him in my arms and feel the warmth of new life against the cooling fabric of an older life. My real job is to dream with him, because it's what I do best. My real job is to condense reams of advice and oceans of experience into the simplicity of a single syllable.

My real job is to hold my new grandson close and whisper to him the most powerful of all words: "Care." That's the best I can offer.

February 11, 2001

❖

DANCING UNDER THE MOON

I SUSPECT THAT THOUSANDS OF PEOPLE LEAVE LOS ANGELES every week to live somewhere else, and on Friday, a day brushed by Santa Anas and laced with falling leaves, one of them was a little girl named Nicole.

Nicole, her father and her mother packed up a yellow Ryder truck, and just as the morning was edging toward noon, they left for Eureka, where the redwoods reach the sea and the air rings with the clarity of chimes.

They leave our house in the glow and silence of memories.

If you will abide a personal column for just this day, I'll tell you how it feels to heed the rhythms of life that determine when movement is required, when, quite simply, it is time to go.

Marty and Lisa moved in with us almost three years ago to buy the time required to save money and to solidify their new life together. Into that new life was born Nicole, my granddaughter.

Ours became a house suddenly under siege. I had not even seen a diaper or a pacifier or a bassinet for more years than I care to remember, and suddenly I was surrounded by them.

I am, by nature, a tidy and efficient man, easily riled by simple disruptions and driven mad by chaos.

My life, when not occupied with writing, is given over to straightening pictures on the wall, putting magazines in neat piles and picking almost infinitesimal pieces of lint off the carpet.

No one in the whole history of Western civilization has been better at spotting lint.

But babies turn households into shambles and shred with singular determination any inclination toward tidiness.

The presence of Nicole in every room, from toy stoves to small, lacy dresses, could have been the very essence of disruption to a man like me.

It wasn't.

There was something special about this girl with the eyes of a pixie and the smile of an autumn morning that almost immediately captured my heart, and as she grew, the attraction increased.

As quick as a hummingbird, as enchanting as a field of wildflowers, Nicole filled the corners of my life with experiences I had not encountered since my own children stopped dragging the cat around by his tail.

Here were my kids all over again in microcosm, learning to walk, learning to talk, reaching toward the upper shelf, trying to sing, demanding the world but settling for a hug.

Nicole is a child of rare sensitivities, as the very young often are, and she defined my moods with a maturity beyond her age. She knew when to laugh with me, when to avoid me and sometimes when to simply touch me.

Moments with her were filled with enchantment.

I saw her one evening on the back deck of our home in the Santa Monica

Mountains as she studied the wonder of a starry sky. She looked for a long time and then turned to me and said, "Let's dance under the moon, Grandpa!"

It was a full moon, and it lit the night with the kind of secret half-light that illuminates dreams and fairy tales, only half-real and vaguely perceived.

Along with my tidiness goes a reluctance to perform. Dancing under the moon was not high on my list of things to do.

But I was being summoned by a poet who saw magic in the union of movement and moonlight, who sensed the exhilaration of that night and the imagery it evoked.

So we danced under the moon, Nicole and I, me with my clumsy feet and her with her butterfly grace....

Dances end. Moonlight fades. Wind shakes the liquidambar trees bare, and time flickers past like fireflies in the night. Fridays come before we know it.

And on this Friday it was time for them to leave.

I'm terrible at goodbyes. My wife is able to articulate all the emotions I am too tongue-tied to express. I stand like a fool in the midst of last moments, hoping the wind that touches their faces will say my love and the sun that shines on their new life will warm their memories.

This is a difficult column for me to write, but write it I must and write it I will because there is universality to the rhythms of life we must all heed, observing rites of passage that clock our rush to darkness.

Our house will be tidy again and the pictures straightened and the magazines piled neatly on the coffee table, but the flow and the magic are gone and that saddens me.

I just don't feel like dancing under the moon anymore.

November 5, 1988

THE DOG THAT ATE TOPANGA

I AM SITTING HERE WITH MOUNDS OF THINGS TO WRITE ABOUT that will enlighten future generations and change the course of human history, but I'm going to put that aside for a moment and instead say goodbye to a dog.

His name was Hoover and he glared at me for the last time the other day, nuzzled me to say the glare was all show and then closed his eyes forever.

It wasn't a bad way to go.

Every old dog faces death sooner or later. Hoover was 18 by human standards. Everyone has a different idea of what that means in dog years, but he was up there, that's for sure.

My wife, Cinelli, brought him home as a puppy. He took an instant disliking to me and tried desperately to get away. In his haste to escape, he ran into a wall.

"Is he blind?" I asked. She shook her head. "I think he's just dumb."

Well, he was dumb all right and not very pretty, with a long pointed nose and beady, close-set eyes that seemed incredibly empty.

Hoover lived well and fell apart slowly, remaining fiercely independent to the very end. His last act of mischief was to maim our cat so badly that it cost me $800 to have her patched up again, and then the coyotes got her.

At the rate I paid to have the cat restored, it was like they were dining at Rex il Ristorante.

There are about 50,000 dogs in L.A. County, and the death of one will not cause any disruptions in the rhythms of animal life. But still, I'll miss the old hound and his annoying mannerisms.

We kept him in a large fenced yard of his own because he had a habit of trashing everyone's garbage can in the area and they'd come knocking at my door with mayhem in their eyes.

He also had a habit of sleeping in the middle of the street, forcing cars to stop and drivers to get out of their cars to chase him away. They'd have to do that two or three times because Hoover would return to the middle of the street as they were getting back into their cars. Then, finally, he'd tire of the game and saunter off triumphantly after having caused someone an incredible amount of misery.

I wanted to get rid of the dog almost from the first moment I laid eyes on him. He was impossible to train, was never housebroken and barked in a high-pitched falsetto that caused neighbors to believe I was beating him.

When we fenced a portion of the yard for him, he spent his life scratching at the door to get in. Most dogs will scratch for, say, 15 minutes and give up. Hoover would scratch steadily for hours at a time, and such was his persistence that he wore a hole in the door. It's still there.

He disappeared once and I thought he was gone forever, so I wrote a touching column about the old dog that vanished in the rain. But I'll be damned if he didn't return, causing me no end of embarrassment. It was one of the few times I saw him smile.

I'm looking for a new dog now. An online service says that the ideal pet for me would be a Jack Russell terrier. The breed was created by a British preacher obsessed with sin and fox-hunting.

I'm not interested in flushing foxes or owning a dog that can recite the 29th Psalm. I just want an animal that can learn a few commands, bark at burglars and not urinate on the rug. His religious beliefs are his own.

Cinelli came home one day recently dragging what looked like a clump of used rags at the end of a rope, and when I asked what it was, she said it was a dog. I damned near died.

"I'm not having another homely animal in the house," I said.

"His name is Dave."

"I don't care if his name is Franklin Roosevelt, he's as ugly as a manatee and he's not staying."

Dave had a bark that sounded as though he was saying "wow" in a kind of low-pitched voice. Wow, wow, wow, wow … he went around the house wowing and mumbling. Thank God we were only watching him for a sick friend, and when she got well a couple of days later, Dave went home.

Just after Hoover died, we saw a play called "Sylvia" that featured Stephanie Zimbalist as a dog that barked by saying "Hey!" I told Cinelli that was the dog I wanted, but she said if I thought I was going to spend my life sitting around scratching Stephanie Zimbalist's stomach, I had another think coming.

I'm still looking, but no matter what I come up with, I'll always have a place in my memory for an old dog with a long pointed nose and close-set eyes who stood alone and proud until the day he died.

March 18, 1997

CHAPTER FIVE

ON THE ROAD AGAIN

"The road less traveled is the one we're taking next."

—CINELLI THE DARING

COME BACK TO AFRICA, ROTER

WE WERE BOUNCING OVER ROADS SO POTHOLED AND RUTTED that I was even beginning to miss the Hollywood Freeway when our driver turned to me and said, "You a roter?"

I smiled and nodded because by then I realized that if I asked what he meant, it would just get complicated and we'd never understand each other anyhow.

I, you see, speak mostly English and the driver was speaking mostly Swahili. I felt like a Mexican housekeeper trying to understand the lady of the house.

"What did he say?" my wife asked.

"I don't know," I said.

"Then why did you nod yes?"

"It's an ethnic trait," I said. "When in doubt, smile and nod. Go ahead, test me. Ask me to dust the furniture."

We were in Tanzania.

I realize that's difficult to understand since my column has appeared regularly during my absence, but some things, like astral projection and metaphysical writing, are not meant for mortal comprehension.

Trust me.

We spent three weeks in Africa and, contrary to my own dire predictions, I loved it.

There is no place I have ever been, with the possible exception of an Oakland bar called the Hollow Leg, that is more surreal in its beauty.

Sunsets are not simply sunsets, they are fire in the sky, with burning reds so brilliant they hurt the eye.

Lions are not merely lions, they are absolute masters of their environment, striding through the Masai Mara with all the magnificence of storied royalty.

When a lion hunts, even the wind stops blowing.

The Serengeti. Kilimanjaro. I see them in my dreams. I understand now why Hemingway loved Africa so. It glows. Gleams. A diamond in the sun. Causing short sentences. Few nouns. Occasional verbs.

The toughest part was getting into Tanzania.

Passing through customs was a little like trying to deliver pizza to the Kremlin. The very air shimmered with suspicion.

To begin with, there were four different lines at the Kilimanjaro Airport and no one readily available to direct us to the right one.

When I was finally able to locate someone to ask which line we ought to be in, he said, "All of them."

Oh.

I feel guilty whenever confronted by authority, regardless of its national origin. By the time I got to the guy who checked suitcases for contraband, I was in a cold sweat.

"I know he's going to strip-search me," I whispered to my wife.

"I don't think they do that at airports," she said. "Anyhow, why should he?"

"Because I look suspicious."

"Relax," she said, "you're a tourist, not a rhino poacher."

"Occupation?" the customs officer asked.

"Tourist!" I said, quick as a wink.

My wife cast her eyes heavenward. She was grateful that at least I hadn't said I was a rhino poacher. I tend to crack under stress.

"You work as a tourist?" the customs officer asked, surprised.

"Well no," I said, falling completely apart, "I'm a, er, journal ... that is, I'm a real estate agent."

He stared at me. My mouth twitched. It always twitches when I lie.

I had been told not to say I was a journalist because in Africa, they believe journalists are only a notch above people who tear tusks off living elephants.

"A real estate agent?" the customs officer asked.

I nodded too eagerly.

"Passport!" he commanded.

"Gladly!" My hand shook.

He looked at my passport and then he looked at me, and I was thinking, Dear God, I'm going to die in Africa tied to an acacia tree and eaten alive by red ants.

"I'm a personal friend of Alex Haley," I said. My voice quavered.

"You know," he finally said, handing me back the passport, "you ought to try and get some rest. You look pale."

"I can go?"

"Go, go," he said good-naturedly.

My wife took my arm. "I'm not sure you're going to make it out of the air-port," she said.

Africa.

First Tanzania, then Kenya. There was nothing I didn't like about it. The people. The culture. The weather.

I even liked the lesser kudus. Not as much as the greater kudus, of course, but they were all swift and free and grand in the sweep of mountains and meadows.

"I knew you'd like it," my wife said.

It was her idea to go in the first place. I whined and objected and fell to the floor when she first mentioned it. Now I can't remember why. It is the nature of the writer, I suppose, not to go gentle anywhere.

Our driver in Tanzania was named Shabani and he was special.

We were saying goodbye at the airport. He must have determined that I hadn't understood his question back on the road, so he asked it again.

"You a roter?"

I answered once more with a smile and a nod.

But this time he persisted: "What do you rote?"

153

"Oh," I said, realizing, "that kind of wroter!"

The tourist agency had found me out, I guess, and had informed Shabani.

"Well," I said, "I wrote a column. I mean I write a column. But," I added quickly, "not a very important one."

He smiled and shook my hand.

"Come back to Africa, roter."

Count on it.

October 22, 1987

❖

SNOW ON THE GREAT WALL

IF I CLOSE MY EYES AND LET MY MIND DRIFT BACK A COUPLE OF weeks, I can still see the Great Wall of China dusted with silver in a gently falling snow.

It was the first snow of the season in Beijing, and it gave the wall a mystical appearance as it snaked upward over the hills into a gray mist.

Always when I think of the trip from which we have just returned, I will think of that scene, glowing like a water-brush painting in that place of the mind where we store significant memories.

That, of course, isn't all there is to China and it wasn't all we saw during a three-week odyssey. We bounced around to half a dozen towns, saw the terra cotta army of Xian, cruised the Yangtze, shopped in booming Shanghai and spent more hours waiting in airports than I ever hope to spend again.

We also witnessed snippets of repression under a Communist regime that although mellowing, remains firmly in place over a people whose inclinations seem anything but warlike.

The Chinese, in fact, are the sweetest of individuals, both amused and tolerant of the well-meaning Westerners who try with somber intent to absorb in a few days what it took 6,000 years to build.

All those images will fight for space in memory's cluttered cabinets, but

154

the one that will always emerge will be that of the Great Wall in the silver snow. Dominant impressions always linger.

Which brings me to L.A.

When you're a newspaper columnist, the city you cover is rarely out of mind. I went about as far away as I could and was still confronted with impressions of L.A. by people who don't know it at all.

To them, we're either Disneyland, Hollywood or bloody murder.

What they know is what they pick up in tidbits of information. They might know, for instance, that Demi Moore is trying hard to adjust to life after Bruce Willis, but they know nothing of our struggle to emerge as the new American cosmopolis of the 21st century.

They see us as giddy, celebrity-obsessed, potentially violent people whose main export is a Coca-Cola culture that includes baggy pants, loud rap music and KFC.

But they love us anyhow.

Because their history is rooted in the very dawn of civilization and ours is a tick on the cosmic clock, they also view us as boisterous children on the world scene, kicking and screaming for attention while they wait patiently for us to reach adulthood.

But at least all the rhetoric of the Cold War is gone in the China we saw. The people reach out with willing hands, past memories of the Red Brigade and the Cultural Revolution, to embrace a globalization that includes us all.

Even L.A.

Their curiosity about us is insatiable, but their information is minuscule. In conversations with those who spoke English, I tried to capsulize what L.A. really is today, but that was an exercise in futility. It would take volumes.

Neither could I tell you in these few words what Shanghai is except to offer a slim visual impression of its crowds, its sea of bicycles, buses, taxis and motorized rickshaws down a glowing Nanjing Road in a city gone mad building new skyscrapers.

With a population of 14 million, Shanghai is China's largest city, the Paris of the East, the Pearl of the Orient, and is roaring toward the millennium at full throttle.

By comparison, L.A. putters ahead, unable to get it all together enough to build an adequate public transportation system, much less spike the sky with a dozen new towers of commerce.

I explained to those who chuckled at our "downtown" that unlike Communism that rules from the top, we rule from, well, the bottom. Democracy is the real people's government, and it takes longer to get where we're going. But, I promised them, we'll get there.

If I were coming to L.A. for the first time the day we flew home, my impressions would be mixed: the open attitude of its people, the sweep of its shoreline, the glowing expanse of its ocean ... and, against all that beauty, a young policeman shot to death in the line of duty.

I would simultaneously see L.A.'s grandeur and hear the words of a little boy saying goodbye to his policeman daddy. I'm sitting here even now hearing those words as the image of the Great Wall fades.

I'm back and I'm still trying to form an impression of the city whose streets I endlessly walk.

December 8, 1998

❖

LOOKIN' FOR MY ROOTS

HISTORY IS FILLED WITH THE EFFORTS OF THOSE WHO HAVE braved the unknown in search of new lands, new oceans, new ideas and ultimately new peoples. Christopher Columbus and Marco Polo come to mind. OK, Charles Kuralt too.

Let me make clear, however, that even had I lived during the Age of Exploration, I would not have been found at the helm of a sailing ship riding the rolling seas in search of India or struggling through a Peruvian jungle looking for souls to save. If where I planned to go didn't offer reasonably pleasant accommodations en route and at least a four-star hotel upon arrival, I wouldn't have gone. I feel the same about traveling today.

156

I realize this sets me apart from a growing trend. An increasing number of backpacking teenagers and old people barely able to walk march bravely through Europe, Asia and Africa every year, bursting with the kind of high spirit that must have motivated the early explorers. I say let them.

I am perfectly content to view the world from a revolving cocktail lounge atop the Hyatt Regency and ponder from a distance the travails of an adventure-seeking populace.

Given such limitations of spirit, I couldn't believe it was me driving in endless circles around the piazzas of Italy, guiding a rented car through streets of France too narrow for bicycles, and maneuvering across perilous, rain-slicked bridges that spanned deep gorges in Spain's Pyrenees.

How did that happen, you ask? I'll tell you. We were looking for our roots.

First, allow me to introduce my wife, the former Joanne Cinelli. In a less repressive era, she would have been aboard the Pinta, the Nina or the Santa Maria, calling upon the terrified crews to sail on, despite their fear of oblivion at the edge of the plate-shaped Earth. Trust me when I say the woman has incredible energy and insurmountable spunk. She probably should have married Jacques Cousteau.

I describe her indomitable love of adventure to explain how we happened to have driven 4,000 miles through Italy, France and Spain last autumn, when only a few weeks before I swore that the most adventuresome I would ever get on any trip would be to take a subway in a foreign land, and only then if the taxis were being driven by known serial killers.

I'm not sure when we began talking about meandering through Europe. I only recall I said firmly and in a tone not intended to tempt debate that I would absolutely never drive in a foreign land in any manner of vehicle. Period. I won't even drive in Cleveland.

The next thing I knew I was pulling away from Milan's international airport in a car I had never driven before, looking for a hotel I had never heard of on a street that didn't exist, with Cinelli saying, "Isn't this great?"

What had finally broken my resistance came on a day I was stretched out on the couch in my underwear watching a football game. She stood over me for a moment and then said in a tone meant to convey irony, "Alex Haley

157

would be proud."

Haley is an old friend who badgered me for years after he wrote "Roots" to trace my own genealogy. "You know," he said once, "the Portuguese were slave traders. Maybe your ancestors sold mine."

When I said I wasn't Portuguese, he looked at me doubtfully and asked, "Well then, what are you?" Listen up, Alex.

My father was cholo Mexican who learned to drink and fight on the streets of Guadalajara. My mother's family was from the Basque coast of Spain. Her great-grandfather was Alfonso Larragoite, the first of the Basques to journey to America.

Cinelli's father was born in a village in northern Italy called Santa Lucia, and it was her contention that we ought to at least see where our souls would rest when the end came.

"Also," she said, "wouldn't you like a nice, chilled martini at Harry's Bar and American Grill in Venice and maybe Florence? Close your eyes and dream along with me. I see a frosted glass...."

That argument got us started on a free-floating odyssey that included a sort of search for her Italian and my Basque roots, and a quest for the perfect martini. I found the martinis at Harry's, but we were less successful in the search for the places where our souls would rest.

To begin with, we discovered there are 38 Santa Lucias in northern Italy alone, and Cinelli's father, Augustus, had not communicated to her precisely which Santa Lucia he had left at age 11. My wife is no wilting lily when it comes to asking questions, however, and in the five Santa Lucias we visited, she managed to convey what she was seeking.

At times, whole families of Italians gathered around us in an effort to figure out what it was the Americans wanted. A European phrase book helped very little, since there was no single phrase I could find that encompassed a search for roots. The best I could come up with was "How long have you been here?" (*Da quanto tempo e qui?*) and "May I introduce Miss Phillips?" (*Posso presentarie la signorina Phillips?*) Neither phrase, of course, would do.

"I guess we won't have time to visit the other 33 villages," Cinelli said as we drove away from the fifth Santa Lucia. I froze. There was that look in her eyes. She was thinking, "But maybe if we hurried…."

"Naw," she finally said, "on to the Basque Country."

Generally, I was looking for a Larragoite, which, as I said, was my mother's maiden name. I am forced to admit that for this quest, I had less than Alex Haley's enthusiasm, because the more we drove the more I was beginning to enjoy simply being there, generally lessening my interest in whatever antecedents had preceded me on this treadmill called life.

While our daily adventures were far less jeopardizing than those, say, of Vasco da Gama, it wasn't always easy finding the kind of hotel I deemed acceptable. I'm sure Vasco had the same problem. We played it by ear every night, with Cinelli navigating us on the autostradas and the back roads, where we mingled with the people as often as possible, toward what end I'm not sure.

Not all of the hotels were four-star and some were even two-star, but they were all what we Americans call charming, which is to say quaint, clean and cheap. Part of our mingling included eating where the real people ate. Not at restaurants listed in guidebooks, but in little places on dark streets where Americans rarely set foot. This was especially true in a small restaurant in southern France called Cassoulet, which is also the name of a Basque stew.

It was in Toulouse, which calls itself the Gateway to the Basque Country. There are several claimed gateways, a requirement for which appeared to be an abundance of shops that sell berets. I didn't buy one. They all seemed to be worn by old men who walked around with their flies half-zippered, and I'll be damned if I was about to join that crowd.

We ordered the cassoulet because Cinelli felt I might like an introduction to the kinds of chow my ancestors thrived on, other than tacos and refried beans. What the Basque stew consists of doesn't sound ominous: white beans, garlic, pork, mutton, sausage, and bits of goose or duck. I'll eat any of those things. My only restriction is that what I eat must be dead. In Rome once, I was served clams that cringed when lemon was squeezed on them. I don't eat things that cringe.

The waiter, a sour little man named Leo, discovered I was part Basque and insisted on bringing us a Basque favorite, *chiperones*. I said sure, what the hell, but what he brought turned out to be squid in its own ink. Add to the list of food I won't eat anything served in its own ink, whether it is squid or a daily newspaper. *Chiperones* looks very much like spiders in a soupy mud.

"It's not so bad," Cinelli said, tasting it. "Just close your eyes and imagine it's … well … imagine it's…." She shrugged. "I can't imagine what else it could be."

I sent mine back. Leo seemed disappointed but promised we would enjoy the cassoulet. "It keeps the sheepherders warm on cold winter nights," he said. "You will like this very much."

Once more, Leo was wrong. The mutton skin still had bristles of hair on it, and while the sheepherders may have indeed been warmed by the bristled collation, I was left cold. Cinelli had ordered chicken, which she generously shared with me. Thank God, it was featherless.

Our next stop was Lourdes, another Gateway to the Basque Country.

The city where Bernadette saw the Virgin Mary in a vision has turned into a kind of ecumenical junkyard. Like the commercial success of Graceland, where the ghost of Elvis Presley abides, spiritualism means big bucks. Gift shops are a growth industry in one of Catholicism's most sacred cities. Proprietors hawk their heavenly trinkets along the Rue de la Grotte like carnival pitchmen calling you to see a two-headed snake.

I got sick in Lourdes. It was a 12-hour stomach upset that kept me from dinner that night. As we drove away the next day, Cinelli asked, "Why is it that in a city where lepers are made whole, you get sick?"

I had no answer.

We arrived at Spain's Basque Coast in the rain. Here, at last, hard by the Atlantic, was the place of my ancestors. Even street and city signs were in Basque as well as in Spanish. Now I could begin asking about Larragoites.

For those who know little about the Basques, they are traced through the pre-Christian era of Europe to tribes in northern Spain and western France. The origin of their language remains a mystery. Over the centuries, they have resisted the Visigoths, the Franks, the Normans, the Moors, and they are still resisting the Spanish, which will give you some idea from whose roots I draw my churlish nature.

At the risk of jeopardizing a sour reputation, I liked the Basque Country. At least partially responsible for that was the luxurious, five-star Maria

Cristina Hotel, which, while it might have lacked the charm and economy of a pension in Italy, did offer the kind of luxury we were ready for after 3,000 miles on the road. We were in San Sebastian, a real Gateway to the Basque Country (or the Basque Euskardi), a city that somehow manages to embrace both Gothic cathedrals and modern high-rises with equal grace.

The Basques have always been farmers, sheepherders, shipbuilders and fishermen, and all of these traditions were evident as we wandered the narrow, cobblestoned streets of San Sebastian's Old Town looking for a Larragoite, much as Diogenes sought an honest man. No Larragoites were listed in the city's telephone directory, but an English-speaking, elaborately uniformed doorman at the Maria Cristina suggested we "ask around."

That sounded reasonable, though less than scientific. Had Alex Haley simply wandered through West Africa "asking around," I'm sure he never would have come up with Kunta Kinte. But Haley had 12 years and we only had a remaining week to locate any European heirs of Alfonso Larragoite.

This took us not only through San Sebastian and its environs, but also into the Pyrenees on a twisting mountain road to a village called Lesaca, about 40 kilometers north of Pamplona, where the bulls run. I, of course, objected that such a trip would be perilous and no doubt useless, but Cinelli said we'd see Lesaca if she had to drag me there by my *orejas*. That means ears, but I'm sure she would have dragged me there by any other available protrusion.

I'm glad we went.

Lesaca emerged from a misty rain like Broadway's hamlet of Brigadoon, the mythical Scottish village that appeared for only one day every 100 years. There was a magical quality to this village trapped in time: narrow roads, brick and adobe buildings, verandas draped with colorful fall flowers, stone walls, women in bright colors and men who wore their berets like they were born in them. Their flies, I am pleased to report, were tightly zippered.

Up until we reached Lesaca, we had asked about the name Larragoite without success. We visited a government building, a library, several excellent restaurants that served their beef dead and hairless (I got to really like Basque food), and a number of *tabernas*, which, while they produced no information relative to my past, did provide booze, music and brotherhood.

I had almost decided that the Larragoites of Basqueland, like the Cinellis of Santa Lucia, would have to wait for another time to be discovered by the Martinezes of L.A. when, in a *taberna* of Lesaca, a miracle occurred.

A patron who heard us talking said something in Spanish, which included the word "Larragoite." Then he pointed to an old dog sitting in the middle of the room.

"The dog's name is Larragoite?" I asked.

The man, puzzled, smiled and half-nodded.

I turned to Cinelli. "I may be part beagle."

"I'm not sure that's what he's saying," she replied, "but if it is, there's no reason to be ashamed. He's a very fine dog."

Interpreters seem to exist in every friendly town, and Lesaca was no exception. Another patron explained that the dog was not a Larragoite but was owned by a man named Claudio Larragoite who lived in the mountains at the end of a dirt road. Although Claudio was rarely seen, the dog visited frequently. Urged on by Columbus' spiritual heir, which is to say my wife, we slid and fishtailed up the dirt road to its very end, stopping occasionally to ask passersby if they knew of one Claudio Larragoite. They did not.

I wish I could say we at least glimpsed a Larragoite running naked through the woods like a Basque version of Bigfoot, but we didn't. Although on sunnier days Cinelli would have led me through the forest calling Claudio's name, it was beginning to rain harder. There was a real danger that our dirt road might be washed out, so we reluctantly turned back. That is to say, she was reluctant. I was perfectly happy to be on a paved highway again, though the little town of Lesaca rests gently in my memory.

As we drove off, we noticed the old dog from the *taberna* trotting toward the mountains in the rain. Cinelli opened the car window and called to it, "Say hello to Cousin Claudio!"

Sorry we missed him.

March 18, 1990

THE BOYS OF AUTUMN

THEY WERE A POTBELLIED ARMY OF MEN IN THEIR 60s, BALDING for the most part and slow of step. One was in a wheelchair, one used a cane and several had hearing aids.

They had returned to a country as tourists where once they had fought as warriors, and were trying to remember what it was like four decades ago when artillery roared like thunder and shrapnel fell like rain.

We were in Korea. This isn't exactly an L.A. column, I guess, but if you'll indulge me for a day, I'll tell you what it's like to go back to a war zone whose images continue to haunt dreams long after the battles have ended.

There were 80 of us, mostly from Los Angeles, on a reduced-rate trip sponsored by the U.S. Navy League, Korean Air Lines and others. It was handled by Olympus Travel in L.A.

The idea was to thank those of us who had fought in that strange and distant encounter that is recalled, if at all, as a footnote to the larger war that preceded it.

We were, as President Harry Truman put it, a police action. Some still regard it as a conflict, not a war, as though by gentler definition its memories are less harsh and its dead less gone.

But while time may have blurred details of combat we once thought we'd never forget, the impact of the war is still with those of us who made the trip back in time to Seoul and Inchon and Panmunjom and Yangu and Chunchon.

I saw a man cry who had never cried before. I saw a widow search for the exact place where her husband had died. I saw a son trying to reconstruct the last days of a father he had never seen.

It was an odd assortment of veterans who made the nine-day trip, reflecting on the caprice by which war thrusts men together. There was a Los Angeles cop and a Presbyterian minister, a restaurateur and a medical doctor, a milk truck driver and a college professor.

Some were retired, some weren't; some were in good health, others in pain. A few brought grown children with them to see beyond words what Daddy was talking about all those years a long time ago.

Emotions ran the gamut among the veterans from bombast to grief, but, always, there was an underlying frustration with the notion that their time of fear and pain amounted to nothing. Korea was still divided. The North was still an enemy.

I heard one tattooed old soldier rage against the obscure forces that make one war important and dismiss the other; that line the streets with flags and flowers for those who fought in one war, and turn their backs on those who fought in another. Who chooses? Who decides?

But, at least the Republic of Korea — South Korea — endures, and we may have had something to do with that. The major cities bustle with commerce. The villages once torn by battles are thriving towns. Only the old remember the war. Only the old should.

"I came to look," Catherine Giles said to me, "to see where he died. It was too long ago, but I've always wanted to know."

She was talking about her husband. It was said without tears, but it was apparent that the sadness had never gone away. Their life together had ended too soon. She felt incomplete.

"There was a mine explosion," she said, looking toward the distant mountains. "One piece of shrapnel hit him. One piece of shrapnel...."

The colors of autumn lay over the high ground that edged Hwachon Reservoir. Bright reds and pale yellows gleamed in the muted sunlight of an overcast day. This was the place of my memories.

I had been here as a young Marine in battles that had almost destroyed a regiment of men I had come to know as brothers. It has been calling me back ever since.

The reservoir lies now in the demilitarized zone north of the 38th Parallel. We were there with special permission granted through the Korea Times and its publisher, J.M. Chang.

I stood on a mountaintop 3,000 feet high and looked over a vista of almost surreal beauty, of ridge lines cascading back into the distance in muted tones of blue and gray, of autumn colors so bright they were blinding.

I tried to remember how it had been back then, trudging past the stepped rice paddies to reach the foot of the mountains, and then charging up their steep slopes in the face of gunfire.

They were days of drums and bugles, of victories so sweet they can never be achieved again; of fear so deep and elemental, it can never be repeated.

But I couldn't re-create them that day on the mountaintop, and it's just as well. The war is over and the dead long buried. I sensed an acceptance of that among those who made the trip back in time. Perhaps now they will rest easier in their dreams.

The drums are silent, the buglers gone.

November 13, 1993

A NIGHT TRAIN TO VIENNA

I HAVE RETURNED TO THIS BIG, SPRAWLING, TENTACLED OCTOPUS of a city thinking about Paris and Vienna and a train hurtling through the twilight at 190 miles an hour.

I'm also thinking about a walk along the Seine on a day as bright as heaven and about listening to a string quartet playing "The Blue Danube" on a frosty Vienna night with the Danube right outside our door.

Poetry is written about the kind of vacation we took, Cinelli and I, from L.A. to Chicago to New York to London to Madrid to Paris to Vienna.

I'm a guy from East Oakland happy with a cheeseburger and a dry martini, but my wife is a lover of culture and longed to see the great art museums of the world.

They sprawl like castles of creative history guarding the works of Monet and Cézanne and Picasso and Renoir and Van Gogh and so many others that I've got to concentrate hard to isolate my memories of them.

Their ghosts swirl like ribbons of mist through the Art Institute in Chicago, the Guggenheim in New York, the Tate in London, the Prado in

165

Madrid, the Louvre and D'Orsay in Paris, the National Gallery in Vienna.

There were other art galleries too, sandwiched between the big ones, but I can't remember their names. I can, however, remember a small cafe on the Rue de Rivoli where I sipped cognac on an amber-colored night and tried to forget the octopus that is L.A.

This city is so damned much with us.

I mention the night train from Paris to Vienna because that ride through the countrysides of France, Germany and Austria convinced me that you can't escape L.A.

Ten thousand miles away from here, we struck up casual conversations with two travelers who boarded the train at separate stops and — can you believe this? — one was a biochemist from Woodland Hills and the other an Austrian hippie who once worked in Topanga and still has a girlfriend in Calabasas.

I mean, we're out in the middle of nowhere, and these guys appear like pop-up figures in a birthday card and tell us they're our neighbors.

That's not all. In the International Herald-Tribune, which I picked up as often as I could, there was no escaping stories about O.J. Simpson, the Menendez brothers and Heidi Fleiss, and on CNN they never stopped profiling the LAPD.

"If we ever got to a remote corner of the universe," Cinelli said as we knifed through the foothills of the Alps, "there'd be someone there from Burbank and a television special on the La Brea Tar Pits."

But even if you can't escape L.A., running off to foreign places offers new perspectives on where we live. All those great cities I mentioned represent an old world of late dinners and classical music, existing comfortably in their own rich history.

L.A., on the other hand, is like Alicia Silverstone in "Clueless": young, sexy, modern and beguilingly naive, a triumph of image over substance, more worried about what to wear than what to think.

In a more specific comparison, we're about 50 years behind all those ancient European cities in terms of public transportation, but when we try to finally build a subway, protests mount, tunnels collapse and streets cave in.

166

If we were an ancient city and tried to build a castle, the turrets would topple off during the ribbon-cutting.

But even so, it's good to be home.

As we flew in over L.A. at twilight, its streets glowed like flecks of magnesium from the Valley to the ocean, and the headlights of its cars on the freeways were jewels of lights laid on velvet.

The beaches shone with their own luminescence and the last rays of the sun splashed the sky with ever-softening pastels. The surf sparkled and the mountains rose into the darkness like walls of a ... well ... castle.

"We don't need the Vienna Woods," Cinelli said as we drove home, "we've got the Santa Monicas."

I think about that now as I roam the city, the memory of a night train to Vienna growing dimmer, like the details of a dream blurring into shadow.

We're a city in the midst of change, convulsed by crime and circumstance, tearing down and building up, blowing horns and beating drums, trying to figure out who we are and where we're going.

L.A. is on its own kind of night train, hurtling through history to some unknown destination, flashing past forests of trauma, climbing mountains of despair.

So I'm coming aboard again after six weeks away, curious about the destination, entranced by the passengers, ready for the ride. Cinelli said it best: "The honeymoon's over. You feed the dog, I'll do the dishes."

Auf Wiedersehen, Vienna. *Au revoir*, Paree. Good morning, L.A.

November 28, 1995

RAIN IN THE RAIN FORESTS

FOR SOME REASON, IT HAD NEVER OCCURRED TO ME THAT IT might be raining in a rain forest. I knew it rained at one time or another, which is why they call it a rain forest, but I never expected it to rain with me actually in it. It wasn't until we were slogging through the jungle entanglements of Panama's Chagres National Park and it began pouring that I realized it could rain whenever it pleased, which it did with great frequency.

My second misconception regarding rain forests was that I thought I would be seeing them from the glass-enclosed top deck of a luxurious air-conditioned bus, while a guide pointed out interesting features through a PA system. Wrong again. Had I known we would be in the forests themselves trying to make our way through thick growths of vines and trees and ferns and palms in storms that rattled the world with lightning and thunder, I might not have mentioned Panama.

To backtrack a bit, we were itching for someplace to get away for a while when I suggested Panama. I was thinking of a trip through the canal, a city tour, dinner at fine restaurants, sunny days on tropical beaches and that luxury ride through forests alive with harpy eagles and howler monkeys.

The first few days were pretty much what I'd anticipated, but then came the rain forests, which my wife, the explorer/adventurer/death-defying Cinelli, could hardly wait to enter. I knew it wouldn't be a bus ride in the park when our guide, Peter Garcia, pointed to a log on the shore of Madden Lake and said, "Climb aboard!"

"That's a tree," I said.

"It's a dugout canoe," Peter explained.

"Isn't this great!" Cinelli said.

Oh, my God.

I had never ridden in a tree before, and though I got wet, it took us to where we wanted to go, which was at the edge of the jungle itself. Being dry really wasn't an option in Panama at that time of year. Not only was it the rainy season, but also the humidity was at the drenching level every day, storm or no storm.

We hiked up yellow-clay trails as slick as ice, crossed knee-deep streambeds and plowed through thickets where, I'm sure, snakes and jaguars watched our every move. Panama supposedly has more kinds of birds than anyplace else in the world, but I never saw one. Peter shouted, "Look, a toucan!" gesturing toward the forest beyond the stream. I ooohed and aaahed but later admitted to Cinelli I hadn't seen anything. I was just trying to please Peter.

After what seemed like hours, we reached our destination, which was a waterfall. If you've ever seen more than one waterfall, you know there's not a lot of difference between them. A waterfall is a waterfall is a waterfall. Big deal. Let's go back.

Going back meant crossing the lake again, this time in a sudden storm. Lightning struck all around us. Thunder roared. Peter stayed calm, Cinelli loved it and I waited patiently to die.

We made it to a village of Empera Indians, where we were greeted by half-naked people whose ways hadn't changed for thousands of years. I've seen topless women before, but never in a rain forest. It was a new experience. They fed us fish in a large, one-room cabana where, Peter explained, "they ate, slept and procreated." Although not, of course, at the same time.

Having survived that, Cinelli, now stimulated by her jungle challenge, wanted to fly to one of the nearby San Blas islands in the Caribbean to experience other feats of human endurance. I fought it for two reasons. I think of small planes the way I think of dugout canoes. Neither is actually meant as an instrument of human transportation. Also, we would have to fly through thunderheads that ate small planes.

Peter suggested instead a lodge in the jungle called Burbayar, which means "spirit of the forest" in the language of the Kuna Indians. Owned by a Basque who calls himself Inaki, it consists of a series of cabanas on about 100 acres of land at the edge of the Nargana Forest, a pristine area protected by both the government of Panama and the Kunas. The jungle embraces Burbayar as its own.

The idea of a lodge pleased me, and the idea of more jungle pleased

Cinelli. The only way to reach Burbayar was in a four-wheel-drive vehicle on a strip of land that defied the term "road." For an hour, we bounced over ruts as deep as chasms and slid to the edges of jungle cliffs that dropped into green oblivion. Getting to Burbayar was the emotional equivalent of reaching an outpost in Antarctica.

It was worth it. We slept in individual thatched-roof cabanas that overlooked the forest and gloried in the peace that lay like soft music over the lodge. The rain whispered rather than roared. The jungle glistened. We hiked through a rain forest again, but by now I was able to perceive its beauty and not its peril. When it came time to leave, after three days of deep serenity, I realized we had journeyed to Paradise.

I hear the jungle calling even as I write, a dream place very deep inside of me.

October 7, 2002

❖

CONFESSIONS OF A TRINKET JUNKIE

IT SEEMED RIGHT, SOMEHOW, THAT I SHOULD HAVE A FLASH OF inner recognition in a gift shop across the street from Vatican City. Even though my flash had nothing to do with religious awareness and though there were no theological visions involved, the ambience for sudden realization was correct.

I was buying a miniature likeness of Pope John Paul II for my sister Emily in Oakland, who, as she likes to say, is a Very Devout Catholic. I capitalize the phrase only to indicate the tone in which it is said.

The likeness of the pontiff was full-bodied and about 3 inches in length. Its feet contained an adhesive substance so that one could affix the Holy Father to a dashboard where he could gyrate to the movement of the car, because of the rubbery substance out of which the likeness is created.

No comparison is intended, by the way, to those miniature hula dancers that are meant to sway suggestively with a similar automotive movement. It wasn't the pontiff's bottom that swayed, if memory serves, but his out-stretched arms, as though he were blessing the multitudes.

The flash that came as I purchased the pope was recognition that I was finally buying the ultimate trinket, and I do not say that lightly.

The swaying pontiff was without a doubt the most unusual artifact my wife and I would find in a month spent traveling through England, France and Italy, visiting every gift shop in sight.

When there were no gift shops in the immediate vicinity, I searched until I found one, as tour-bus drivers honked for me to hurry and other tourists aboard the bus grumbled their unhappiness in half a dozen languages. I hadn't realized until then how lyrical cursing can sound in Japanese.

If I'm an Ugly American, I don't mean to be. I just can't help myself when I travel. I'm a gift shop junkie.

I say that with an appropriate sense of uneasiness, because there is a kind of addiction involved. When a man walks into something as vast and beauti-ful as the Louvre and instantly asks where the gift shop is, you know he has a problem.

"You're buying more and more junk," my wife said to me one evening in our room at the Hotel Elysees Marignan in Paris.

I was sitting on the floor with my day's purchases. Spread before me were mementos of our trip thus far: coasters, towels, woolen stocking aglow with the Union Jack, wooden soldiers, a Winston Churchill mug, and even a kitchen knife purchased at Stratford-on-Avon and said to have been used by the Bard himself. "These are treasures of which memories are made," I said.

"Infant-sized T-shirts that say 'France is for Louvers' in Algerian across the front?"

I had picked them up in Fontainebleau, on a side street near an Algerian restaurant where we ate huge bowls of couscous with chicken and something brown in a bowl. Usually I don't eat brown things, but I didn't want to upset the Algerians. I don't know where we stand with them.

"They're for our grandchildren," I said.

"We have three grandchildren and you have 14 infant-sized T-shirts," she said. "You plan on selling some to other grandchildren in the neighborhood or are you going to buy additional grandchildren in France who will fit the T-shirts?"

"I like T-shirts."

She leaned closer to look at my collection of trinkets.

"Do you also like miniature toilet seats?"

I think I got that on the Left Bank. It's a small, pink toilet seat with a cardboard backing into which one can slip photographs. You lift the little toilet seat and, *voilà!* there's Aunt Zulema.

"It's for pictures of our loved ones," I said. "The French are very imaginative."

"Not for any loved one you share with me. Store it with your genuine-ivory Eskimo rock."

I had almost forgotten the rock.

We were on vacation in Point Barrow, Alaska. I'm not sure why we'd chosen Point Barrow. It was 20 below in the pale sunlight, and an arctic wind cut like a whaling knife. But there we were.

We dragged our luggage over an icy road from the airfield to discover that the Top of the World Motel had no record of our reservations.

"Sorry," the desk clerk said, slamming the book closed.

The last plane had left for Anchorage. We were stranded in a frozen wasteland. Top of the World offered the only accommodations in town, and quite possibly the only accommodations north of the Arctic Circle.

A motel employee was, in effect, telling us to sleep outside in the snow and thus sentencing us to death by Popsicle-ization.

I don't recall what I said to her, but I am certain it had something to do with the life expectancy of a desk clerk in combat with a desperate tourist. The way I saw it, it was her or us.

"All right," she said, "no need to get snippy. I'll put you in a temp."

I didn't know what a temp was, but at that point I'd have slept with the stuffed polar bear in the lobby.

"A temp is fine," I said.

"Absolutely no alcoholic beverages in the room," she said.

"I wouldn't dream of it," I said, thinking about the martini flask in my suitcase.

I felt a moisture on my chin.

"You're drooling," my wife whispered.

The genuine-ivory Eskimo rock came next. We had walked a few miles to a coffee shop on the Beaufort Sea when it began to snow. The world went instantly white, so I insisted we return immediately to our motel.

There was one taxi in Point Barrow, operated by a thin, sallow man with yellow eyes set dangerously close together. My mother never trusted close-set eyes.

"Get in," he said, without moving from behind the wheel.

He wore jeans, boots and a soiled white T-shirt. Rolled up in the sleeve of the T-shirt was a package of Marlboros. It was as hot in his cab as it was cold outside. I felt like I was in Hell.

Had Yellow Eyes not existed, someone like Tennessee Williams would have eventually created him.

"Got something for you," he said before the cab even moved.

I thought, Oh, my God, a drug dealer!

I was trying to figure out how to tell him I don't put anything in my nose that can't be mixed with vermouth when he handed me a small piece of what he said was ivory.

He didn't say ivory from what, but since there are no elephants in Point Barrow, I figured it had to be from the tusk of a sea lion, if there are sea lions in Point Barrow.

"Five dollars," Yellow Eyes said.

"That's nothing more than a piece of white rock!" my wife replied. "We're not paying five dollars for a white rock."

She is absolutely fearless in situations of that nature. Part of the reason, I feel, is that women realize instinctively that anyone with homicidal intentions will go for the man and not for his mate. It is a kind of unwritten law among felons.

The cabby turned to face us directly and glared. His mouth twitched. I wrote a television movie once in which I created a homicidal maniac whose mouth twitched moments before he killed.

"Sure looks like ivory to me," I said quickly, handing him a five.

Years have passed. We survived Point Barrow. I brought back a red T-shirt from Pepe's Mexican restaurant, which was the only restaurant in town, and the genuine-ivory Eskimo rock.

"What's this?" my wife asked.

We are once more seated on the floor of the Hotel Elysees Marignan, surrounded by trinkets.

She held up what appeared to be a piece of bent wire with springs on either side.

"I think it's an ancient intrauterine device."

"A what?"

"An adjective of or pertaining to..."

"I know what an intrauterine device is, and that is definitely not one of them."

"I've only seen pictures."

"Did you buy it at the flea market?"

We had been at what we described to the cab driver as *puce marche*. It was supposed to be the famous flea market of Paris. Instead, I think we described a market for fleas.

It was raining when we got there, but that didn't stop me. Paris is definitely not Point Barrow. I bought a cheap Statue of Liberty whose head lit up. It is made of a silvery material that chips, exposing an even cheaper brown substance underneath.

I loved France. Even its good stuff seemed trinkety. But Rome is gift-shop heaven for people like me.

I found a detached purple hand on the Via del Corso that even now hangs over my desk, pointing down at me like Michelangelo's finger in the Sistine Chapel. And a small mirror edged in seashells glued to cardboard.

"That," my wife said, observing the seashell mirror, "may be the ugliest trinket you have ever purchased."

But then as she thought about it, she added, "No, the porno from Pompeii is uglier."

She was using ugly in the spiritual sense. The porn is contained in a book called "Forbidden Pompeii." It contains illustrations of 102 erotic statues and paintings found in Pompeii after it was buried by the eruption of Mt. Vesuvius in AD 79.

I thought it was a travel book when I bought it. A tour guide who hustled us along momentarily blurred my sense of propriety.

"Step lively," he kept saying, "you never know when she might erupt again!"

I bought the book in haste and studied it with amazement. I have never seen so many ... well ... positions in my life.

The next day I discovered the miniature pope. It made me feel cleansed after Pompeii. From porno to pontiff. The Romans understood the therapeutic value of moral balance.

It was my last trinket in Europe, by the way. We crammed everything into suitcases and carry-on bags and headed homeward.

As we winged over the Mediterranean, my wife cried out, "I've got it!"

"It was probably the raw clams," I said. "We'll treat it with antibiotics in New York."

"I know what the mystery trinket is!"

"The ancient intrauterine device?"

"It's a collar-stay! You bought a genuine ancient collar-stay!" She shook her head and half-smiled. "Taken again, Martinez."

She snuggled down and closed her eyes.

No problem. I'll put it with the genuine-ivory Eskimo rock. They can be friends.

October 18, 1987

EATING OUR
WAY THROUGH EUROPE

IT WAS OUR LAST NIGHT IN EUROPE. WE WERE AT A RESTAURANT IN Rome called El Presidente. I can't tell you exactly where it is because I can't tell you exactly where anything is in Rome, and neither can the Romans. That's why the empire fell.

"Ummm, this is delicious," my wife was saying with a brave smile.

Moved by generosity and goodwill, she was eating a clam that moments before had been alive on her plate.

"You ate it?" I asked, impressed.

I had never seen anyone eat anything live before.

"I had to," she whispered back. "Giorgio is watching."

I glanced to the left and, sure enough, there was our waiter, Giorgio Fontani, smiling and observing us in a spirit of anticipation.

Giorgio was not only a waiter but also our personal tour guide. He was giving us a feast in his restaurant and he desperately wanted us to be happy.

My wife smiled back and ate another live clam.

"Eat one," she whispered, "or you'll hurt his feelings."

I looked down at my plate. It was the biggest clam I had ever seen. I squeezed lemon over it as Giorgio had suggested. God help me, the clam cringed.

I shoved the plate away.

"I'll be damned," I said, "if I'll eat anything that cringes."

"You've got to. Think of NATO."

"What's NATO got to do with it?"

"The alliance is based on the mutual goodwill of our peoples."

"If Italy joins the godless enemy because I don't eat a clam, the alliance was on shaky ground to begin with."

"Just fake it," she said.

I happen to be an expert at deceit and trickery, which is why they gave me a column, so with a display of theatrical gluttony that would have pleased both

Hadrian and Nero, I tore the unfortunate mollusk from its shell.

You could almost hear it scream.

Then, hands dripping with olive oil, I tore others from their wretched shelters, all the while smiling and chewing and wiping my grinning mouth with the back of a greasy hand.

"Don't overdo it, for God's sake," my wife whispered. "This could get disgusting."

All of the clams ended up, of course, not in my stomach but in my napkin, where for the sake of the Atlantic alliance, they died shell-less but at least undigested.

Giorgio, no doubt impressed, came for the empty platter.

"*Devo cambiare treno!*" I said with gusto.

He seemed perplexed for a moment, then shook his head no and went off to get the next course.

"Why did you say that?" my wife asked.

"I told him the clams were delicious."

"You asked him if you had to change trains."

"Wrong! I got it right out of the...."

I opened my Berlitz European Phrase Book. She was right.

"Well," I said, "it's good to know we don't have to change trains."

The feast lasted four hours. I don't know what I ate, except for the pasta. I know that none of it is recommended on the Pritikin Diet. Even the napkin was soaked in butter.

That was but one feast of many.

We ate and drank for three weeks throughout London, Paris and Rome. My wife displayed restraint and good sense, qualities of which I have never boasted.

I ate everything but the live clams and drank liquids I would normally not soak my feet in. I had no choice. I gave up ordering martinis in England when an innkeeper laced one with lime juice and put a cherry in it.

Some things, like highway planning and martini making, are best left to Americans.

Giorgio came to us through our travel agent, who knows the dangers of wandering unleashed through the narrow avenues of an ancient empire.

One street changed names three times in the course of a single block. Others aren't even on the map.

When Giorgio wasn't with us, I led the way. Disaster followed.

On one occasion, we drifted lost half a day down the winding back streets, somewhere between the Colosseum and Vatican City.

"I have the feeling, Toto," my wife said, "we're not in Kansas anymore."

We were looking for the Piazza Navona, where a restaurant called Tre Scalini served ice cream known throughout the NATO alliance as the best gelato in the free world.

"Don't worry," I said. "I've got a fix on it now. We go down Via Cestari and turn left at the Pantheon."

She stared at me.

"What's the matter?" I asked.

"I don't know," she said. "There's something basically wrong with the phrase 'Turn left at the Pantheon.' Would Caesar Augustus have said that?"

"He would if he were giving directions to Tre Scalini."

We finally found it. We turned left at the Pantheon. Well, actually, right.

There were two peace demonstrations in Rome. They were, of course, anti-American. Someone actually wrote "Yankee Go Home" on a wall.

That bothered Giorgio. He loves Rome and wanted us to love it too.

The night we left Italy it was raining. We stood in the rain after our feast and said goodbye. Giorgio hugged us. Then he said, "Yankee, come back." I liked that.

Arrivederci, Roma.

November 10, 1986

CHICKEN DANCING
THROUGH TOWN

IT OCCURRED TO ME, AS I WAS ON THE DANCE FLOOR FLAPPING MY arms and clucking like a chicken, that I would never do this in America.

I would not suddenly leap to my feet pecking and high-stepping hen-like through a fashionable Parisian restaurant and think I was having a good time.

I would instead realize instantly that I was probably suffering a seizure due to the mad chemistry of jet lag and the excesses of foreign leisure.

Why else would a dour man in a solid blue suit take to dancing the wildly kinetic "chicken" with a room full of German tourists?

Afterwards, for God's sake, we even oompahed together. Man, I never oompah.

Something happens to a man when he becomes a tourist. Surging adrenalin short-circuits the synaptic conjunctions of his brain and he inexplicably begins to peck and flap his arms.

I say he because women are immune to that kind of pathology. Instead, they are knocked askew by the see-and-buy syndrome.

Wives who at home worry over a fluctuation in potato prices suddenly begin loading up on French perfume at $150 a drop because they are in Europe.

But even that, I suppose, is one hell of a lot better than chicken-dancing across a crowded restaurant.

The sole redeeming factor of my otherwise odious display is that when we left the restaurant I told them I was Syrian so as not to shame America.

For the past three weeks, as you might have guessed, my wife and I have been vacationing in Europe.

While you were having a good time at Lake Isabella fishing in the scum, we were dining on grouse and kipper pâte in London, cruising the Seine on a starry night in Paris and standing amid the 2,000-year-old ruins of Rome.

But, hey, I'm not knocking your vacation, I'm just telling you about mine.

Someday you can amuse me with stories about how you sat around the old Coleman stove having chili dogs and Budweiser beer and singing "Someone's in the Kitchen With Dinah."

I would not even mention the fact that we strolled the Via Condotti or boated the Seine except that it is in the fine tradition of newspaper columnists, even those who have not made it downtown yet, to swagger and boast about their holiday, which you might know as vacation.

I have never been able to do that before. This year, however, my wife got tired of my whining about how I've never been any farther than the ruins of Oakland, so she snapped a leash on me and led me off to wondrous places.

We decided against a packaged tour because tour groups generally include nice old ladies from Omaha and she does not believe that nice old ladies from Omaha are ready for mad-dog columnists in their midst. They do not understand maniacal fury in Omaha.

"A tour group would be all right," she explained, "except that you don't actually like anyone. I can't depend on you to be civil."

"Trust me at least to remain nonviolent," I said.

"I tried that before. You chewed through your muzzle and bit a Christian."

We therefore agreed to commission Woodland Hills travel agent Marsha Calig to create a personal itinerary for us. She did and it was perfect.

When we arrived at the major cities, we arranged short tours, which afforded my wife an opportunity to bask in the wonders of Stratford-on-Avon, Pompeii and the palace of Versailles, and gave me a chance to study other tourists.

Forget the Germans chicken-dancing off the wall and the turbaned Middle Easterners fearful that they would be mistaken for terrorists and beaten senseless by British gentlemen carrying umbrellas.

What intrigued me were the Japanese. They cluster.

We were in the Louvre when one particular group of Japanese tourists marched by.

"Will you look at that," I said to my wife.

She turned, expecting another painting of rare beauty.

"Where?"

"There. The Japanese tourists."

They were moving in a cluster through a room full of Renaissance art. There were about 40 of them and they were grouped together like atoms.

"We are standing before the Mona Lisa and you're asking me to look at tourists?" she asked.

"The cluster never seems to break up," I said. "Even when they veer suddenly or turn a corner it remains a single entity. It must be from living on those little islands."

"I can't believe you are standing there staring at 'clusters' with all this beauty around us."

"It's just that they're somehow so … well … awesome in their clustering. I know how the Marines must have felt at Iwo Jima. *Another cluster of Japanese coming over the rise!*"

"You were pretty awesome yourself last night. Another chicken-dancing Yankee coming over the table!"

I guess she's right. But it is still pretty unnerving to be suddenly confronted by a cluster of Japanese tourists bearing down on you.

One cluster went temporarily out of control and almost ran me down. Thank God I am still fairly nimble. I simply chicken-danced aside and let them cluster on by.

November 6, 1986

CHAPTER SIX

SUNSETS AND WINDS OF FIRE

*"Los Angeles exists between ocean and mountains
And in places of the imagination where
Whimsy and fantasy abide."*

—ELMER TEENEZ

SOUTHERN CALIFORNIA SUBLIME

IT HAS BEEN SAID THAT WE WILL NEVER BE CONTENT WITH THE weather until each man makes his own. True. I complain constantly that there is no real weather here, only a flat, enervating sunlight that saps the spirit and diminishes creativity. Even Oakland has weather.

But for a few days last week and part of the week before, we were witness to a combination of weather and color that painted our town with brush strokes that not even Monet could equal. It began with a sunset so intense it seemed artificial, streaks of pastel golds and reds in a fiery mix that burned into the scattered clouds above it.

I was on a balcony at the Getty when I saw it, startled by what seemed to be an abrupt burst of color, as if the horizon had suddenly exploded. I waited until it had subsided, then stopped along PCH on the way home to watch darkness descend like a dream over the ocean, the last traces of sunset melting into the Pacific.

While I realize that it was not a performance meant especially for me, I was moved to begin noticing the intricacy of color and weather, one blending into the other in remarkable displays of dependency, creating a glory isolated only for a few moments and then, like drifts of a passing memory, gone.

The next morning, fog embraced the Santa Monicas, creeping over the hilltops in billowing strands of silver that added a sheen to the trees along the canyon roads and down the slopes of the valleys. I don't know why I hadn't noticed before how autumn dresses the mountains in a harmony of shades that glow in the dampness of the passing mists. The leaves of the trees — elms, liquidambars, pomegranates and buckeyes — responded to the cool moisture with a chromatic affirmation of fall that could move a poet to tears. It wasn't the fierce autumn colors of the Adirondacks, but it did at least contribute a moment of splendor to a city that hungers for seasons.

Then the rain came, quickly and unexpectedly, tapping on the roof like a hesitant drummer, then building into downpours to signal with gusto its return to the land of eternal sunshine. I couldn't believe, even as the sky darkened, that it would actually rain. Heavy clouds moved in, then broke up, leaving diagonals of sunlight slicing through the darkness to illuminate flowers still braving the weather change. Then it poured.

It was a storm of modest proportions compared with the horror that plagued parts of the East and the South. No tornadoes tore through our cities, killing and uprooting like demons descending from the sky. The winds that followed our rain were more benign than murderous. Trees fell here and there, power lines snapped in the gusts that blew down from the northeast and the lights went out in some parts of town. But the effect of the wind was to enhance what a poet called "the perfect image of the infinite."

It scrubbed the sky into a blue so dazzling it gleamed, and faked our vision into believing that Santa Catalina Island was but a touch away. As it blew, the leaves of fall fluttered like butterflies to the mountain trails, laying pathways of gold for us to wonder at their destination. Then it whisked them away into corners of the poetic infinity that weather creates. The cries of crows riding the wind filled the day with music, completing the chemistry of fusion when weather changes.

Autumn to me is a time between seasons, an unraveling of complexities, an easing of tensions. Even as God's patience is tested amid the bluster of warrior kings, autumn cautions us to wait, to listen, to sigh deeply into the wind and to walk softly on the fallen leaves. This pause between summer and winter reminds us of the transitory nature of beauty and of the fleeting moments of grandeur meant to be absorbed and remembered.

There will be other sunsets and other rainy days, mornings laced with strands of fog and nights lit by starry skies. The wind will blow and the multicolored leaves will grace its currents and settle softly to earth. But they won't come often in a combination of weather and color that set our world aglow for a few days in November. I was moved to regard it as a message from heaven to a troubled world, and to wonder at its timing.

November 15, 2002

❖

RAIN AND THE BARKING DOG

AS I LOOK OUT MY WINDOW OVER THE SOGGY HILLS OF TOPANGA, the sky is blue, the sun is bright and puffy little white clouds drift by like fluffs of cotton on a placid sea. It is a scene of peace and tranquility. I don't trust it.

Any minute now, El Niño will come pounding at the door again and blast us out of our somnambulation and into a state of high stress until the last drop of rain falls and the last whisper of wind fades and the dog stops barking.

Barkley, which is the dog's name, believes rain to be some kind of foreign invader attempting to break into the house, so when it falls, he opens up, running from one room to another, warning the rain away.

Since February 2, according to our local weather-watcher, 25.08 inches of the stuff have fallen on Topanga, a period of disaster that coincides with my vacation. My time off began with El Niño swooping in with almost 2 inches of rain and now that my vacation has ended, sunshine. Go figure.

Instead of catching up on reading or lazing about the house looking over my collection of factoids during the calamity, I was outside cleaning storm drains, setting up a pump and clearing out a culvert under the driveway.

I like rain, but not the kind that sends houses sliding like bobsleds down muddy hillsides. Normally I wouldn't go out into that kind of weather even if Monica Lewinsky were waiting under an oak tree, but I had no choice.

"You're the man of the house!" my wife said over the noise of the storm and the barking dog. "Save us!" Yeah, right, sure.

Factoids are little bits of useless information that CNN Headline News flashes on the screen between reports of disasters. For instance: "Only 0.05% of the population buys bowling shoes," and "A woman in an average day speaks 66,000 words and a man speaks 25,000."

I have been collecting factoids for years for reasons that escape me at the moment. No doubt I will someday be a factoid: "0.03% of the male population collects something that has absolutely no point whatsoever."

Part of the 66,000 words my wife, Cinelli, was speaking at the height of the storm was that the water was rising in our backyard. I looked out and said "Yup" as part of my 25,000 words. She used up two more words by saying, "Do something!"

Twenty-six percent of all German men say they have too much leisure time, which is not my problem. It seems to me I am always doing something, even if after I've done it nothing seems to have changed. I am man at his busiest, endlessly engaged in sweeping sand from the beach.

I sigh and lay aside the factoid I am reading ("600,000 pianos are purchased worldwide each year"), grab my Little Wizard pump and head into the backyard cursing the weather. It occurs to me as I do that I must use about 8,000 of my 25,000 words each day cursing something.

I set the pump in place and shout, "OK, plug 'er in." Then I realize I am standing in the water where the pump is located. Although electrocution is probably not a possibility, I still jump clear as the pump kicks in. Twenty-two percent of all cases of electrocution no doubt involve angry men standing in water staring at their Little Wizards.

We were the Isle of Topanga for a while. El Niño blocked the main boulevard at both ends with slides, but we are a hardy group up here on Walton's Mountain. Give us enough beer, brown rice and cat food, and we'll hold out until Malibu freezes over or the beer runs out.

Meanwhile, my Little Wizard pumps water from the backyard with the spunky tenacity of the Little Engine That Could. I think I can, I think I can…. It grows stronger with each pump. I know I can, I know I can….

I am getting drenched down to my underwear (of which 434 million pairs are sold each year in the U.S.), but that's man's role in a stormy world. On the other hand, nearly 200,000 U.S. women are enrolled in seminars. Mine is standing in the window watching me.

"Why aren't you at a seminar?" I holler, but the dog is barking like crazy and she doesn't hear me.

"Yo there!" I hear someone shout. I turn to see a spry, cheerful old lady striding through the storm followed by her goat. She gives me a thumb's up sign and vanishes into the blinding rain. I'm thinking, an old woman and her goat in the mother of all storms shouting, "Yo there!"? What the hell's going on here? Did I really see it or has living in Topanga warped my perceptions?

I reenter the house snarling and dripping. Barkley looks at me and growls. He has never witnessed pure misery before. It keeps a dog busy barking at rain and snarling at misery. Arf to the rain! Arf to the misery!

"My goodness," Cinelli says in a kind of Mary Poppins tone, "are we all wet and angry! My poor brave dear, out there in all that nasty water. If only rain were vodka, how much nicer it would be for you!"

I dry off and snuggle down with my factoids. The average household spends $27.21 on bananas each year. The average adult has 26 friends. The most popular lunch in U.S. schools is peanut butter. Ham is second.

February 27, 1998

❖

SEEING THE OCEAN AGAIN

I WAS ATTRACTED TO THE MAN BY THE INTENSITY OF HIS STARE. He was standing on the beach at Venice on an early morning, the wind in his face and the waves at his feet, transfixed by something he apparently was seeing beyond the breakers, oblivious to the water that soaked his shoes.

His hair was beginning to thin and he was wearing clothes that seemed as old and rumpled as he was. They hung like rags on a scarecrow.

As I approached, he glanced over at me, turned back to the ocean and said, "Will you look at that?"

I followed his stare but saw only a Pacific turned silver by the coming day.

"Will I look at what?"

I kept thinking he might have spotted Morgan Fairchild swimming naked near the breakwater.

"The ocean!" he said with enthusiasm that seemed about to explode.

Another Venice nut flying on mescaline.

"I've seen it before," I said with a sigh and began to move on.

"You're lucky," the man said. He turned to me full-face and added with pride of accomplishment, "This is my first time."

His name was Hank Ketlin and he had arrived at the ocean that very morning after driving in from a place called Thayer, Kansas. He had never seen the ocean before.

"Have you ever actually been on the ocean?" Hank asked after introductions.

"Well, yes," I said, "many times."

"In a boat?"

"In a boat."

"Hoo," he said, "that must have been something."

He stomped his feet in the surf a couple of times, splashing water like shards of crystal into the diagonals of sunlight that sliced over the rooftops.

I couldn't believe the man. He was like a kid at a birthday party. I had never seen so much emotion in anyone over 9. We are accustomed to cool out here. Cool at any cost.

"I can't believe that horizon," Hank said.

I looked at the horizon. It was one I had seen thousands of times. I tried to imagine it was my first view, but that never works. Wonder is a passing magic, glimpsed once and gone forever.

But still, it was a magnificent horizon at that, wide and sweeping in its scope, tantalizing in its unknowns.

"All my life," Hank said, "I've wanted to see the ocean. Dad was in the Navy during the war and gave me one of those large seashells he'd brought back from Dago."

Dago? San Diego? Do they still call it that? They do in Thayer, Kansas, I

190

guess.

"He used to tell me to hold it up to my ear and I could hear the ocean winds blow." He thought about it for a while and then said, "I think it was ceramic but I still heard the wind."

There just didn't seem good enough reason and there was never enough money to come to the ocean before, Hank told me. But Mary had died two weeks ago and there were no children ("Mary was barren," he explained somberly), so there didn't seem good enough reason not to come anymore. Hank was alone now.

He had just packed up and headed west in his 1972 Chevrolet Nova, pulling a U-Haul trailer and still hearing the ocean winds. He just wished Mary could have been there with him.

"Lookit there!" he said so suddenly I thought he'd spotted a Russian sub. It was a sailboat tacking into the wind, its clean bow slicing through the flying spray.

As we stared, the boat keeled to port, its multicolored mainsail (shades of orange and magenta) sweeping over the wave tips, then spiking upright, teeth to the wind, heading for open water.

"Jesus!" Hank said. He realized what he had said and apologized. "I don't usually talk that way."

"That's all right," I said. "You may be the first person I've ever known who doesn't talk that way."

Hank had seen the ocean on television and in the movies, of course. They showed fairly current movies in Thayer. But this was the real thing. Sea air you could smell and water you could touch. I didn't tell him the sea was toxic and the fish were dying. We didn't talk about the smog that sits along the horizon when the Santa Anas blow.

They weren't important now. A man was seeing the ocean for the very first time, an ocean of expanse and strength and life-giving vitality, an ocean of patience and beauty and dark currents of mystery.

The wonder deserved respect.

But time and magic are fleeting transitions, and Hank had to leave. He was on his way to Long Beach to catch a ferry for Santa Catalina Island. "It isn't really being on the ocean," he apologized, "but it's close."

He pulled himself reluctantly away from the edge of the surf, torn between what he owned that sunrise moment and what he was about to experience. We shook hands. He took one last look at the sea and then strode quickly toward his car.

"Hank!" I called after him.

He turned. I wanted to say something, but I didn't know what. I liked the man. And I liked seeing the ocean, the brand new ocean, through his eyes.

"I'm sorry about Mary," I said.

I'm not sure he heard me. He waved and was gone.

I stood there for a long time, a native Californian, seeing the Pacific for the very first time and grateful beyond words to a man named Hank.

July 4, 1985

❖

THE LAST SUNSET

I WAS DRIVING WEST THROUGH THE CLEVELAND NATIONAL Forest, past wooded groves and small settlements, when I heard the news. A jet had crashed into the sea off Port Hueneme.

I remember the exact moment. It was at sunset.

I was 30 minutes out of Lake Elsinore on a meandering search for columns across the Inland Empire. The route I was taking, Highway 74, winds through Riverside and Orange counties, up and over a summit of about 2,000 feet.

The views from certain high points are awesome in their scope, looking down on open valleys and across to the crisp outline of other ridges, sketched in penciled detail against an early winter twilight.

The scene was especially compelling at this moment. A sunset gleaming with pastels superimposed on a sky cleansed by rain had created an iridescence that was blinding.

Few moments are more magical.

I stopped to stare and to marvel. The car radio was on but barely audible, a murmur in the background. But still I heard the terrible news. Years of being tuned to bulletins train one to pick out the essential words of shattering events amid the otherwise mundane.

A jetliner with 88 people aboard had gone down 45 minutes earlier. The impact of the news was in sharp contrast to the texture of the moment. And for reasons I can't explain, I found myself wondering if those aboard had seen the sunset too.

It was an odd collision of pain and beauty. My first thought was, "Oh, the humanity." It was a phrase broadcast in tears and grief by a young radio reporter, Herb Morrison, as he watched the airship Hindenburg go down in flames 63 years ago.

Oh, the humanity. Has it ever been said better?

There were 88 elements of humanity, men, women and children, aboard the Alaska Airlines jet as it dropped from the sky like a wounded bird and marked its grave with a tower of seawater shooting into the air.

One can only imagine the sudden, gasping horror of the plane's final seconds. Did the passengers know they were going down? Was there a warning? Or did the end come too quickly for the mind to compute its terror?

The search for survivors was already underway by the time I drove out of the mountains and onto Interstate 5. Details of the crash were now coming in snippets of talk, like bits of a conversation overheard across a crowded room.

The flight path. The words of a witness. The function of a horizontal stabilizer. The reliability of an MD-83. The litany of calamity, always the same.

Oh, the humanity.

I don't know how many plane crashes I've covered over the past four decades of newspapering. I don't know how many body bags I've seen or how many fields of wreckage. But I do remember my first.

It was in the mid-1950s. A four-engine turboprop had gone down in San Francisco Bay, and I was there in a small fishing boat out of Point Richmond to report on the rescue effort.

I remember seeing bits of wing and fuselage bobbing like toys on a churning surface. I remember seeing scraps of luggage and clothing. And I remember seeing bodies, torn and mutilated beyond description.

Calamity has a way of imprinting itself on memory. Years later I can still evoke those moments in vivid detail. Time and similar experiences make them no less horrifying.

Radio reports of Monday's crash filled my car for the remainder of my trip from the Inland Empire to L.A.

It was late by the time I reached home and turned on the television. Harsh scenes of tragedy were repeated far into the night. Helicopters hovered over a sea illuminated by searchlights. Emergency vehicles stood ready on the shore. Body bags lay in a neat row along a walkway.

The voices of witnesses became faces. Graphics illustrated the plane's plunge from 17,000 feet. Airport scenes were heavy with a blend of urgency and grief.

I could have gone to the rescue scene, but I didn't. It was enough to have seen the sunset gleaming against the fading day. It was enough to wonder if those aboard Flight 261 had seen the same colors, the same iridescence, the same glory.

It was enough to ponder if, in their last moments, they had been granted one last look at a vision of life they would never see again.

Oh, the humanity.

February 2, 2002

❖

A VAN GOGH KIND OF DAY

VAN GOGH WOULD HAVE LOVED THE DAY. THE SUN WAS A DEEP yellow, the ocean silver, the sky a vibrant blue and the hills a dusting of green.

In one distance you could see snow-capped mountains, in another a misty Santa Catalina. The very air shimmered with color, embracing us in streaks and halos of blinding iridescence.

194

You didn't have to be a Van Gogh to understand at least some of what he understood so well, that we are travelers on a sea of color, small bits of humanity in a glory too complex to explain.

Call it nature, call it God's creation, the name matters little. On its simplest terms, what the world offers in startling array is beauty in so many forms that all you've got to do is stop and look to see it.

I thought about this as I stood in line that shimmery day between storms, waiting to view the works of Van Gogh, the lonely and troubled Dutchman who has stunned heaven and history with his own understanding of the world.

Much has been said of the exhibition in the Los Angeles County Museum of Art's west gallery, a funny little series of small rooms in what used to be a department store. And much of it has been negative.

Sure, Van Gogh was great, they've said, but the wait to get in was too long, the line was unbearable, the crowds were too large, the name of the exhibition wasn't lyrical, and wouldn't it be swell if they had the wheat field and crows, the shoes and the potato eaters all to themselves?

No.

Great art belongs to the people, and I was glad to see them there in such variety and diversity on the day of my visit: ladies who lunch, men who work with their hands, kids with rings in their noses, old people with walkers, the handicapped in wheelchairs.

We were all the colors and languages of a city rapidly becoming the cosmopolis of the future in a line that snaked back through a large tent-like structure into a parking lot outside.

What I saw wasn't a crowd but a celebration of individuals, each a dot or a brush stroke of a painting in progress. What I heard was a melody of languages for a concerto still being written.

Understand this, I hate lines. I dislike crowds. My best times are quiet moments with my wife or writing alone in a room of only distant sounds.

But I'd stand in a line five miles long and cram myself into a closet filled with Japanese tourists to be able to view the smallest work that Van Gogh ever created.

I'm one of the guys, not an art expert. But my wife knows art and has educated me over the years to appreciate what I'm seeing, like a child who, for the very first time, is introduced to a night filled with stars.

I stare in wonder, I absorb with pleasure.

Lines and crowds somehow ceased to matter once when we stood in line for three hours in a wind that chilled the bones to see Cézanne in Paris, and when we fought our way through hordes to view Monet in Chicago.

It's what is at the end of the line that counts.

What the whiners have lost sight of is the genius, the insight, the pain and the splendor that wait at the end of this line. Van Gogh embodies it all in a single self-portrait, an awesome man in a felt hat with eyes that pierce, that follow, that study, that wonder.

Yes, there are crowds. Someone's going to step in front of you, someone's going to jostle you and many are going to block your view. But be still. Hold your ground. Absorb. And soon Van Gogh will wash over you in waves of color so deep and personal that the crowds will vanish and the room go silent.

What I'm saying is come to this exhibition. Drag your old man off the couch. Take a day off from work. Leave the office. Borrow the money for tickets. Bring your kids. Pay a baby-sitter. Drive, take a bus, walk.

This is something special, moments created more than a century ago to linger through time like a sunrise, touching something in each of us, calling us to really see that which glistens around us.

The world is a series of crows and wheat fields observed from different perspectives and filtered through the arcs and flashes of our lives. We mirror ourselves in the art we create.

I think about that now as I write. The day is dark and threatening, the sky heavy with the possibility of rain. It's a Van Gogh sky, and the landscape that lies below the darkness is a Van Gogh wheat field.

It's all there. All we've got to do is pause for a moment and look.

February 5, 1999

THE BIG ONE, ALMOST

I WAS ASLEEP WHEN OUR HOUSE BEGAN TO SWAY AT 4:58 A.M. SUNDAY.

The first thought that entered my head was, "It's an earthquake." The second thought that entered my head was, "There goes the tourist industry."

"Hold still," my wife said.

Cinelli assumes that any movement between the hours of midnight and 7 a.m. must be me wiggling in bed.

She sleeps without moving a muscle. I do not remain in the same position longer than 18 minutes. I sat up and watched her one night. Not a twitch.

I explained the next day it wasn't normal for someone to sleep without rolling over occasionally.

She said, "How can anyone who hums in his sleep talk about normalcy?"

"I hum because I'm happy," I said.

"You hum because you're crazy."

On Sunday morning, she opened her eyes and said, "If it isn't you, it must be an earthquake."

It seemed to go on interminably. Light fixtures swayed like palm trees. Windows rattled. My stuffed barracuda fell from its shelf.

"We don't have an earthquake preparedness kit," Cinelli said. "What would Quirky Quake say?"

That again.

Quirky Quake is a cartoon logo of the Southern California Earthquake Preparedness Project. She uses him to remind me I have done nothing to prepare our family for the Big One.

I should have put aside fresh water and blankets and pinned an evacuation plan to the wall. Instead, I made up a kit consisting of vodka, vermouth, cigars and a can of smoked oysters, and to hell with Quirky Quake.

Paul Flores is director of the preparedness project. He told me once to forget standing in a doorway when the Big One comes.

I couldn't believe it. I grew up trusting doorways. Stand in a doorway in an earthquake, and close your eyes in a nuclear attack.

The thing to do, he explained, was to get under a solid wooden desk. "But hang on tight," he warned, "because the desk might suddenly go shooting across the room."

The doorway theory has been abandoned because during a quake, the door is liable to slam open and closed several times and beat you to death.

Among the casualties was a newspaper columnist who was battered to death by his own door. His wife was too embarrassed to divulge his name but did mention that at least there would be no wiggling and humming in bed anymore.

"It can't be an earthquake," I said as we rolled with the Earth. "The mayor didn't call for calm last night. He always calls for calm before a disaster."

"Also the dog didn't howl," Cinelli said.

That's a joke. Hoover never warns us of anything. Other dogs yowl their brains off. Even crickets crick their little hearts out. Hoover crouches in a corner and stares.

Schopenhauer, the pessimistic philosopher, said, "No good will come from relying on a silent, cowering, staring dog." Hoover also drools. Less good will come from that.

The Earth had barely stopped moving when my sister Emily called from Oakland. "Are you all right?" she wanted to know.

It is part of the Big Sister Syndrome. Whenever anything happens south of Buttonwillow, she telephones and wants to know if I'm all right.

"I'm fine," I say, "I'm drunk and in jail for murdering a whore."

"Thank God," she says.

Emily never listens.

Television was relentless in its coverage of the quake. The same news was repeated until it rang in your head. The same wrecked bowling alley was shown until it was burned on your brain.

We had guests for dinner that evening. One of them said if the media hadn't dwelt on the earthquake, it wouldn't have seemed as bad.

"Turn off the tube," Cinelli said, "death is everywhere."

The woodcarver Barry remembered one quake where a cat was hurled across the room, flat out, like a missile. He hates cats and recalled the incident warmly. "Whoosh!" he said, laughing and moving his hand in a flat line.

A big quake is a carnival for seismologists. They salivate at the first tremor and are in paradise for weeks warning about aftershocks. Lucy Jones and the Caltech Gang. Everybody stay tense, more on the way!

On Monday, the real aftershock came.

The tourist industry is in jeopardy! Radio and television reported the quakes would cause a 4% dip in the number of visitors to L.A. this year.

First the riots, then this. I don't know how they figured the percentage. Perhaps Lucy Jones told them.

My sister Emily telephoned immediately. "I heard about the tourist problem," she said. "Are you all right?"

"I'm fine," I said. "I'm downtown strangling Quirky Quake."

"Thank God," she said.

June 30, 1992

❖

WAITING FOR THE RAIN

IT CAME TAPPING ON THE ROOFTOP JUST AFTER MIDNIGHT, LIKE the hesitant knocking of a stranger at the door.

It was an unfamiliar sound, given the dryness of the season, and at first I wasn't sure what it was. I lay there half-awake listening. And then I realized.

Rain.

Even the name whispers. It should be said with a mixture of awe and reverence, the gift of nature to a thirsty city.

I pulled back the drapes and looked out. A porch light caught droplets of water cascading off the roof. The leaves of the oak trees glistened. There were diamonds in the night.

Tap, tap, tap, tap....

I could visualize the television weather forecasters shaking their heads. The weather, they will declare grimly, has turned bad. Fools, I would say to them, have you no perspective? The weather has, at last, turned good!

"Do you intend," my wife said sleepily, "to sit up all night watching the rain?"

I could.

Henry Ward Beecher referred to the "soft architectural hands" of rain. He knew its power to cleanse and cure, and to carve canyons out of stone.

Only those who don't understand the cycles of time deplore the rain. One should stand in it and feel the centuries to know the intrinsic value of a storm.

Tap, tap, tap, tap....

There is a stillness to the land. Swirls of mist gather into a fog. Moisture shines the silver.

For the first time this season, it's winter.

This is the way the season ought to be. Wind blowing into the fog, scattering it. Earth and sky blending. Crows calling into the breathless morning.

I let the dog out. He's a springer spaniel with ears that flip and flop as he runs. Puddles of water splash up around him. He jumps and spins, a dancer in winter.

"Go ahead," my wife says. "Play in the rain. You won't rest until you do. Just leave your clothes on."

I step into the storm that by now has become a light drizzle. It touches my face with the softness of a child's hand. The softness, as Beecher wrote, with the power to chisel mountains.

Our roof leaks when it rains. Water seeps through pinholes where old construction joins new. Plastic pans catch the drips. Towels soak up the overflow.

Roofers patch things and walk away. No guarantees, they say. The leaks continue. Drip, drip, drip....

The dog runs in and out through his own door. Muddy footprints mark the floor like symbols of an artist's design as the dog races through the house, excited by the storm. He knocks over a pan that catches the drips. The mess is exasperating.

But still....

Rain, like tears, helps to wash away the grief of terrible times. There is redemption in rain. I drive down to the ocean that swallowed Flight 261. Rain has cleansed the air that bore witness to a plane's last moments. The sea, reaching up to the rain, remembers.

I don't underestimate the power of rain. I've seen roads washed out and houses swept downhill. I've seen streets flooded to waist-high depths. I've seen lives lost and property ruined.

But so far, this rain isn't like that. This is a rain that promises spring. This is a rain that dazzles and glistens. This is a dog's winter dance.

I don't know what the weather's going to be like today. Will the storm still tease us with gentle fingers? Or will that strange pale sunlight that has shone most of the winter still cast our city in an eerie glow?

L.A. isn't afraid of rain. I see joggers splashing down San Vicente and along Ocean Avenue. I see volleyball players on a soggy beach. And I know that, despite all, golfers slam balls into the moist air, and tennis players fire missiles across dripping nets.

Only paper flowers, another poet wrote, are afraid of rain.

I come home and stand in the driveway. The softness continues. I love the smell of a storm, a clean mixture of earth and distance. I know as I stand there that I'll go in and write about the rain.

I should move on to other subjects. Not everyone sees poetry in the exhilaration of wet weather. Problems should be explored and people defined. The city cries out for comment.

But still....

I sit at my word processor and begin: It came tapping on the rooftop just after midnight, like the hesitant knocking of a stranger at the door....

February 13, 2000

A TIME BETWEEN STORMS

SANTA ANAS ARE FORMIDABLE WINDS, HOWLING DOWN OVER THE high desert like blasts of hot air from heaven. They wiped the skies clean of clouds and smog over the weekend with a rush of energy that left us all a little dazzled.

I became aware of them in the middle of the night when the branch of an oak tree began rattling against a window. I thought it was rain at first and bolted upright in bed to await the downpour.

Almost instantly I realized it was wind, but the experience reminded me of all the waiting we had done after that roaring killer storm just two weeks ago. And it reminded me of Larry, who is dying of cancer.

I had stopped by to see him during what was supposed to be a lull between storms. He was sitting by a window that looked out toward the Santa Monica Mountains, absorbing all he could of life during the time he had left.

His house had weathered the first storm OK, and now, like everyone else, he was waiting to see what the second one would bring.

"Waiting," he said, coughing slightly, "is the hard part. You never know what's going to happen next."

I'm not sure whether he was talking about the interim between storms or about himself, suspended between life and the unknown.

Later, as I drove around Topanga, I saw how much waiting was actually going on. Nothing was more symbolic of it than a Caltrans truck with a blinking sign that flashed "Residents Only" to traffic entering the canyon.

The blinking was set on a regular rhythm and, like the ticking of a clock in a quiet room, emphasized that the time between calamities is often short.

A highway patrolman sat in his car near the crest that overlooked the San Fernando Valley, waiting for the next emergency.

A bulldozer operator stood near a bridge where the highway had been seriously undermined, waiting for truckloads of boulders.

Volunteers joined homeowners in piling sandbags along Topanga Creek, where a roaring flood tide threatened homes. And when the piling was over, they watched the water and waited.

It was an unsettling time. The sky would alternately darken and lighten, as though God were playing games with those who looked upward.

"Here it comes," we said when the day seemed to go suddenly black and the wind began and a torrent of water spilled from the heavens. But it stopped suddenly and the clouds drifted off and nothing else happened.

"Whatever became of showers?" Larry asked. His face was gaunt and drawn. "It's not raining at all one minute and then it's pouring. Doesn't it sprinkle anymore?"

From his window, he could see the street next to his house. Neighbors had gathered on a corner and were chatting happily. Calamity creates block parties even as it breeds grief.

We are one in disaster. In Topanga, old-timers mingled with yuppies whose very presence they scorn. Yuppies loaded sandbags to save the shacks of old-timers they could never understand.

We honored the human spirit in that storm, even as we shouldered the burden of not knowing what lay ahead.

At my own home, the waiting was evident. As I entered, the televised image of young Adam Paul Bischoff was on the screen, his terrified face above water, his mouth forming the words "Help me."

Rescue workers reached for the boy from bridges that spanned the L.A. River, dangling near the surface of the water, arms outstretched, only to miss him by a sigh.

We watched the screen in horrified fascination to see him swept downstream by the fierce current, a hand rising briefly from the river, reaching backward to where life still existed, and then disappearing.

We watched him vanish, and we waited.

I looked around my house. Towels were piled on a table to soak up the water that seeped into a rear bathroom.

I opened a back door and cleaned a drain that had clogged with mud. On the deck, I emptied toy buckets that had filled with water. And I waited.

The second storm never came. The body of Adam Bischoff was found downstream. The waiting was over.

So why write about it now, weeks later, when the sky is a breathless blue and even the wind has died to a whisper?

Because I realized that night as I listened to the Santa Anas how unnerving the unknown can be.

Waiting, as Larry said, is the hard part. We huddle like children at the door of eternity. And though the storm is gone, the waiting is never really over. We are all, in a way, endlessly between storms.

The best we can hope for is that we endure each one with equanimity and, like Larry, get on with absorbing all the life we have left.

February 25, 1992

CHAPTER SEVEN

WAR AND REMEMBRANCE

"As long as war is looked upon as wicked,
it will always have its fascination.
Only when it is looked upon as vulgar will it
cease to be popular."

—OSCAR WILDE

THE FACE OF WAR

THE FACE OF JOHNNY SPANN STARES AT ME FROM A BULLETIN board next to my computer, torn from the front page of the newspaper a few days ago.

It's a face of such youth and vitality that I can almost imagine his presence in the room, watching the words I write. His smile is open but hesitant, as though there is something he wants to say, a secret he wants to impart, a truth he has discovered.

But whatever his words, they will never be said now. Johnny Spann is our latest hero, offered up in tears by the world's newest nonwar. A CIA agent, he was killed in a prison uprising near Mazar-i-Sharif, the first American combat fatality in Afghanistan.

And now we mourn.

The word "hero" is not a term of my choosing, but one applied by others to explain an atrocity. Johnny Spann was a victim, not a hero. His intent was not to die at age 32, beaten bloody by fanatic militiamen, but to experience life in a new place, to do a job he had chosen to do and then to go home again.

When he did go home, it was in a coffin.

The day we stop thinking of young men killed in war as heroes may be the day we begin wondering why we keep fighting wars. It will be the time to ponder how the human race, alone among mammals, could ever allow such a periodic slaughter of its own future. The morning will come when we'll ask, why do we do this to each other?

I was thinking of Spann as I watched a 1968 documentary called "A Face of War." It follows a Marine company for 97 days during combat in Vietnam, its cameras open to every twist and bloody turn of the fighting.

But mostly it focuses on the faces. And you can see Johnny Spann in every one of them.

Hailed by critics for its "numbing power" and "unbearable poignancy," the film was produced by legendary documentarians Gene and Natalie Jones, who for 51 years as partners, and as husband and wife, have traveled the world in search of the people and places whose images reflect the history of our time. They live now in a hilltop home in Bel-Air, writing of their exploits, surrounded by the art and artifacts they've gathered over a lifetime of travel.

A Marine combat photographer in the Second World War, Gene has been wounded five times over the long course of covering nine wars. He was hit at Iwo Jima as a Marine, then twice in Korea and twice in Vietnam as a civilian. He worked first for NBC and then freelanced with Natalie.

Their work has been nominated for an Oscar and an Emmy, and was notable in the 1960s as a powerful statement against war. "A Face of War" ran in theaters for 14 months and over the course of a year on television throughout the U.S. A small network of stations showed it for 16 hours straight, over and over, as a hallmark of the peace movement.

Few have seen as much of war as Gene Jones. Few have seen so many young faces swept from the world like smoke in a breeze. Few have shared the peril and pain of our young warriors to such a degree.

Generals posture and pontificate like figures in a comic opera, but Jones was close to the humanity of battle. He's the expert on people, not units, at war. And as an expert, he was asked to define it in a sentence.

He replied in a tone flattened by experience, "War is the most terrible thing human beings can do to each other."

What troubles me is how easily we have accepted the presence of this war, this nonwar. The peace movement, if there is one, has been muted by the yahooing out of Washington. We have marshaled not only our military forces, but also our minds into the shape of a weapon ready for battle.

Flags and mottoes do the job. A combination of country-love and battle images from abroad stirs the soul like the sound of trumpets. Drumbeats rally the masses. And the faces of men like Johnny Spann will continue to adorn the front pages of our newspapers, their forever-smiles frozen on film and tape, their words never said.

In his long career of recording the sounds and images of war, Gene Jones has concentrated on faces. "They're the masks of rage and terror that bare the soul," he said the other day in a telephone conversation. "The worst and best of humankind emerge at the point of a bayonet."

All of it is manifested in "A Face of War." We see fear and bravado, courage and nostalgia, determination and pain reflected back in expressions that alter like images in a slide show, shifting quickly from one to the other as situations change.

And all the men remind me of Johnny Spann. Guys from down the block, from across the street, from around the corner.

We'll see more of their faces. We'll hear more of how bravely they died. The word "hero" will be repeated many times to the words and music that will celebrate their youthful courage. But a grim fact remains. Johnny won't be marching home again. And that's the saddest song of all.

December 6, 2001

❖

WHEN NIGHT FALLS

NIGHT WAS THE WORST OF ALL TIMES IN KOREA, ITS ABSOLUTE darkness embracing the potential of a dozen ways to die.

Twilight was almost as bad, because anticipation entered the equation and heightened our awareness of every shape that blurred into ebony and every sound that rustled in the wind.

I knew with certainty that the snap of a twig could be the last sound I would ever hear, the final, single tap of a drumbeat before a bullet.

211

It was Joe Citera's last sound and Pete Mammaril's too, and a hundred others whose names I once knew in the tight camaraderie of war.

The memory of night's menace has lasted 45 years, emerging at unexpected moments like a bird startled into flight, causing an almost physical reaction to keep low and seek cover.

And so it was proper that I should visit the newly dedicated Korean War Memorial as dusk fell over the Washington Mall.

I looked all the terrible memories in the face, held to the scene by a fascination that would not allow me to glance away, staring into the eyes of a warrior-statue whose horror is eternized in stainless steel.

I stared until twilight merged into darkness and the sunset that splashed rainbows on the underside of thunderclouds vanished, and the terrible, drenching heat of an unbearable day became an unbearable night.

The 19 soldiers that compose the memorial seemed to move with the shadows that shifted with the transition from day to evening. Pale green spotlights cast their faces into ever-deepening expressions of tension and anxiety.

The images were haunting. I saw myself there and heard a twig snapping....

Monuments are often larger and grander than realities, assuming heroic proportions in the aftermath of the events they commemorate.

In the case of the Korean War, a hole in history three years wide, that may not be so. It was a confrontation beyond the statistics that were endlessly quoted over the dedication weekend.

Speakers and booklets, needlessly seeking justification for the memorial, never failed to mention that 54,000 Americans had died in a war once dismissed as a police action, as though a euphemism, however often repeated, would erase the flow of blood that traced red ribbons on the snow of an Asian winter.

What I never heard on that weekend was that a total of 3 million human beings from all sides, military and civilians, young and old, lost their lives in the battles that raged up and down the Korean peninsula.

There isn't a monument big enough to recognize that kind of loss, except wherein it dwells on the world's conscience.

I thought about those things as I finally pulled free from the hypnotic state I found myself in, troubled by both the memories of war's endless nights and the murder of those who were its innocent victims.

Even as night deepened, crowds swirled around me at the memorial, creating a surreality of movement over my own memory of being totally alone in the shadows that fell over the front lines almost five decades earlier.

Armies of graying and potbellied men were my company as we walked around the memorial's sculptured squad of soldiers, each 7 feet tall, which seemed to move through time and remembrance up a slight incline toward the Washington Monument that glowed in the distance.

Helmeted, draped in ponchos, their M-1s and Browning Automatic Rifles at the ready, they are frozen in postures of vigilance, looking this way and that, alert to movement, listening to sounds.

One seems to have just turned, swinging to the right, listening. Was that a twig he heard snapping?

Passenger jets from Washington National Airport added to the mystique of twilight, silhouettes against the setting sun, reminiscent of the terrible sunsets created by flashes of fiery napalm once dropped from the skies in bursts of color on seashores, ridge lines and valleys terraced by rice paddies.

They were the sunsets of Inchon and Pusan and the Punchbowl and Chosin Reservoir and Heartbreak Ridge and Hamburger Hill, and of a dozen sweeping offensives with names such as Operation Killer and Ripper and Mousetrap.

The napalm sunsets left behind figures charred in the posture of flight or crouched in fear, the odor of their burning flesh lingering on the breezes of memory that drift occasionally into my sleep.

If I talk too often of memory, it is because so many of them were evoked during the two days I spent at the Korean War Memorial.

I was reminded a dozen times over of the war and those who fought it with me, especially on the sweltering night of my arrival with the presence of a small piece of cardboard left at the head of the memorial.

It said simply, "F-2-7, 1st Mar. Div."

There were many such notes left in the area of the monument, either around the marching soldiers or at the foot of a 164-foot-long granite wall, on whose face was etched the ghostly images of war's participants.

But the one that caught my attention was the handwritten F-2-7 notation, because it meant Fox Company, 2nd Battalion, 7th Regiment, 1st Marine Division. Seeing it was an affirmation of my past. It was my company, my battalion, my regiment, my division.

I had been there. I had honest to God been there.

I never discovered who made the F-2-7 sign or found anyone from Fox Company, but it really didn't matter. We were all warriors in the same battles, confined to a peninsula about half the size of California, oddly companionable in the mutuality of our war.

We looked for faces, we looked for names, we looked for combat insignias at the memorial, and we talked endlessly to each other, the way old soldiers do, about how close friendships were and how quickly they ended in sprays of fire and lead, or in the single drum tap of a sniper's bullet.

There was a completion to all this, a closing of the circle, final recognition that, yes, there had been a war and we had been in it and now everyone knows that.

There were no parades and bugles when we came home. No crowds cheered, no storms of confetti and streamers fell from tall buildings.

The troopship William Wiegel that returned me to San Diego docked, prophetically, as night was falling. But if we expected family to meet us, none was there, because there had been confusion about where the ship would land and when.

A small detachment of Marines waited as we docked and led us to buses at the end of the pier. There wasn't even a band.

The buses took us to the Marine Recruit Depot, where I had entered the corps two years earlier. I was told as we were mustered out the next day that I couldn't leave the base because records showed I had never returned a pillow issued when I was in boot camp.

But then they looked in my eyes, where visions of blood and hell still dwelt, and knew that no goddamn pillow would ever stop me from leaving that base. The Marine Corps in its wisdom wrote off the pillow and sent me to my Cinelli, my wife, who waited.

There was no such silence or insensitivity on the long weekend of the memorial.

The president spoke, bands played, flags fluttered, fireworks lit the cloudy night and everyone marched on parade. There was even a thunderstorm.

You couldn't ask for a better acknowledgment of an effort at arms. If it seemed a little excessive, that's OK too.

It was for Joe Citera and Pete Mammaril, who heard the drum taps 44 years ago, and Adolph Brunn and Don Weiland, who made it home, and for all of us who felt so alone when our ships docked at piers notable for their emptiness.

The Korean War never really ended. Tensions continue to bristle along the border of a divided country. I saw it firsthand during a visit a year ago. Nothing has changed.

As a result, we have been unable to feel that anything was over or that we were truly home. We have been suspended in history and vilified by our own memories, leaving a war neither won nor lost, and 3 million people dead.

But now, if nothing else, the monument tells us our pain is acknowledged and the brutality of our war is recognized. To that extent, we can slip out of the uniforms of our memories and rest easily with our terrible encounter.

Finally there has been a tribute. Finally, a parade. Finally, a band. I can say with a satisfaction I never anticipated that after decades adrift in nights I can never forget, I'm home at last.

August 1, 1995

THE CRUSHING WEIGHT
OF GOODBYE

NOW COMES THE HARD PART, AFTER THE FLAGS AND CANDLES, after the speeches, after the angry hubris of a wounded nation. Now come the goodbyes.

We see tears and kisses at homes, at airports and at docksides as our young go off to those places where there are no speeches, only vast areas of uncertainty and death.

Terrorists left a hole in our nation where the twin towers once stood, and now they are leaving another, the space occupied by those who now must abandon families and jobs to make war on shadows.

Saying goodbye to them is hard to do.

Those of us who have been there know that war takes on a different tone when the troopships leave the shore. Pain replaces patriotism in combat, and shouts of vengeance become the cries of those whose lives are left in the shattered paths of moving armies.

Henry Miller wrote, "How different war would be if we could consult the veteran instead of the politician." As a veteran, I'm here to tell you a little something of what I know about it.

I was a small child when the Second World War began, but I remember as though it were an hour ago saying goodbye to a brother-in-law drafted into the Army. We were at a train station in Oakland on a drizzly morning, and a sadness as gray as the skies lay over those who had gathered there.

About 100 draftees and their families clung to each other in embraces that only a strident call to duty could end, and war creates the most strident of calls for the most terrible of duties. When it was time for them to leave, my brother-in-law touched my shoulder and said, "Take care of your sister," and disappeared onto the train.

That moment, with its grayness and its finality, became a part of the boy growing up, a memory defined as much by its loneliness as its drama. I walked away from the station feeling as though something had been torn from inside me that would never be replaced.

Years later, as Marine reservists were called to action, the scene would be replayed in much the same way, but this time I was the central character in a cultural passion play that has repeated itself so often in human history.

That memory too is strong. The same sister I had accompanied to a train station just 10 years earlier was now saying goodbye to me. My wife, barely 20, was clinging to me the way my sister had clung to her young husband just a decade before.

This time it was the war in Korea. This time it was a train station in San Francisco. This time we were wrapped in ribbons of fog that chilled the morning air. But the differences became less significant in the fields of conflict.

My brother-in-law had come back physically whole but emotionally wounded. Horror had created an emptiness in him. He died an old man, unable to talk about the blood that shrouded his memories in deep red until the very end.

The war in Vietnam was next, and we said goodbye to other young men, my nephew among them, whose expression I remember as one of bewilderment as he boarded a plane. There had been a party the night before. The goodbyes were noisy as a rock band played, but now they were quiet.

He went off to war a promising golfer, shelves filled with amateur trophies, and returned wounded, barely able to walk, his goal of turning pro ended by the shrapnel of a single grenade.

What do they teach us, these repetitive goodbyes? Nothing, apparently. In my lifetime, America has lost more than a half-million young men and women on fields of combat in Europe, the South Pacific, Korea, Vietnam and the Middle East. Millions more, military personnel and civilians, have joined them in death around the world.

And yet, once more we stand at the points of emotional embarkation, kissing our soldiers and sailors goodbye, waving a last wave, crying tears of fear and sadness. Are the lives we give to this new cause worth the grief?

We look back to the Second World War and say yes, it prevented a new dark age. But the others? Korea remains divided, and Vietnam is in the hands of those who were our enemies. In the Gulf War, we saved Kuwait, but Saddam

Hussein still owns Iraq.

The politics of war play on a different plane than its realities.

Nothing said it better than a Bill Mauldin cartoon just before Korea. It showed two very old and wizened men at their club, sunk into deep leather chairs. One is remarking to the other, "I say it's war, Throckmorton, and I say let's fight."

I think about that today as I remember the face of a friend who was dying in my arms, holding in his own intestines, his eyes staring into mine, pleading, wondering, seeing something I couldn't see, and then at last collapsing into himself.

All I could think of saying to him as his life ended was a tearful "good-bye." It remains today, as it was then, such a lonely word.

September 24, 2001

❖

LEAVING PRIVATE RYAN

I HAVE NOTHING LEFT FROM THE KOREAN WAR BUT A DIARY AND a camouflage helmet cover.

The diary is in a drawer somewhere, and the helmet cover has been turned into a lampshade that sits on a shelf in my writing room, which my wife refers to as the Chapel, so many sermons emerge from it.

I got rid of my Marine uniform as quickly as I could because I just didn't want any lingering connections to that part of my life, except for the camou-flage helmet cover that somehow stayed with me.

There are enough images in my head and enough dreams in my nights to remind me of that war, that conflict, that police action, 50 years ago, and now there's even a movie.

I realize that "Saving Private Ryan" isn't about Korea, but war is war and hell is hell and it all came flooding back as I watched the film amid a tense and silent audience.

The Second World War was history's last great, patriotic battle, and Steven Spielberg and writer Robert Rodat made the most of it in "Private Ryan." Every war after VJ Day was bothersome, time-consuming and even downright annoying, but old Double-U Double-U Two was, well, fulfilling. The battle scenes in the film are about as realistic as you can get, from the terrifying confusion to the immense and drumming silences, from the roar of exploding artillery shells to the terrible screams of the dying.

But I kept wondering as I watched it all, where was Private Ex?

That was what we called anyone whose name we couldn't remember or didn't want to think about, the guy among us with no special identity. Unlike a movie where major characters are pretty well defined, war is composed of a lot of grunts whose faces blend into the background. One of them was Private Ex.

He was a fat little man from Nowhere, U.S.A., who had no friends and hardly spoke to anyone. Someone said he'd delivered mail in a small town in the Midwest and had no relatives. He never got mail of his own and wasn't included in most activities.

I remember him especially when we limped back into regimental reserve one summer day, all shot up and war-weary. He was off by himself as usual, just kind of sitting there doing nothing while the rest of us drank beer and tried hard to forget that which was not forgettable and never will be.

We had a hospital corpsman with us who was good at hypnotizing and making his subjects act like damned fools. It was our primary form of entertainment so we asked him to hypnotize Private Ex.

Ex agreed to it because for a moment at least he was a part of something. The corpsman put him under and said when he came out of it he'd have a little candy-striped dog in his arms named Pogie. And then he snapped his fingers.

Private Ex looked around for a moment, and then began petting his imaginary dog and talking to him in loving terms. He held the dog like a mother holds a baby, radiating a warmth we'd never seen in him before.

There were laughs all right as the candy-striped dog did tricks and fat little Ex romped around like a kid. But then someone went to grab the dog, and

Ex spun around and knocked him on his ass, screaming, "Don't touch him!"

As we thought about it later, we realized that the guy probably had never owned anything in his life, and that nonexistent dog was dearer to him than anything we could possibly imagine, a lonely man with a warm possession.

It got even more serious when a captain came by and, demanding that the game end, tried to approach Ex. He also got decked. The corpsman had been trying his damnedest to snap Ex out of it but nothing was working, and when he tried again, Ex ran to his tent and came out with a loaded .45.

He stood there with one hand clutching his candy-striped dog and the other holding that .45, daring us to try to take his dog. His whole life existed in that imaginary world, clutching the one thing that made him real.

The corpsman worked for an hour and finally got Ex's attention and brought him out of it OK. We went back to our beer in silence, and Ex just sat there like he always had, looking alone.

That's the way war is sometimes. Not just shot and shell but an awful isolation of spirit. It's in that singularity of existence that we learn about ourselves and glance briefly into the souls of others in the raw awareness that reality provides. It's an emptiness that lingers long after Private Ryan has gone home.

July 31, 1998

❖

ANOTHER PLACE, ANOTHER TIME

IT'S ALL BEGINNING TO SEEM FAMILIAR. THE TEACH-INS, THE candlelight vigils, the marches, the chants, the confrontations.

The sounds and the scenes float through memory like tendrils of smoke, evoking images of other places, other times and other threats to the human family.

What's going on this time is that we're organizing for peace again, to stop a war before it starts. The world waits in breathless anticipation to see if our cowboy president turns Iraq into a heap of ashes.

Old campaigners and young first-timers alike are waving no-more-war banners in the faces of those in the bomb-first, talk-later school of thought, who in turn are waving flags in their faces and demanding that we not forget 9/11.

Peace workers gather in increasing numbers, utilizing the electronics that didn't exist four decades ago, when, after years of trying, they succeeded in helping to end a war — but not until after more than a million people had died.

There were just bullhorns in the 1960s, and a lot of yelling. Now there are fax machines and e-mail and cell phones, humming away in a cooler climate of protest that is forming, as someone has said, "under the radar."

Former state Sen. Tom Hayden, in the streets back then, is on the podium now. "We will create a new peace movement," he promised at a rally observing the first anniversary of the destruction of New York's twin towers. He challenged the flag-waving militarism that followed the attack and warned, "We must not allow the Bush administration to turn September 11 into a national promotion of war."

It's a danger, all right. Patriotism fires the spirit to seek righteousness. Tears form. Fists clench. A young man, tense with anger, said to me that we had to get over there and teach them a lesson. Them who? He wasn't sure, but he knew that Iraq must be involved. His passions ignited by the drums and bugles, he was ready to march, as others have marched before, into the fields of war. Only after he's there will he discover that beyond the music and the oratory lies a reality filled with pain.

I have mixed feelings. If we can believe Bush, and I'm not sure I can, Iraq builds for the day it, and others we call terrorists, will destroy us with a hidden arsenal of nuclear, chemical and biological weapons. "We waited too long to stop Hitler," the hawks warn. "We can't wait that long this time."

War is high drama in which presidents and generals take center stage. It allows them to strut and posture and wave swords of words, knowing that at least a percentage of the audience will cheer. Ego and vengeance drive the military plot. "Give me enough medals," Napoleon Bonaparte said, "and I'll win any war."

I don't trust politicians, and I sure as hell don't trust generals. But if there is truth in the supposition that Saddam Hussein plans to equip a secret army

221

for Armageddon, can we afford to wait? Can we even afford to negotiate with one whose hidden agenda could plunge us into a new dark age? The only way to appease a tiger, it is said, is to allow oneself to be devoured. Are we ready for that?

I'm for peace. I don't care what it takes. And so are a growing number of those telling Bush to at least wait for an international coalition. Wait for a United Nations mandate. Wait for the U.N. weapons inspectors to do their job. Wait because rage engenders rage and vengeance creates more vengeance, until it all burns itself out in the smoking ruins of a postwar world. Wait for a year and avoid a century of anguish.

A CBS/New York Times Poll indicates that two-thirds of those asked want the weapons inspectors to go in before any military action is taken. A CNN/USA Today/Gallup Poll shows sentiment for invading Iraq down from 57% in September to 53% today.

As the terrible scenes of the twin towers falling grow distant, we're pausing to consider the consequences of what we might be about to do. And we're beginning to ask ourselves how many hundreds of thousands of lives we are willing to lose in a war to avenge the 2,800 who died in New York.

I loathe terrorism and the convoluted logic that says it's OK to kill children to advance a cause. But I also question the same twisted rationale that says it's OK to kill the babies of the terrorists in response. The losses are terrible in both instances.

I keep thinking of those we love who must exist in a world we have created and how they would fare in any kind of apocalyptic confrontation. The thought is chilling. Disarm Iraq by force if all the proof is in and it's the only way to stop a madman. But weigh carefully the cost.

Rather the rising voices of a growing peace movement than the screams of the innocents who will suffer if war comes.

October 10, 2002

MEMORY LINGERS ON

I AM AWASH THIS GRAY MORNING WITH MEMORIES OF JOE CITERA, a 19-year-old Marine who died during the Korean War, a lifetime ago. He'd be my age now, maybe retired and with grandchildren. I'm sure Joe would have married after the war, because that's what he talked about most. He wanted what we all wanted, a wife and kids and a life that had meaning.

Two things got me thinking about Joe the other day. One was the disclosure by North Korea's Kim Jong Il that the country has a secret nuclear weapons program.

I thought to myself, God, not again. Wars end in other places; why do the lingering threats of hostilities never cease in Korea?

An effort to organize was the second event that revived memories of Joe. I was sorting through a pile of stuff trying to get things in order when I came across his photograph.

It was one of those large studio shots, with Joe in gaudy Marine dress blues, a uniform furnished specifically for the picture. None of us had uniforms like that. We laughed at the image of a white hat and those blue pants with red stripes down the sides in a muddy foxhole.

But that was long ago, and I'm not laughing anymore.

The Joe Citera who looked out from the photograph was a face that has burned itself in my memory like the brand on a horse. He was a tall, loose kind of guy with big ears and a self-amused smile that never failed to fit the moment. I remember that grin during the worst times of the war: Joe glancing across at me during a withering mortar barrage and rasping in a Durante voice, "I wonder what the poor people are doing?"

He had an uncanny sense of timing when it came to lifting our spirits. He'd have made a great stand-up comic, appearing on stage in a dungaree cap, his ears sticking out and that faint smile on his face, talking about what it was like to be a private in the Marines. I can still hear him saying, "Oh, the sad indecencies of war," while trudging up a hill under a relentless sun, loaded down with combat gear.

We thought of him as a buffoon when he first joined the company, a clown among warriors, but he proved himself one day under enemy machine-gun fire when he rose in the face of that firestorm to bring out a wounded comrade. After dragging the man into a ditch, Joe popped his head up and hollered, "Ya missed!" We knew then he was made of special stuff, balancing courage with humor in the face of terrible odds.

His sister, Mary Fruehwirth, sent me the photograph and some letters her "Joeboy" had written from Korea when I was doing a magazine piece on the war. They were a close pair, raised by relatives after the deaths of their mother and father. She referred to him as a kid in a letter to me, then explained, "That's all he really was when he joined the Marines on his 18th birthday, Oct. 18, 1950. He was killed Sept. 12-13, 1951. He never really had a chance to grow up into a man."

Joe's letters to her were filled with an underlying loneliness. "Write every day!" was scrawled all over them. "Send plenty of candy, cookies and cake!" He was a high school dropout and his letters, written in pencil, were replete with misspellings, but that wasn't the measure of the man. What characterized this kid from Greenpoint, Brooklyn, was his grace under fire. In one letter he wrote, "How's everything at home? We're getting a lot of mortar and sniper fire here. Well, that's all for now."

The only time I saw Joe truly sad was when he talked about wanting a girl-friend to write to. Someone to love. He didn't have one, he said, because his ears stuck out. Who wanted a guy with big ears? "I'll have them fixed someday," he said to me in a quiet moment. "Then you'll see one handsome son of a bitch."

Joe was hit by machine-gun fire on a hill called 749, but even then he came through. Although badly wounded in a night assault by the Chinese, he yelled for us to hold on. When the enemy hollered, "All Marines from California go home tonight," he shouted back, "What about Brooklyn?" He died at dawn, and as we moved on up the hill, we posted a cardboard sign that said, "To Joe Citera, Hill 749. He held our luck as long as we needed it."

I'm sending the photograph and Joe's letters back to his sister in New Jersey. I don't need pictures to remind me of Joe. He's a ghost that just won't go away. *October 25, 2002*

ALL THE BRAVE YOUNG WARRIORS

THEY SLID FROM A HELICOPTER FIVE STORIES TO THE GROUND, dropping like tethered birds of prey and scattering in directions of the storm winds that blew around them.

Once on the ground, they turned from the "tether" — a rope dangling from above — to face unseen enemies, guerrilla fighters as invisible in practice as they might be in reality.

Then they returned to await their turn to do it again, and again and again.

The scene was an open field at Camp Pendleton, a sprawling military complex of 125,000 acres just north of San Diego, home of the storied 1st Marine Division.

The large gray helicopter, its twin rotors stirring up the hurricane of wind and dust, hovered over the field, and from its opening came the "birds" — young camouflaged warriors practicing the techniques they could be called upon to employ under hostile conditions.

The exercise was performed for the media as a way of demonstrating the capabilities of these "new" Marines to strike with the speed of cobras in areas of combat where large forces can't operate.

For instance, in Afghanistan.

We were there with our cameras and our notebooks watching as the young men, mostly in their early 20s, fast-roped and then rappelled from the belly of the chopper in the storm-wind setting.

And we listened to them boast, as young warriors will, that they were ready for anything. As they spoke, we could hear the chatter of small arms fire somewhere and the distant boom of artillery, underscoring their bravado.

It was all so familiar.

This was routine training, but there was nothing routine about the situation that has suddenly placed this 60-year-old camp on high alert. Terrorism was on everyone's mind, and the young warriors were edgy.

"When Bush says go, we go," one Marine said, crouched on the edge of

225

the field, watching the Sea Knight helicopter circle over the dry hills to return for another drop. "That's why they call us the 911 Force."

"But our families worry," said another, adjusting the vest that held his combat gear, everything from ammo to a first-aid kit. "My mother keeps calling."

Their names are Guesta, Ward, Mayfield and McKinley. Furlong, Grasmuck, Rackley and Lawler.

They come from Alabama, Michigan, Florida, Texas, California and New York. Three of them are from the same hometown. All bear the Military Occupational Specialty number 0311, the MOS of basic infantry, backbone of the Marine Corps.

"They're ready all right," an instructor said as he stood over a group of 10 Marines who knelt in the dirt, waiting for the helicopter to return.

His name is Sgt. Thomas Quinn. During the past year, he has trained 250 men to drop from the sky in an exercise of quick deployment.

"I sign their 'graduation' cards," he said. "That makes me responsible for seeing that they're ready when they leave here. Their lives are in my hands."

The big chopper settled into the dust storm. "All right," Quinn shouted over its roar, "let's rock and roll!"

The machines of war are large. The helicopter, an ancient cargo carrier, seemed to dominate the sky it occupied. The deep thrump-thrump-thrump of its rotors and the overpowering smell of its aviation fuel filled the senses.

In battle, tanks join the chaos, bombs explode, machine guns fire and men shout to be heard above the roar. Confusion often replaces the precision refined in training, which is why special units, such as Marines, train so hard.

But there is no way to accurately duplicate war in a camp-based exercise. Combat introduces variables that can never be anticipated. The machines seem even larger in a battle, more awesome and dangerous. And one realizes, amid the smoke and the noise, that humans are the most fragile elements of the fight. We are the heartbeats in the steel.

I said this all seemed familiar. I trained at Pendleton a half-century ago. We climbed up and down the sides of ships back then, troop carriers anchored off the coast. We trained out of foxholes and charged up hills with bayonets.

We anticipated hitting the beaches or taking the high ground, not dropping like eagles from the sky. Combat helicopters came later.

It's a different Marine Corps today in some ways, but in other ways the same. We, too, were 20 and 21. We, too, knew we would be sent overseas to fight. Camp Pendleton was as tense then as it is today, but we felt ready. We boasted. We were, after all, Marines.

But how different it was when we got there.

Guesta, Ward, Mayfield, McKinley. Furlong, Grasmuck, Rackley and Lawler.

If they only knew.

September 27, 2001

❖

WE COULD HAVE BEEN FRIENDS

I THINK I WOULD HAVE LIKED DANNY PEARL.

I think I could have sat down with him in a quiet corner of the Red Dog and had a drink with him and talked about … well … nothing.

There haven't been too many people in my life whom I could talk nothing with, if you know what I mean. Not cosmic events, but small kinds of occurrences that blow into a room like puffs of smoke and then vanish out a window.

I think I could have laughed with Danny Pearl. From what I read and heard of him, he had a quirky sense of humor, an ability to understand fun when it was time for fun. He had the look of a guy who could kick back and open up.

And I think I could have sat in silence with Danny Pearl. That's important, maybe even more important than being able to discuss nothing with a guy, being comfortable enough with each other that you can just sit there without talking and still be company.

My old pal Belcher was like that. We drank together, talked together and laughed like madmen together. For years we carpooled at 5 a.m. to the old Oakland Tribune, where we both worked, sometimes not saying a word for the 45 minutes it took to get there. We could ride in silence together.

I think Danny Pearl could have been like the Belch, one of the old-school kinds of reporters who understood the idiosyncrasies of life, even as he clung to its values.

Belcher died in 1987, alone with the cancer that ravaged him. Danny Pearl died weeks ago, alone with the killers who took his life for no good reason at all.

Now I miss them both, one a good friend, the other a man I didn't even know.

I was thinking about Danny Pearl the other night as I watched the closing ceremonies of the Winter Olympics: all those flags of different nations in one gigantic flow of color and all the athletes from everywhere mingling together and hugging each other. And I began wondering what Danny would have thought of it all.

I have to admit I felt a kind of rush, not from the pageantry, but from the idea that nations aren't just nations but are also people too. And maybe the mingling of the individuals, the people, would cause them to wonder at some future date why people were always shooting at each other, always killing other people.

It would have been one of the more serious conversations I'd have had with Danny Pearl. I'd have told him how I felt, and probably he'd have laughed a little and chided my efforts to try to reshape the world.

But then he'd have understood the idea of close associations, and how difficult it would be to shoot someone you knew.

I think I could have had heavy conversations with Danny Pearl as well as light ones. Belcher and I were able to bring each other to the edge of tears over, well, big things, like love and humanity and the passage of time. I suspect, as I think back on it, that a lot of the emotion may have grown in direct proportion to the number of martinis we drank, but at least it was there to begin with.

If Danny Pearl and I had been sitting there watching the closing ceremonies of the Olympics and maybe having a drink or two, I'd have asked him if he thought all of that would be worth dying for.

All the pageantry and hoo-ha, all the music and the flags and the hugging and the words, and before that little Sarah Hughes, iridescent and beautiful in her youngness, soaring over the ice like a bird in flight.

"What about it, Danny?" I'd have said. "Would you give your life for their right to skate and hug and talk and sing and be a giggly teenage girl in that brief flash of triumph?"

We'd have talked about it long after the Olympic torch had been extinguished and the pageantry had turned to party and the news shows had gone on to something else.

I think the gist of Danny Pearl's response would have been that it's too bad you had to die for anything at all, especially a big carnival like the Olympics. But maybe what it was supposed to represent, a kind of union of the world, would be worth giving your life for, the idea that humanity is one and the world is small. The idea of tomorrow.

And then we'd have gotten into all the other kinds of things that were less gigantic and flamboyant than the Olympics that were also worth dying for. Like a walk in the park. Or coffee with a friend. Or being in love. Or seeing a movie. Or raising a child. Or demanding respect. Or sleeping in peace.

Or just being able to talk together, or laugh together, or ride in silence together, or cry together.

I'd have liked Danny Pearl, because I'm sure that he valued the freedom of being able to do the small things we hardly ever think of. In a way, he died for them. He went down like a soldier, but one whose weapon was words and whose goal was not conquest but the information that leads to knowledge, and the knowledge that leads to truth.

No doubt about it. I'd have liked Danny Pearl.

February 28, 2002

THE TRUTH ABOUT LIES

A MAN I KNEW IN THE KOREAN WAR OFTEN BOASTED ABOUT THE girl he left back home. She was blond, she was beautiful and she loved him dearly.

He spoke just as frequently about a wealthy father, a mother who doted on him, and brothers and sisters who idolized him.

We didn't notice at the time that he never seemed to receive any mail, and we accepted on faith his reason for refusing to show pictures of his pinup-caliber girlfriend. Their love, he explained, was just too private to share.

Then as we were returning home aboard ship, the pale lights of San Diego in sight, he turned to me.

"That stuff I told you," he began quietly as we stood at the railing. "About my girl? My family? It was all lies. I made it all up."

It was evening, but I could see by the lights of the ship that there were tears in his eyes.

"I've got nothing," he said. "I've got no one." He left the railing, and we never spoke again.

As I thought about it later, I realized that his confession was the symbolic abandonment of the enclosed world that had been ours for all the months of war. The surreal community that war creates was in the past. He had to face what was real.

And so it is with Bob Kerrey.

Much will be made of Kerrey's admission after 32 years that human conflict contains brutalities that no one cares to confront. In his case, it was leading the slaughter of women, children and old men during the war in Vietnam.

A former Nebraska senator and governor, Kerrey confirmed that he had led the raid — but only after news reports gave him no choice but to admit it. He was a Navy SEAL commanding a seven-man team that attacked a village called Thanh Phong.

They began shooting, Kerrey said, when they thought they were being shot at by Viet Cong soldiers. It was only later they discovered that their "enemies" were unarmed civilians.

Kerrey won the Bronze Star for the engagement. He and his men remained silent about the true nature of the incident. Later, he won the Medal of Honor in a battle that cost him part of his right leg.

Relieved that the truth about Thanh Phong had at last been made public, Kerrey says he has been haunted by the incident all these years. He hadn't even told his family about it. Notwithstanding that he "feels better already," more is being revealed. A member of that SEAL team and a Vietnamese woman who claims she was there talk of throats slashed and a systematic massacre rather than a firefight.

Kerrey denies their charges and responds in the lofty tone of one forgiving himself. "My highest responsibility," says this once and future presidential candidate, "was to deliver the men back to their mothers, fathers and loved ones."

High responsibilities, first as humans and then as warriors, are often in conflict on the field of battle. The most charitable soldiers are frequently the ones who die first. The wary and the brutal survive.

It is this truth of war that creates lies. Survival is the instinct upon which war spins. Do what you must to stay alive and atone for it when old age comes knocking at your conscience. "Shoot first," is the way a Marine gunnery sergeant put it, "and pray later."

Kerrey's confession is significant because of his political standing, and it will likely cloud his future endeavors. Were he less prominent, the heat of controversy his admission created would likely cool in a matter of months.

How quickly we have forgotten, for instance, that less than two years ago, a dozen ex-GIs admitted that they were part of an American army unit that systematically gunned down 300 civilians in the South Korean hamlet of No Gun Ri just after the start of the war. They were afraid they might have been infiltrators. The Army investigated but did nothing.

Thirty years before that it was the Vietnam War revelation of a massacre at My Lai by American soldiers. A search-and-destroy mission took the lives of 300 innocent villagers. The attack was led by Lt. William Calley, who served three days in a stockade and three years under house arrest for a mass killing.

And that's all.

In both cases, the incidents remained terrible secrets until participants and journalists brought them into the open.

Lies are not just falsehoods, but also awful truths never revealed. We hide in dark places those events we don't have the courage to confront. We become as afraid of the memory as we were of the reality.

War is not a parade. It's not flags flying and drums beating and heartbeats quickening to the tempos of martial music. It is composed both of the horrors we conceal and the horrors we reveal. It is fear and pain beyond anyone's ability to describe. That incidents of brutality can occur in the overheated atmosphere of combat is understandable but never forgivable.

So how do we handle the revelation by Bob Kerrey, the war hero, that he made a "mistake" that cost innocent lives? I was thinking about it when I went to bed last night. And I was thinking about it at 2 a.m. and again at 4 when I got up to prowl the house, images of combat clawing at my mind.

We tell lies at war individually and collectively, to justify our actions and to placate the demons that pursue us thereafter. My lonely friend left his fantasy world behind by telling the truth. Bob Kerrey kept silent until the truth was thrust upon him.

Whether he is beyond redemption will probably be for history to decide. But, meanwhile, the least he can do is return the Bronze Star awarded him for the lie that began at Thanh Phong. Mistake or not, there ought to be no medals for savagery.

April 30, 2001

CHAPTER EIGHT

ENDINGS:
JUST PASSING THROUGH

*"Time is a river which carries me along, but I am
the river; it is a tiger that devours me, but I am the tiger;
it is a fire that consumes me, but I am the fire."*

—JORGE LUIS BORGES

NO SAD SONGS FOR US

I AWOKE EARLY THE DAY MY BEST FRIEND DIED, AND I DON'T know why. I sat out on the deck and watched a pale dawn wash through the sky, heavy with a fog that lingered in the mountains and dripped from the oak trees.

It wasn't until later that his wife called to tell me that Jerry Belcher had let go the pain and fear that accompany cancer, and cold silence lay where an immense energy had burned.

He was the Nick I wrote about when he was told two months ago that he was going to die, so it was no surprise when the end came.

I saw him for the last time a week ago, a gaunt and skeletal man on a rented hospital bed in the living room of his home, barely able to talk but still able to peer at me closely and whisper, "Where in the hell did you get that jacket?"

It was an affirmation of our ties: a friendship rooted in combat, bound in steel and tested each time we were together, even the last time.

I took his hand and sat next to him and we just looked at each other, half-smiling. Then I said it was a Penneys Outlet sale jacket and he said, "I thought so."

I didn't cry and he didn't cry, because that's not what our bond was. We had truth between us, and truth is closer and deeper and stronger than tears.

No sad songs for us, my friend.

Belcher was my confidant, my competitor and my critic for 30 years, with a wit like the sting of a wasp, and 10,000 times we battled over trivialities elevated to supremacy in a wash of dry martinis.

These were no casual debates. We clashed over who was fastest and who was best and once even over who wasn't best, for reasons lost in the blurry past.

I argued that his command of words far surpassed mine, and he argued that my style of prose towered over his, and to prove it we decided on a write-off.

We stalked through the rain from a bar called the Hollow Leg toward the city room of the Oakland Tribune across the street.

But halfway there we realized that in order to prove the point, we would have to leave the judging to others, and that was an intrusion neither of us could abide, so we returned to the Hollow Leg and called it a tie and toasted the storm.

We could tolerate the wounds we inflicted on each other because ours was the combat of young lions in the process of maturing, but we knew better than to seek judgment from those who could not begin to fathom our truths.

They were good days. We drank too much, but by God we communicated, and that's rare between warriors.

The Hollow Leg was our special place, and whoever wrote slowest on a given day would have to holler, "Save me a place at the bar!" as the other headed out the door.

It was a shout of concession, but only for today. There was always tomorrow.

When I came to L.A., Belch followed a couple of years later. But he was never really happy here.

He missed the wind and the rain of San Francisco, and the boozy camaraderie that typified its journalism. The Times was bigger, slower, colder. The kind of flaming rewrite he had become accustomed to up north was nonexistent down here.

Priorities were shifting. Times were changing.

We talked about it in a quiet moment, this time at a bar called the Redwood, when it was late and there was no one left but us and nothing to offer but truth.

He wanted to go home again and I talked him out of it, because this was the top, this was why we had written all those words a lifetime ago, to be here, where the muscle and the money were.

Belch was never convinced, but he began dealing with misery in his own way. He quit drinking and quit smoking and started seeing a shrink. It helped at first, but then his emotional problems deepened and after a while he was taking mood-lifting drugs.

We talked about that too, and he told me once they'd given him the wrong prescription and he began hallucinating that he was seeing Ed McMahon in his living room.

It saddened him, I think, not so much that he hallucinated, but Ed McMahon? He would have preferred Ella Fitzgerald. Belcher loved jazz.

Later, McMahon led a St. Patrick's Day parade in Beverly Hills, and I messaged Belch that I had finally seen him in person too. Jer flashed back a memo, "Are you sure?"

When they told Belcher he was dying, I took him to the Wellness Community in Santa Monica, where cancer patients draw on each other for the strength and style to face the uncertainties ahead, and I think it helped him.

I was with him often in the two months that followed. We talked about the people we'd known and the stories we'd written and the deadlines we'd beaten. We talked about the weather in San Francisco, and he looked at me and said quietly, "I wish it would rain."

On the day he died, his wife said, "I never saw anyone fight so hard to live. He said to me when he found out about the cancer, 'I don't want to die a wimp.' By God, Al, he was never a wimp."

I'll miss Belcher more than I have ever missed anyone, but the truths we discovered together are still stronger than tears. I'll just say goodbye, Jer.

And save me a place at the bar.

September 10, 1987

THE DEATH OF BEAUTY

WHEN FRESNO POLICE DETECTIVE AL MURRIETTA ASKED WHY THE big interest in the murder of a Hollywood beauty queen, I had no immediate answer.

"Aren't girls like her a dime a dozen down there?" he wanted to know. "Why all the fuss over this one?"

We were talking about Jill Weatherwax. Her case has been in the newspapers, in a magazine and lately on television. She was murdered a year ago at the age of 27 and her body dumped in a vacant lot behind a Fresno animal shelter.

I should have told Murrietta that it doesn't actually happen that often. But when it does, it's the Black Dahlia case revisited. A beautiful young woman comes to Hollywood to make it in show biz, gets used and then gets killed.

That's putting it in shorthand cop-reporter terms: life and death distilled and simplified, shorn of anything but a series of tidy, relevant facts. Girl comes west, girl gets used, girl gets done in.

But there remains a haunting quality about each case — the beautiful, vulnerable innocence of a life ending in despair and violence. What goes wrong in the dreams of stardom that become nightmares of reality?

Mystery is an element of eternal interest. We don't know what happened to Jill Weatherwax any more than we know what happened to Elizabeth Short, the so-called Black Dahlia, an actress wannabe murdered half a century ago.

We only know that beauty came to Hollywood and the beasts got her.

The beasts sometimes dwell in beauty's own drive to succeed. That may have been the case with Jill Weatherwax. Born in Fenton, Michigan, a onetime apple-growing empire about 60 miles northwest of Detroit, she displayed talent and ambition early on, singing along with her musician father when she was, as a friend has said, no bigger'n a grasshopper.

Outgoing and strikingly pretty, she was a cheerleader in high school, won beauty contests, studied dancing and modeling, and wrote music.

"She was energetic and vivacious," her older sister Julie said in a telephone interview. "The world was a wide and wonderful place to her, just waiting to be explored."

A career in acting as well as music was on her agenda, so she came west to the place where acting and music and dreams converge, an ideal fantasy intersection for a young woman bursting with starry self-confidence.

At first, there was promise. Through an agency she met an old-time manager who introduced her to Ciro Orsini, an international restaurateur who had opened a place in Los Angeles called Ciro's Pomodoro. They fell in love.

Orsini let her sing in his restaurants here and in London, and helped her win a Miss Hollywood crown in 1991. He also introduced her to Hollywood character Hal Stone, who produces a female boxing-wrestling show.

She sang in Stone's national revue and produced a couple of Orsini-financed CDs, but was never good enough to make it beyond the charity of her friends. She knew that. And that's when her life began to unravel.

Frustrated at her failure to make it, Jill turned to booze. Stone says Orsini found her "uncontrollable" and their romance cooled. What happened thereon becomes murky. She moved in with a troubled brother in Oxnard and began an affair with an ex-con known as Butch.

Somehow, and no one knows how, she ended up in Fresno. Witnesses saw her with three men on the night of March 25, 1998. Some hours later, her stabbed and beaten body was discovered in a vacant lot habituated by prostitutes and their customers.

Stories abounded that Jill Weatherwax had turned from booze to drugs, and to support the habit had become a hooker. An autopsy showed enough alcohol in her system to make her drunk, but no sign of narcotics.

Detective Murrietta doesn't think she was a full-time prostitute. "Maybe she just got herself in a jam and needed money to survive," he says, not unkindly. "So she turned to 'Mother Nature.'"

Orsini, who stays in touch with the family, has offered a $30,000 reward for the arrest and conviction of her killer or killers. He's contacted psychics and an Indian medicine man to help with the case. Stone investigates each lead. The metaphysics haven't helped. The case remains unsolved.

So why the big interest in Jill Weatherwax? I'll know what to tell Murrietta the next time we talk: She was young, she had dreams and, in the way that dreams drive the young to us, she was one of ours, and she's gone. Beauty was lost. The beasts had won.

May 12, 1999

❖

ARMIES OF THE NIGHT

RAIN CLOUDS HOVER LIKE A SHADOW OVER THE CITY AS I WRITE, reflecting back the mood of a village that has lost a son.

The air is wet and hot and uncomfortable as though nature, by its ageless perceptions, were aware of the sadness that has somehow embraced us all.

An officer is down. His name is Filbert Cuesta.

I realize that in an age that counts its dead in multiples of millions, the death of one man will not alter any of Earth's rhythms or stamp a lasting imprint on history.

At best, our names are written on sand, and sooner or later the ocean reaches up and washes them away.

Cuesta's widow will go on, his two small children will grow, other officers will fall, and the memory of the event that took his life will fade as time moves relentlessly forward.

Then what's the point of all these words? I think that something ought to be said about those who venture out into the nights of the village to protect us from the wildness that exists there.

As warriors in an army of atonement, they face what any soldier faces, shifts of endless boredom broken by moments of sheer terror…. But when the boredom explodes and terror is afoot, anything can happen.

In the company of peril, no one is safe.

Eulogies will attend the ritual funeral for Officer Cuesta and some will call him a hero. I'm uneasy with that. He was a cop doing his job, and if there's an element of heroism in that, OK I guess, but it's not what the word was intended to mean.

The truth is, he was shot through the head while stopped on a dark street waiting for backup, ambushed by thugs making their mark by killing a cop.

Heroics are generally based on confrontation, not duty. Cuesta was robbed of even the opportunity to confront, to march into gunfire to protect the innocent or to risk his life to save a city.

Only his partner, Richard Gabaldon, heard whatever last sounds he made. Only his partner witnessed his last startled look of life.

And now the black bands, and now the motorcade, and now the bag-pipes.

What took Cuesta's life was a combination of events that bear heavily upon the public conscience, the easy availability of guns among them.

There are those who say that if we all had guns, the bad guys who terror-ize us would be less inclined to test our mettle.

Cuesta had a gun. So did Gabaldon. But so did those who waited in the shadows for the patrol car to pass and then, in a moment of stupidity and sav-agery, pulled a trigger.

The guns cops carry are of little value when killers move like guerrilla armies through the night. We saw how poorly our bombs and cannons did in Vietnam against shadow troops. We lost that war. Will we lose this one?

Cops aren't always good guys. There are brutal, redneck racists among them, liars and thieves and killers and rapists who have darkened the good name of the constabulary throughout history.

I have written more than once of these uniformed Neanderthals and take back not a word of it. If I have seemed harsher on them than on others, it is only because more is expected of those who proclaim to protect and to serve.

Perhaps commitment, if not heroism, lies there.

We demand more of our guardians than we do of each other. They must be cleaner and braver and somehow purer than the rest of us. They've got to be firm but friendly, wary but approachable, armed but not dangerous.

We've got to be able to trust them, to hide behind them, to assure our-selves that in the end society's needs are better served because they're out there.

We have given them our sons, and now our daughters, because there is a kind of nobility in what they do when they deliver babies, save lives or stand between us and evil in the conduct of duty.

Perhaps therein lies a new and different definition of the word "hero." To perform one's duty in the face of danger can require a quieter courage, subduing an instinct to hide for the sake of a higher moral imperative.

Part of Cuesta's duty was to check out a noisy party, to recognize gang-bangers and to call for backup. He was doing that duty when evil took his life. The sky darkens in his memory. The city weeps.

August 11, 1998

❖

FLOWERS AT THE FENCE

AUTUMN IS COMING. I CAN FEEL IT IN THE EARLY MORNING AIR that frames the day's heat, a crisp tingle that chills the sunrise. I can see it in the leaves beginning to fall from the trees that grow in our yard.

It is the first day of school for my friend Nicole, and that too signals the fading days of summer, a mark on the calendar of a child's growth that helps chart the seasons of our lives.

Nicole is 10, and I watched her go off to the fifth grade with a hug and a wave, loving both the challenge and the conviviality of a classroom that calls our young to the knowledge that waits.

I see her turn for a final moment and smile before she enters the schoolyard, and the smile lingers on the vivid air even as she disappears among her gathering friends.

I think about that look, and as I do her face becomes that of a young boy, the smile emulsified on film, frozen in time, and I realize with a start that I am superimposing the face of Juian Coronel on that of my granddaughter.

This was to have been his first day of school too.

Instead he lies among the statistics of more than 5,000 children killed each year in this country by accidental gunfire, another small body wrapped in the tears that society sheds for its young.

And the mounds of flowers placed against the fences of gunfire's victims appear once more in the City of Angels. The candles of remorse flicker in the cooling twilights of autumn.

The photograph of Juian Coronel, the last one we will ever see, appeared in newspapers and on television, the sweetness of his face looking out at a world that waited with who knew how many wonders.

There is an easiness to his smile, the same kind of innocence that radiates through Nicole's smile, and the eyes glow with anticipation. One can imagine that moments after the picture was taken, Juian spun away and raced toward the adventures that each moment holds for a boy of 11.

But the running stopped, and now we grieve.

Exactly what happened just after midnight last Friday remains unclear. There was a gun in the house and Juian alone, or with a brother, probably thought it was unloaded. It wasn't. By the time paramedics reached his home in South-Central Los Angeles, he was dead.

That death is unlikely to cause even the tiniest disruption in the rhythms of the days that structure our lives. One small boy disappearing from the face of the Earth is not apt to create a large emptiness in space.

Some will grieve, I among them, who cry for each child's death on the planet's face or among the city's numbers, but most will go about their business grateful, if they think about it at all, that the child who died wasn't theirs.

I just keep seeing that face on the trembling air of the coming autumn and wondering how we could have saved Juian's life.

I won't belabor the statistics of gun deaths. You've heard them all, and so have I. And by hearing them too often they become yet another accepted peril among the 10,000 that exist in today's violent society, each one indexed with a body lying in blood.

However the lines of the death graphs may swing upward, there is at least some consolation in the efforts being made to end the tragedies that the click of a trigger can create. The banning of bullets, Saturday-night specials and assault rifles won't bring anyone back to life, but it might save another life somewhere down the line.

There are miles to go in the effort. With a gun in every fourth house in L.A. County, getting rid of them won't be easy. But get rid of them we must.

I realize that when this appears I will hear from those whose advocacy of firearms is a bluster of rationalization rooted in antiquated constitutional rights and the need for self-protection.

Cross their paths with mischief on your mind and they'll blast you into hell. They're always ready, guns nearby and loaded, their right to fire an unquestioned credo in the conduct of their scary nights.

When morning comes, the weapons of their survival are slipped into drawers, placed on shelves or stuck in closets, maybe loaded, maybe not, until the night comes again … or until a child's hand reaches out.

The tragedy of Juian Coronel's death is multiple. However one argues over guns, a reality exists. The boy is dead, his parents accused of criminal storage of a weapon, his three siblings placed in county custody.

The truth is sad, simple and undebatable: An entire family died last Friday night, and a gun did it.

September 10, 1996

❖

A LAST ACT OF DEFIANCE

ON THE DAY JERRY RUBIN DIED, I CALLED HIS HOME TELEPHONE number for comment from someone close to him.

No one answered, but his message machine clicked on and Rubin's voice exploded in my ear, full of the relentless energy that characterized his life.

"I'm back in town and looking forward to talking to you and everything's great and I'll call you back and make your day fantastic!"

By the heat in his delivery, Rubin could turn the simplest phrase into a call to arms, and his telephone message was no exception. It said, Stand by,

America, Jerry Rubin's comin' at you!

It was a voice on the brink of doing, a message from the soul of those who rebel and defy, whose clenched fists glorify the commandments of freedom that allow them to rage.

That's why I liked him.

Although later in his life he would slip into the warmer robes of affluence he once scorned, Rubin remained true, at least, to his insuppressible nature, defying even his own past and those old rebels who mocked his new standards.

And, at the end, he perished defying the most modest of regulations, traffic lights, in favor of dodging cars to cross a dangerous thoroughfare.

Struck by an automobile, he lay in the street like a fallen flag and died two weeks later, leaving us his voice and his memory to ponder.

I began writing about Rubin 25 years ago when he was a screaming Yippie. He and Abbie Hoffman had come to symbolize a time of fire in the streets and violence at the barricades of those who demanded a war's end.

Rubin's voice at the trial of the Chicago 7 still rings in history's ears, mocking the process, challenging the Establishment and daring authority to silence his rage.

He was, as a reporter put it long ago, a radical's radical who could never be silenced, the very epitome of those who shout defiance.

I met him last February in his $5,000-a-month high-rise condo, still a living superlative, the salesman's salesman, a network marketeer, hustling health powders instead of world peace ... but with no less stridency than he displayed a quarter of a century before.

The meeting took place because I had written about another Jerry Rubin, the Venice peace activist, and the ex-Yippie Rubin had telephoned to demand clarification. The Venice Rubin, I had said, was out of work and needed money. The Yippie Rubin was incensed.

"They think it's me!" he said over the phone, in a voice that managed to be both pleading and uncompromising. "My landlord thinks I can't pay the rent! My girlfriends think I'm broke! You've got to clear this up!"

I knew it was a gimmick to get him back into print, but in gimmickry often dwells the stuff of ideas. I got the two Rubins together. Before the Venice Rubin could even sit, the Yippie Rubin fixed him with a stare that could melt steel and said, "I want you to work for me! I want every Jerry Rubin in America to work for me!"

The Venice Rubin sat quietly as his namesake, a man he deeply admired and was often mistaken for, paced the room, answered telephone calls, promised wealth and demanded that I heed every word he uttered.

He was, for that instant, the Rubin we all remembered: not a "people's capitalist" in pinstriped suit, but the bearded, wild-eyed, frizzy-haired kid in jeans whose rage and rhetoric helped end a war and bring down a president.

Watching Rubin last February was to watch the energy of social activism abruptly redirected, a transformation so total and miraculous it belied the very existence of the Yippie who had cursed what he was to become.

In his new persona, he loved America, hated drugs and believed that power belonged not so much to those who seized it as to those who could afford it. He understood the irony and gave it the finger.

Even that was true to his character. He was defying every word he had once uttered, and the smoke of that defiance filled his penthouse that day we sat together, the Venice Rubin, the Yippie Rubin and me.

As I look back on it, I realize that Rubin, the eternal Yippie, was what he had always been, part hero and part hypocrite, and totally defiant of both elements of that nature.

At his best, he was a kid in the streets, burning flags and raising hell, and saying what had to be said in the context of his era. I would wish him now to rest in peace, but this wasn't the kind of peace he was seeking.

Instead I'll say to those who remember, raise a fist and bow your head. A rebel lies uneasy in his grave.

December 3, 1994

REQUIEM FOR A CLOWN

FOR A MAN WHO HAD SPENT HIS LIFE MAKING OTHERS LAUGH, Martin Ragaway's final observation seemed a bitter punch line to 35 years of comedy writing.

Kept alive by tubes at St. Vincent's Hospital, unable to speak, he gestured for a pencil and a pad and wrote laboriously, "Game's over, we all lose."

Then, his body ravaged by cancer, Ragaway closed his eyes and was dead at 66. Or 62. I never did know his real age.

"How old are you?" I asked impatiently when I first met him a few years back in a Studio City bar called Residuals.

Ragaway had been sidestepping the question for an hour, telling jokes, making comments, waiting for laughs. He had the quick, furtive moves of a chipmunk, and even sitting still seemed in motion.

"S-Sixty," he finally replied with a slight stammer.

"You don't look it," I said in false praise.

"O-k-kay," he shot back, "59."

Before I could respond, he was out of the starting blocks again and halfway around the track with, "You hear about the widow in Miami Beach? She meets a guy and says, 'I've never seen you around here before.'

"He says, 'I've been in prison for 34 years. I poisoned my wife, cut her into small p-pieces and put her in the garbage disposal.'

" 'Oh,' she says, 'then you're a s-single man!' "

Ragaway never stopped entertaining. He told stories, he repeated anecdotes, he made up gag lines. Sometimes he stammered, sometimes he didn't. The faster he talked, the less he stammered.

He had his own newsletter, Funny, Funny World, composed of jokes, offbeat news items and comments on the news. He began by sending it to friends. In a few years it had a circulation of 10,000.

It was another way of telling a story, of defining with wry insight the nature of the existence he would ultimately call a game. Ragaway was a man obsessed with laughter, the ultimate entertainer, the quintessential clown.

Then why didn't he leave us laughing?

I last saw him three months ago. I didn't know he was dying. None of his friends did. He didn't look well, but he never looked well. That's what made my false compliment seem funny to him back at Residuals.

The face was pale and craggy, the eyebrows arched in a sad and quizzical expression, his hair dyed a funny auburn. Only the eyes were bright and riveting. Only the eyes were alive.

He talked about his years of comedy writing the last time we met, about how he churned out gags for Skelton, Benny, Hope, Gleason and a lot of others you wouldn't remember if I told you.

There was a biographical quality to his monologue. He wanted me to remember. The cancer he had secretly fought for almost two years was winning.

Ragaway had written for radio first and then television. He produced scripts for 400 sitcom episodes, or maybe 800. He told different stories. "All those episodes," he'd say with incredulity, "and I'm s-still able to dress myself and t-tie my own shoes."

He loved making people laugh but hated laugh tracks, and it drove him crazy when sitcom actors couldn't deliver the lines he sweated to create. Of one particular performer he'd say, "She's so dumb she thinks a d-double-entendre is a strong drink."

"My father was always entertaining," his daughter Jill said. "At a dinner party he'd sneak a look at a matchbook cover he'd written words on during the day to remind him of jokes. When we'd see the matchbook cover come out, we'd say, 'Oh, oh, here it comes.' Then he'd start in."

Ragaway's last note perplexes fellow comedy writer Bill Larkin. "It didn't seem like Marty. He was always up. His only goal in life was to entertain. But maybe being up and entertaining just covered his real attitude. Who knows?"

Humor is born in dark places of the soul, masking anguish with a tilt toward absurdity. The humorist defines not only human folly, but also his own dreadful inadequacies, and to come face to face with them is to look the devil in the eye.

I think at the end Ragaway was observing life's ironies more than its futilities. He was acknowledging that we all play a game we can never win, no matter how well we play it.

"Humor," he once said to me, "is based on little realities. Everything's a joke."

Last week he must have realized the joke is ultimately on the clown.

April 25, 1989

❖

A WISE AND GENTLE SPIRIT

I DREAMED THE OTHER NIGHT I WAS SITTING WITH JOHN ESPEY on an evening as sweet as heaven, drinking a chilled white wine and talking about paper towel dispensers.

We were on the veranda of the home he and Carolyn See once occupied on a hilltop in Topanga, overlooking a ridge line that was slowly melting into the deepening twilight. I was intense and serious, and John was relaxed and amused but thoroughly involved in the discussion.

We had both used the same men's room somewhere on different occasions and had noticed that the paper towel dispenser didn't work right. When you took one paper towel, it was supposed to pull the one behind it into position and it didn't.

Digging out a second towel was a small annoyance, and I wasn't going to do anything about it but complain. John, on the other hand, had researched the problem and had discovered how the process was supposed to work and why it didn't.

He was about to explain it to me when the dream ended.

I'm not making this up. It was a real dream I had the night after John's memorial service. I had been thinking all afternoon what I could write about him and went to sleep with that on my mind. And there it was.

John Espey died last month at age 87 as gracefully as he had lived, without rancor or self-pity, but his death leaves me frustrated. We can't afford to lose men of his stature.

Scholar, teacher, storyteller, world traveler and wit, he was the smartest man I ever knew, and among the gentlest. I am not erudite enough to have discussed anything with him, but he made me feel that I was, that I had something to contribute to his life, or at least to that moment.

I think that John's egalitarian attitude was what the dream was all about. I had probably broached the subject of the paper towel dispenser, and rather than tossing it aside as the babble of a fool, he had listened and reacted.

His was the kind of intelligence that understood compassion as well as irony, and fun as well as scholarship. I heard that said many times as we sat in the cool shade of a giant pepper tree at his memorial service one sunlit afternoon.

He was a Rhodes scholar who sang to the English classes he taught for 25 years at UCLA, and composed whimsical haiku for a depressed colleague. He wrote a heavyweight tome about the poet Ezra Pound, a children's book about Algernon the Cat and memoirs that won rave reviews.

His children remember him using chewing gum to fight an infestation of gophers because he had researched the gopher problem and that was one of the solutions. It didn't work. He had also read that human urine would drive the rodents away.

"I'm not sure it worked," one of his daughters said at the memorial service, half-laughing and half-crying, "but he tried it and they never came back."

I met John through Carolyn See, a novelist I had admired for some time and whom I am privileged to call a friend. She and John had lived together for years in a relationship that warmed the rooms they occupied.

They lived in that hilltop home I was talking about, but moved out of Topanga not too long ago, leaving a hole in a community that embraced them both. Carolyn's daughter Lisa, who became John's daughter too, is also a celebrated author, making them a unique and gifted family of writers.

The memorial service was held at Lisa's house. John's two daughters from an earlier marriage spoke and so did Carolyn's two daughters, one of whom, Clara, composed a list of things she hadn't known until John Espey entered her life.

"I didn't know how to watch birds," she wrote. "I didn't know how to feel safe. I didn't know how gentle a man could be. I didn't know the importance of style or finesse. I didn't know how much you could love someone you weren't related to."

"He made everyone feel they were special in his life," Carolyn See said later. "His last concern was for his students. He said he had given his all but didn't think he had done enough."

That was John Espey, the charity of his final thoughts directed at others, a glowing last light in the darkness that finally engulfed him. We radiate attitudes to those who surround us, and what he radiated was a generosity of spirit that burned to the end of his life.

Ultimately, we are judged by those we love and who love us. There were many who loved John Espey and who relied on both his warmth and wisdom to fulfill themselves. Who else of his standing would have bothered over paper towel dispensers with a college dropout, and who will do so now?

October 18, 2000

❖

A CITY WITHOUT ITS POET

HE SAW SAN FRANCISCO AS A DREAM CLOAKED IN FOG, A MAGIC city part Paris and part Brigadoon that didn't exist anywhere else in the world.

It was a mystical island of beautiful people, soft jazz and cognac-colored nights. Laughter never stopped there and parties never ended.

No one loved San Francisco more than Herb Caen and, quite likely, no one ever will again. He was its poet and its prophet for almost 60 years, and when he died Saturday, a lyrical voice was silenced.

Even when his column was strictly three-dot gossip and not an essay of love to his city, there was still a poetic quality to it, a rhythm that echoed the clang of cable cars and the mournful bellow of foghorns on the bay.

He called his essays corny and his itemized name-dropping "the stoop

253

labor of newspapering," but we all knew he loved what he was doing because you can't write a column the way he could unless you do.

I began reading Caen in college, and when I wrote for the student newspaper at San Francisco State, I tried to emulate him. But trying to copy a master is an exercise in futility. I dropped the effort before the term was over.

He was Mr. Three Dot and no one could ever do it better.

Beyond his qualities as a newspaper columnist, Caen was a nice guy, the way Jack Smith was a nice guy, despite the levels of fame each had achieved.

When I began writing a column for the Oakland Tribune in 1963, one of my first fan letters was from Caen.

He didn't know me from nothin', but began reading me right from the start and welcomed me to the world of commentary with the grace of a maitre d'.

I learned later that he did a lot of that, but the recognition was no less meaningful to someone just getting started in an area of newspapering that is simultaneously compelling and terrifying.

He invited me to lunch occasionally at places like Banducci's in North Beach, where writers like Alex Haley and Herb Gold used to go. Caen made it his job to introduce me to all of them.

He pointed out the best places to eat in San Francisco and said you could always tell if a restaurant was any good by the quality of its veal.

I only remember him coming once to Oakland, where, he joked, veal hadn't been invented yet. We ate at the old Sea Wolf in Jack London Square, and when I asked him to define Oakland, he said it was the only city in the world that could make a square out of Jack London.

It was not so much a put-down of Oakland as an elevation, by comparison, of San Francisco, because Caen would often admit in less competitive moments that San Francisco probably only existed in his imagination anyway.

That didn't stop him, however, from saying to me when I left the Bay Area for L.A. that I'd better take a box lunch because there was no place to eat south of Santa Barbara.

Caen's influence reached down here through his friend and contemporary Jack Smith, and when I came to the L.A. Times, it was Smith who became one of my biggest supporters.

They were alike in many ways, those two masters of commentary, even though their writing styles couldn't have been more different. Both were gentlemen of the highest order and totally selfless when it came to their colleagues.

Smith lobbied on my behalf when, after about a 10-year hiatus, I decided I wanted to write a column again, only this time in L.A., not Oakland.

A few years later, when Chronicle columnist Stanton Delaplane died, Caen lobbied for me to take his place in San Francisco but understood when I turned the job down.

We both knew that the movement and the muscle in newspapering had shifted south, and the place to be if you were in journalism was down here. San Francisco may have been a precious jewel, but we owned the jewelry store.

"San Francisco has grown old disgracefully," Caen would write, "from raving beauty to crone. Los Angeles is far ahead of us. It's outta sight."

But the city he created will never grow old and ugly. It continues to exist as the fog-cloaked dream that emerged from the sometimes hard, sometimes airy poetry of one who saw it clearer than anyone else.

The deaths of Jack Smith and Herb Caen leave me feeling alone and uneasy in the joy and pain of writing a newspaper column. I miss them both. They were golden.

Researching this piece online, I came across the Chronicle home page that contained a recorded message by Caen. It said simply, "It's great to be in touch with all of you!" And it was great for all of us, those many years, to have been in touch with him.

February 4, 1997

THIS ONE'S FOR JACK

I WAS SITTING AT MY WORD PROCESSOR THINKING ABOUT WRITING a tribute to Jack Smith when I noticed a piece of lint on the carpet near my desk.

It wasn't the biggest piece of lint I had ever seen, but it was there nonetheless. I stared at it for a while and then looked away, hoping it would be gone when I looked back.

That happens sometimes. Lint has powers not granted to other small things. It is able to appear and disappear at will, and that has always fascinated me. I spend a lot of time picking up lint.

I stared at the computer screen for a while, thinking about Jack, his sweetness and his talent, and then turned quickly again to confront the lint.

It was still there, but vanishing. I think it has something to do with the movement of sunlight in a room, but I'm not sure. I couldn't stand it anymore. I got down on my hands and knees to go for the lint when my wife, Cinelli, walked in.

"What in God's name are you doing?" she asked.

"I'm writing a tribute to Jack Smith," I said.

"On your hands and knees? You look like a grasshopper."

"I'm taking a lint break."

"Not that again."

Cinelli hates it when I pick up lint. Well, "hate" isn't the right word. It annoys her. She finds it in my pocket at clothes-washing time and has to remove it piece by piece. She says it makes her feel like a chimp picking fleas off its mate.

"Are you going to hunch down there forever?" she asked, wondering if at last I had taken total leave of my senses. "Write the Jack Smith tribute. Then I need you to take out the garbage."

"A tribute like this can't be hurried. I have to come up with new superlatives. All the usual ones have been preempted. I need powerful adjectives to summarize Jack."

I'm not sure a superlative is an adjective. Grammar has never been my strong point. You'd have known, Jack. You always knew things like that.

"Look," Cinelli said suddenly, "I don't have time to stand here while you crawl around on the floor. I've got to fix the dryer. Taking out the garbage doesn't seem too daunting a task. Think of it as increasing the blood flow to your brain. It'll help you write."

I remember before my heart bypass surgery when Jack tried to cheer me up. He'd already had his bypass, and it worried me because equipment failure had deprived him of oxygen during the operation. "Well," he said, "it may have caused brain damage, but don't worry. That doesn't impair the ability to write a column."

"There you go," Cinelli said, helping me up. "Now will you take out the garbage? It's been sitting by the front door for a week. The smell is making the cat sick."

I recall reading in one of Jack's essays how much he disliked taking out the garbage. It seemed somehow demeaning. I fight it too. Once I went for 91 consecutive days without taking out the garbage. It was a new record. In terms of resistance, I was the Babe Ruth of garbage-averters.

Like Jack, I'm not crazy about cats, either. I really believe they try to suck the breath out of babies. After a few drinks once, I challenged my son to see who could bowl the cat farthest down a hallway. He declined. I won by default.

Back to Cinelli. We were face to face. It was garbage-challenge time again.

"You know that lifting garbage hurts my back," I said with the kind of whine that causes mothers to turn in alarm.

It's too bad Jack never heard me whine. I mean, I am a journeyman whiner. I learned it as a private in the Marines and, later, as a reporter. He probably did too. I'll bet he was one hell of a whiner at home.

"Sometimes," Cinelli said, sighing, "I get awfully tired of your bad back, your bad heart, your bad leg and your bad attitude."

I love that woman, Jack, the way you loved Denny. We were, I am, blessed with special people to lead us through life. They suffer our inadequacies lightly.

"I can't help it," I said, raising the whine level a notch. "Feel sympathy for a damaged veteran."

"All right," she finally said, "I'll take out the garbage, you look for lint. When I'm finished, we'll pick fleas off of each other."

"I'll never forget you for this," I said. "Now I can write the tribute to Jack."

Cinelli lifted the garbage bag, then turned to me. "I think," she said wisely, "you already have."

She knew and I knew what was going on. We had engaged in the kind of small moment Smith wrote about so well. In its way, it was our tribute. So is this column.

We did it for you, Jack.

January 12, 1996

❖

BLOSSOMS BY THE SEA

THEY LAY AT THE FOOT OF THE CLIFF LIKE FALLEN FLOWERS, amid the flattened boulders and gentle surf, two young women who had given up on life.

Their names were Amber Hernandez and Alicia Hayes.

The likelihood is that they had deliberately plunged to their deaths down the steep cliff for reasons yet to be determined.

They were found a week ago, small bodies near the vast expanse of the ocean, at the point in San Pedro where Fermin Park juts into the sea.

While those who knew them weep and wonder, the girls vanish into a mass of statistics that register the suicides of 5,000 young people each year in a nation that is becoming increasingly dangerous for children.

Amber was 14, Alicia, 15.

I visited the site of their deaths on a morning that, by its melancholy darkness, seemed to grieve for them. A cold, gray fog blanketed the shoreline like a funeral shroud, damping the hues of even the brilliantly colored bougainvillea that blossomed in the yards overlooking the Pacific.

I was drawn to the scene by the deaths of the girls and by the suicides last March of two other young people, Christopher Mills and Heidi Chamberlain, both under 16, who had jumped into oblivion a few miles north.

Standing at the edge of the cliff, listening to the laughter of children from below that tinkled like wind chimes in the gray morning, I wondered: What makes our kids decide to kill themselves?

The question evokes an unsettling memory. Years ago, at a camp in the Sierra Nevada, a young man I knew tried to hang himself from the rafters of a cabin a group of us were occupying.

We were 13-year-olds from poor families being taken on a weeklong outing in the mountains. There were a half-dozen of us in the cabin. It was night. We heard a noise from the corner bunk and flashed lights into the area.

What we saw in the confluence of our flashlight beams remains fixed in my mind: the boy hanging by his neck, his eyes staring into emptiness, his muffled sounds of strangulation filling the enclosure.

We cut him down and called for help. He recovered and weeks later I asked why he'd done that. He shrugged, smiled self-consciously and said, "I don't know." We never talked about it again.

Suicide is the third leading cause of death among teenagers in the nation, behind accidents and homicides. The American Association of Suicidology estimates that every hour and 40 minutes, a young person kills himself.

Why? I asked that question of Dr. Jay Nagdimon, the clinical psychologist who is director of the L.A. Suicide Prevention Center. The answers seem obvious: drugs, depression and a failure at interpersonal relationships.

But I suspect that at least part of what takes them to the edge of their lives is the violence that has permeated our society like an evil vapor.

Movies are violent, television is violent, music is violent, sports are violent. We blow up, stab, smash and shoot down to a degree never before witnessed at a single time in a single place.

By our obsession with violence, we make death seem easy. Even a kid can do it.

Thinking back, I suppose I went to the edge of the sea where Amber and

Alicia had died because a few days earlier I had seen the flipside of youth in commencement exercises at Whittier College.

I was on stage at the ceremonies and could look across at a different sea: the faces of those about to leap not onto the rocks, but into a future far from the cliffs of Point Fermin.

I heard the stories of their struggles and studied the faces of those who, despite everything, would not give up, who often clung to the edges of life by their fingertips, who bellowed defiance at despair.

I kept wishing as I shared in that moment with the graduates that I could have spoken to Alicia and Amber, before they crossed the dark barriers of their final decisions.

I wish I could have told them that there are ways out of misery, that those of us who have stood at the edge and turned back have tasted a sweetness of life that we otherwise would not have known.

It's too late to tell them, but maybe you can tell your own kids. I have plans too. I'm going up north for a couple of weeks to see my friends Travis and Shana, who moved to Washington a few months back.

I'm going to hold them close, these two little wonders, and tell them about hope and love and the glory of life … and about some flowers that lay at the edge of the sea on a sad and overcast day in May.

May 31, 1996

TAKE HER SWEETLY, TAKE HER GENTLY

HE RECALLS HER WITH LAUGHTER AND WITH TEARS, HIS BELOVED Betsy, so filled with the tradition of the stage that she honored it to her last breath.

Her real name was Beatrice Colen. She was the wry, roller-skating carhop in the old TV series "Happy Days," a woman never without a comeback, always owning the last line.

She died last month at age 51, still in character.

"She was sweet and she was funny," says her husband of 22 years, Patrick Cronin. "She died as she lived, and she never said, 'Why me?' "

We are in the living room of their Westside home. The day gleams with intensity, its skies swept clean by blustery winds.

As he talks, Cronin must fight to maintain his composure. Laughter and grief are tight companions here.

"When she learned she was dying, she said, 'I don't expect you to remain celibate,' " he remembers. "Then she added quickly, 'I've picked out three fat ladies for you in Encino.' "

He laughs wildly at the memory, then pauses, half-smiling, his eyes filling, still remembering.

"Near the end, I leaned over her and said, 'You can't die!' I loved her so much."

Semi-comatose, she still managed to open her eyes and say, "Why the hell not?"

Surprised at her quick response and at a momentary loss to respond, Cronin finally replied, "You haven't given me the phone numbers of the fat ladies from Encino."

"She drifted back to sleep," he says, his voice catching, "then five or six hours later awoke again and whispered, 'Sorry, Pat. They've moved to Ventura.' "

In so many ways, this is a show biz story, laced with dramatic love, with history and with that shiny tradition of the show going on.

Betsy was the granddaughter of George S. Kaufman, the Pulitzer Prize-winning playwright who co-wrote "The Man Who Came to Dinner."

She and Patrick, also an actor, met while he was a drama teacher and she a student at Philadelphia's Temple University. She was 18, he, 25. While still a student, she was stricken with Hodgkin's disease. It was cured with massive radiation, but the treatment planted a time bomb that was to explode years later.

Betsy went on to win a role in "Happy Days" and later in "Wonder Woman." Cronin came to L.A., as he says, "with a thousand bucks and an unemployment claim." In 1977 he landed a role in Kaufman's "Merton of the Movies" at the Ahmanson.

Betsy's mother, Kaufman's daughter, asked Betsy to go to rehearsals of "Merton" to be sure it was done right. There, Betsy saw her former teacher. They met, they talked, they fell in love. A month later they were married.

But that's only part of the story.

Told they could never have children, they defied the odds and became the parents of two sons, James, now 17, and Charlie, 16. Both attend a private school, Brentwood High.

A robust kid, Charlie plays tackle for the school's football team. James, his father says, is also a jock, but upon meeting a girl studying drama, decided the drama department was a good place to be.

After winning a small part in "Macbeth," James was given the lead role of Sheridan Whiteside this year in a George S. Kaufman play. It was "The Man Who Came to Dinner."

Kaufman's spirit hovered over their lives like a shadow from the grave.

Betsy, meanwhile, had been diagnosed with lung cancer, which later spread to her brain. It was the result, she was told, of the radiation treatment years earlier. Her days were few.

"We told the boys the truth," Cronin says. "We didn't tell them Mom had the flu."

She desperately wanted to live long enough to see her son perform in her grandfather's play, but she knew she wouldn't. James wanted to give up the play to be with his mother. She refused to let him.

Only days away from death, she told him he had to fulfill his obligation to his audience and his fellow actors. He had to go on. The play was to be on a Thursday. Charlie was to be in a football game on Saturday. He too wanted to give it up to be with her.

Cronin remembers her words to them: "She said, 'If you really want to remember me, don't use my death as an excuse for screwing up.' " He cries openly as he finishes. " She said, 'You will honor me with a good life.' "

Betsy Colen died the night James played the lead in her grandfather's play, honoring the tradition she was born into.

At the end, Cronin held her and said, "Lord, take your servant. Take her kindly, take her sweetly, take her gently."

She left this world still in his arms.

December 19, 1999

❖

BILLY'S LAST HEARTBEAT

SHE REMEMBERS IT NOW, EVERY DETAIL, AS THOUGH IT WERE yesterday: the stillness of the night, the muted light of the room and the soft, fading beat of her brother's heart. And she remembers the silence when his heart stopped.

Only hours earlier, Billy Fucile had said to his family that he loved them and then, as though in final recognition of his own emotions, whispered, "How powerful those words are."

They were his last words. His body ravaged by AIDS, he slipped into unconsciousness. His sister, Tricia, sitting next to him on his bed, put her head on her brother's chest.

It was after midnight on August 10, 1992. The night passed slowly. Tricia dozed. Then at 4:45 a.m. their father, who had watched Billy's breathing grow shallow, awakened her to say he thought the end was near.

263

It was then that Tricia Hopper, her head still on her brother's chest, became aware of the fading beat of his heart … and then the silence.

"In some ways it was special," Hopper remembered recently, her voice catching. "He died so gracefully and left us with such a powerful feeling."

Two years later, she translated the power of that emotion and the compelling memory of her brother's last heartbeat into a play that has been performed before thousands of high school students throughout L.A. County.

Its message: AIDS is an equal-opportunity scourge.

Billy Fucile, who was gay, was 32 when he died. A clothing stylist and AIDS activist, he was especially close to his big sister Tricia in a family of four boys and three girls. She was six years older.

They shared a love of music and movies and talked for hours on the phone, exchanging as well their joys and their problems. When Billy was found to have AIDS, Tricia was devastated. When he decided in the fading days of his life to end all medication, she understood.

When he died, she was there.

Afterward she sought help through therapy to guide her through her grief. A therapist suggested she do something in Billy's memory using her creative talent. An actress, she began studying writing. After two years, she had created a one-act play, "The Closet."

It's the short, powerful story of a family not unlike her own. A central character is the ghost of a boy named, appropriately, Billy, whose presence adds both humor and high drama to the performance.

Billy has died of AIDS, and his remaining family — a mother, father and sister — and friends must deal with it in their own special way: with love, with guilt, with memories and with a need to do something!

Messages and warnings are intertwined with very human reactions in a play that could have only been written by someone who was there … listening to that last beat of her own Billy's heart.

"The Closet" was first performed at Hopper's neighborhood church in Palos Verdes, then, months later, for educators and AIDS workers at a community theater in Torrance.

By then, Hopper and her husband, who owns an engineering company, had created a nonprofit organization called Timeless Educators Inc., and proposed producing the play before high school students.

The request won Los Angeles Unified School District approval, and since then the play has been performed 200 times at 75 high schools. Actors trained as HIV/AIDS peer educators play the six parts and discuss the play and its subject with students who attend the performance.

"High-risk behavior, abstinence and HIV-prevention discussions are taken as far as each school will allow," Hopper said. "The optimum is to discuss all facets of sexuality."

The actors are paid minimum wages from small grants and from funds either supplied by the Hoppers or donated by those who have seen the play.

Tricia was Billy's big sister in life and identifies with the mother, Karen, in "The Closet." Both the real Tricia and the fictional Karen lived through each moment of Billy's decline, the Billy in life and in the play.

Tricia was with him when he visited friends dying of AIDS, knowing that was his future. She was with him when he worried that God would reject him because he was gay. She was with him when, nine days before he died, he said, "I just don't want to do this anymore" — and stopped his medication.

What gives the play strength is not only its subject, but also its underlying reality. It takes the beating of a single heart and empowers it to become a message meant to fill the hearts of us all.

January 22, 1999

❖

THE PURIFICATION OF COOL

HE WAS THE ESSENCE OF COOL, ON STAGE WITH A DRINK AND A cigarette, a swinging, singing, ring-a-ding kind of guy who could croon midnight into a romantic fantasy.

His music was after-hours music, when women with perfumed hair snuggled up to guys in tuxes and Frank filled the starry sky with a voice as warm and sweet as honey in hot rum.

There was a quality to that voice we had never heard before or will ever hear again, something more than just perfect resonance and phrasing and the seamless beauty of a compelling ballad.

There was Sinatra behind it, a composite of the magic that God gives to only a few people in each lifetime, a man who could stand alone in a spotlight surrounded by 10,000 people and dominate the room.

I saw him walk through a casino in Las Vegas once, when the marquee that announced his presence said simply "Frank," and the crowds parted before him like the Red Sea for Moses.

He didn't have to say anything, and it wasn't that people were afraid of him, but rather they realized instinctively that you did that for a king, you opened the way. After he had passed, you closed again and stood there watching him disappear into the crowd, occupying the space he once owned.

At Matteo's, a restaurant on the Westside where Sinatra used to hang out when he was in town, they ushered me to a corner booth once, and informed me in a reverential whisper that it was where Frank sat and should he wander in out of a summer night I was to move. It was the least I could do.

I was still in high school when Sinatra began sending teenage girls into screaming fits the way the Beatles would a generation later. It was the beginning of a love-hate relationship that would never change.

I didn't really admire Sinatra the man, at least not some of the time, not when he was calling newspaper reporters and columnists the kinds of names that even today you can't print, now that almost anything goes.

But there were times, too, when you heard that he'd do things like buy a school bus for some kids in a poor district without the usual kind of hype that accompanies celebrity giving, filling a need, not fattening an ego, and you had to respect him for that.

And there was the time he called off his lawyers who were warning a saloon singer named Nick Edenetti to stop using Sinatra's name in a show where Nick did a kind of Sinatra takeoff, wearing a skimpy-brim hat and a trench coat tossed over his shoulder. You liked him for that too.

Edenetti sang "Make It One for My Baby" the way Frank did, trying to emulate the voice that no one could really copy, and setting up the spots so that in a certain light he looked a little like Frank. Sinatra saw the show and afterward said to Nick, "You got balls, kid." It was the emotional equivalent of a papal blessing.

At Matteo's, Larry Cullen was Frank's special waiter for 24 years, and remembers him as the master of class and generosity, sipping a dry martini at Station 8, the corner booth, dining on veal Milanese, and then afterward going into the kitchen to sneak a smoke and tip the cooks and the dishwashers.

"He was a sweet man at important times," the comic Shelley Berman said, recalling a night when Sinatra praised him from the stage. "He loved to talk boxing," bail bondsman and ex-lightweight contender Joey Barnum said, remembering the night he sat at Frank's booth. "But I never saw him without a drink in his hand."

That was it, you see, the drink and the cigarette. We all drank and we all smoked back then, when Sinatra began chronicling his own years in a ballad that took us into the twilight of his life, cloaking us in a sense of time and mortality that bordered on the mystic.

"When I was 17, it was a very good year...."

He was cool and warm at the same time, if you know what I mean, smoothly bridging the gap between the up-yours, I'm-doing-it-my-way guy and the singer who could translate dreams into music and embrace love as though he'd invented it.

We saw him in concert in Oakland once, my wife and I, and up until then she wasn't a Sinatra fan, not the way I was. There's a saying in show biz, probably emanating from San Francisco, that says, "When you think you're good, play Oakland."

Frank did, standing alone on a small stage, isolated by a single spotlight, selling moonlit walks and soft summer nights and the snap of recognition between two people who had never met but would never part.

"Strangers in the night, exchanging glances.... Lovers at first sight, in love forever...."

When the concert was over, I could see the change in my wife's attitude. She had never seen anything like that before, one man casting a spell over thousands with almost effortless sorcery.

She sensed the magic the way we all did, and I guess that's why a lot of us guys wished secretly we had that power. It wasn't just the cool or the mellow or the talent; it was the complexity that created the whole, the persona that hallmarked the lovers and the lonely who came out when the sun went down.

Frank showed us how to be cool and showed us how to grow old, and in the end he showed us how to die. It was simple. He did it his way.

May 16, 1998

❖

A FALLING STAR

IT STREAKED ACROSS THE SKY LIKE A FALLING STAR IN A ROAR OF fire and thunder, leaving contrails of glowing debris in its wake.

Thus died the shuttle Columbia and the humanity in its trust.

We were transfixed by the incongruity. This wasn't the way the journey was supposed to have ended. Not seven lives lost in a flash of flame on a day as bright as heaven, but the conclusion of a routine flight by a spaceship that had flown many times before.

The order of orbit, reentry and landing had been fixed in our minds since the first flight of the same shuttle 22 years ago: a speck in the sky, a pair of sonic booms and then a seemingly effortless glide to Earth.

But not this time.

While the families and friends of crew members waited at Cape Canaveral and we watched with almost bored anticipation, the streak of light that was Columbia, a vehicle entrusted with seven human lives, gave up its trust to fire, and the journey was done.

"A space shuttle contingency has been declared," said an amplified NASA voice, in a tone as dry as a Texas desert. The whole world seemed to hesitate in the stunned silence that followed. Columbia had been lost.

Twice now we have been witness, either in person or through the cold eye of television, to shuttles — and lives — lost in bursts of fire and smoke. Seventeen years ago, it was Challenger, doomed by icy weather and an innocuous piece of technology called an O-ring.

The post-apocalyptic scenes are always the same. Expressions of horror followed by disbelief, tears, condolences, promises to move on with our explorations in space, then the pondering. How could it have happened? What went wrong?

Accusations and investigations are the result of public disasters, reducing lives to computer images, memos, what ifs and months of enough rhetoric to fill an auditorium. Words, words, words.

What this moment truly amounts to is that the seven men and women who died were explorers, and in the history of exploration, things have gone wrong. The unexpected has a way of intruding on the best laid plans. Did someone err? That's always a risk. Humans make mistakes. Did machinery fail? That's possible too. Ships sink, planes crash and spaceships explode.

Although disaster may cause us to hesitate on the brink of seeking new worlds or new ways of thinking, there can be no abandonment of the quests. Columbus, Magellan, De Soto, Ponce de Leon, Lewis and Clark, and every test pilot, deep sea diver and Arctic adventurer who challenged the unknown carried with them not just the knowledge of risk, but also the responsibility of moving us forward. We owe them.

Husband, Ramon, Brown, Anderson, Clark, Chawla, McCool. We took their loss personally, as well we should have. Shared grief reveals the existence of human empathy despite dangerous hostilities that continue to characterize our species. We are not totally reduced to savages yet. We can still cry.

Oddly and tragically, by dying, the seven astronauts who rode Columbia into oblivion have achieved a level of heroism that would not have been theirs had the ship simply landed and they walked away. It's a peculiarity of human nature to accept discovery as routine once the shine wears off.

But horror has a way of fixing itself in history, and those who rode an awesome vessel of exploration to their doom will be remembered. They were us, with smiles and kids and mortgages and backyard barbecues and things to do once their spaceship, 16 minutes from Earth, settled to the ground.

Like the flight of Icarus, something went wrong. Mythology merged with reality as wings melted and our best efforts failed. Icarus had reached for the sun. We were reaching for truths beyond our earthbound existence. Both journeys ended in fire.

I remember seeing Sputnik almost half a century ago, a small dot in the night sky, and being awed by the very notion that we had lofted a man-made satellite — our own moon! — into orbit around the Earth. We were connected to each other then as we are now, our sensibilities linked by the wonder of an event larger than our best dreams or our worst nightmares.

In 1981, my wife and I packed our kids into a camper and braved the crowds at Edwards Air Force Base to watch Columbia, completing the first space shuttle flight in history, land smoothly to wild cheers and flag-waving. Now, I watch as images of Columbia, a falling star, flash in endless replay across our television screens.

I saw it born and I saw it die, and the loss hurts.

February 7, 2003

END

INDEX

abortion, 105–7
Abrams, Bob, 62
abundance, 90
acid trips, 29
ACLU, 35, 37
activism
    abortion, 105–7
    AIDS, 263–65
    animal issues, 49–52, 97–100
    anti-death sentence, 88–90
    chemical sensitivity, 75–77
    gay rights: Morris Kight, 14–17
    Jane Fonda, 85–87
    Jerry Rubin (ex-Yippie), 246–48
    Jerry Rubin (Venice peace activist),
        77–79, 247–48
    peace movement, 85–87, 210,
        220–22, 247
actresses, 85–87, 261–63
Afghanistan, 209, 225
Africa, vacation in, 151–54
AIDS, 263–65
Alaska, travel in, 172–74
Alexander, Lamar, 38
Allen, Tina, 38
Allred, Gloria, 79
Almodovar, Norma Jean, 67–69
Altman, Sidney, 65–67
Alvarez, David, 101
Alzheimer's disease, 11
"America's Dumbest Criminals," 10–11

animal activists, 49–52, 97–100
animals, love of, 65–67
anniversaries, 116–18
annoyances, 55–57
Anzur, Terry, 84–85
Archimedes, 17
Arkoff, Sam, 40–42
"Arlo" (animal activist), 49–52
Arnold, Danny, 41
art museums, 165–66, 180–81, 194–96
artists, 33–35, 195
Ashe, Victor, 39
autumn, 186

babies, 113–16, 130–32, 140–42, 143
Bach, Travis, 123–25, 127–29, 137–40
bail bondsman, 9–10
Bailey, Bruce, 25–26
bananas, 189
Barkley (the dog), 66–67, 187, 189
Barnum, Joey, 9–11, 267
Barrow, Carla, 64
Barry (the woodcarver), 198–99
bars, 12–14, 48–49, 238
Basham, Mark, 19–21
Basques, 158–62
beauty, 195
beauty pageants, 62–64
beauty queens, 240–42
Beecher, Henry Ward, 200
Begley, Ed, 79

Belcher, Jerry, 227–28, 237–39
Berman, Shelly, 267
Bischoff, Adam Paul, 203–4
Black Dahlia, 240
Bloom, Robert, Jr., 88
Bonaparte, Napoleon, 221
Boosler, Elayne, 98
Borges, Jorge Luis, 235
Bostic, Melanie, 88–90
Bounitch, Pavel, 58–59
bowling shoes, 188
boxers, 9–11
Broder, Albert, 52–55
Bronze Stars, 231, 232
Broude, Alice, 12–14
Brown, Jerry, 17–19
Bruce, Lenny, 60–62
Brunn, Adolph, 215
Bukowski, Charles, 7–9
Burbayar, 169–70
burn victim, 19–21

Caen, Herb, 253–55
California Abortion Rights Action League, 105–7
Calig, Marsha, 180
Calley, Lt. William, 231–32
Camp Pendleton, 225–27
cancer, 202–3, 237–39
canoe trip, 168
Captain Kazoo, 52–55
capital punishment, 88–90
car chases, 83–85
"care," 142
Castaic Elementary School, 123
Catholics, 134, 160
cats, 257
celebrities
    as activists, 79, 106
    mothers of, 60
Chagres National Park, 168
Challenger space shuttle, 269
Chamberlain, Heidi, 259
chemical sensitivity, 75–77
Cher's mother, 60
chewing gum, 56–57
Chicago 7, 247

chicken dancing, 179, 181
child abuse, 113–16
children. See also Martinez family
    birth of, 114–15, 116, 140–42
    first steps, 130–32
    gun deaths, 244–46
    homelessness, 93–95
    hunger, 91
    Jeffrey, wrapping presents, 111–13
    murder of, 100–101, 113–16
    teen suicide, 258–60
    touring D.C., 127–29
    touring New York, 125–27
China, vacation in, 154–56
chores, 117
Christmas: wrapping presents with Jeffrey, 111–13
church bells, 56–57
Ciro's Pomodoro restaurant, 61, 241
Citera, Joe, 212, 215, 223–24
civil liberties. See rights
clams, live, 51, 176–77
"The Closet," 264–65
clothing stores, 57–60
clowns, 249–51
coffin sales, 72–75
Cohen, Mickey, 13
Colen, Beatrice "Betsy," 261–63
Columbia space shuttle, 268–70
columnists, 253–55
comedy writing, 249–51
comics, 60–62
compassion, 141
Coronel, Juian, 244–46
country-western music, 119
courage, 15–16, 35–37, 232
Cronin, Charlie, 262–63
Cronin, James, 262–63
Cronin, Patrick, 261–63
crowds, 195–96
Cuesta, Filbert, 242–44
Cullen, Larry, 267
customs officials, 152–53

Dana, Marie, 65–67
dancing under the moon, 142, 144
Daugherty, Phyllis, 98–99

Dave (the dog), 146
Davies, Tammy, 33–35
D'Chartoy, Elisabeth, 58
death. See also murder
    and 9/11, 102–4
    after car chase, 83–85
    Beatrice Colen, 261–63
    Billy Fucile, 263–65
    Bud and Christina Emerson, 24–26
    and coffin sales, 72–75
    drowning in flood, 203–4
    Frank Sinatra, 265–68
    gun statistics, 245–46
    Herb Caen, 253–55
    Hoover (the dog), 145–47
    Jack Smith, 254–55, 256–58
    Jeff Langley, paramedic, 31–33
    Jerry Belcher, 237–39
    Jerry Rubin, 246–48
    John Espey, 251–53
    Martin Ragaway, 249–51
    plane crash, 192–94
    space shuttles, 268–70
    teen suicide, 258–60
    things worth dying for, 228–29
    in war, civilian, 230–32
    in war, friends, 212, 215, 218, 223–24
    war statistics, 212, 217
death penalty, 88–90
Delaplane, Stanton, 255
DeLuise, Dom, 79
Diaz, Roberto, 100
Direct Casket, 73–75
disabled people, 28–30
disfigurement, 19–21
documentary on war, 210–11
dogs
    attacks and activism, 97–100
    barking at rain, 187, 189
    Barkley, 66–67, 187, 189
    Dave, 146
    as heirs, 65–67
    Hoover, 56, 117, 145–47, 198
    hypnotized soldier and, 219–20
drive-by shooting, 95–97
drug addicts, 28, 33–34
drug dealers, 97

drug use, 29
Dutch rub, 134

earthquakes, 197–99
Eason Monroe Courageous Advocate
    Award, 35, 37
Eaton, Bill, 13–14
"Ecology House," 76
Edenetti, Nick, 266–67
El Niño, 187–89
Emerson, Bud, 24–26
Emerson, Christina, 24–26
Emily (sister of Al Martinez), 132–34,
    170, 198
emotional wounds, 217
end of the world, 57
English teachers, 35–37, 251–53
environmental illness, 75–77
equality, 39
Esiquio, Daniel, 124
Espey, John, 251–53
Europe, traveling in, 156–62, 165–67,
    170–71, 174–81

"A Face of War," 210–11
factoids, 188–89
families. See also Martinez family
    daughters, 109
    homeless, 93–95
    and hunger, 91
    John Espey and Carolyn See, 251–53
    and war, 216–18, 226
fear, 100, 102–4, 131
fiction and reality, the line between, 83–85
fire, 19–21, 24–26
first steps, 130–32
Fiscus, Kathy, 84–85
flags, 127–29
flea markets, 174
Flockhart, Calista, 48
Flood, Michael, 91
flooding, 202–4
Flores, Paul, 197–98
Fonda, Jane, 85–87
Fontani, Giorgio, 176–78
"Forbidden Pompeii," 175
"Forrest Gump," 129

free speech, 60–62
freedom, 36–37, 128, 229
Fruehwirth, Mary, 224
Fucile, Billy, 263–65
Funny, Funny World, 249
furniture restoration, 69–72

Gabaldon, Richard, 243
Galbreath, LaDonna, 28–30
gamblers, 71–72
garbage (taking it out), 256–58
Garcia, Peter, 168–69
Gay, Janice, 88–90
Gay, Kenneth, 88–89
Gay and Lesbian Pride, 16
Gay and Lesbian Resistance, 16
Gay Liberation Front, 16
gay rights movement, 14–17
genealogy, 156–62
generals, 221
generosity, 22–24
Ghuman, Sharonjeet, 123
gift shops, 170–75
giggles, 125–126
Giles, Catherine, 164
Goetz, Bernhard, 131
goodbye, 216–18
Goodwill Industries' Special Projects
    Program, 30
gophers, 252
Gossett, Lou, Jr., 38
governments, 141, 221
graduation, 123–25
Graham, Billy, 61
Great Wall of China, 154–56
Green, Max, 68
grief, 269
Gulf War, 217–18
guns, 95–97, 243, 244–46

Hadji, Ala, 124
Halaby, Charles, 71
Halaby, Jorge, 71
Halaby, Marc, 71
Halaby, Nick, 69–72
Haley, Alex, 38–39, 153, 157–58, 161
Haley, Nannie, 38

"Happy Days," 261
Harris, Doris, 88–90
Harris, Lanell Craig, 88
Harris, Loyal, 22–24
hatred, 85–87
Hawn, Goldie, 70
Hayden, Tom, 85, 221
Hayes, Alicia, 258–60
helicopter accident, 31–33
helicopter training, 225, 226
"hellit," 138–39
Hermes, 58
Hernandez, Amber, 258–60
heroes, 39, 209–11, 242–44, 269
Hicks, Ruby, 25
hip, 47–49
history, 127–29, 141
Hoffman, Abbie, 247
Holbrook, Melissa, 124
Hollow Leg, 238
Hollywood beauty queen, 240–42
Hollywood Walk of Fame, 60–62
Holmes, Joe, 101–2
homelessness, 22, 93–95
homework, 135–37
homicides. See murder
honor, 35–37
Hoover (the dog), 56, 117, 145–47, 198
Hope, Bob, 79
Hooper, Tricia, 263–65
House Un-American Activities
    Committee, 36
Hubbard, Frank McKinney, 109
Hughes, Sarah, 229
Human Relations Commission, 14, 16
human spirit, 203, 220
humanity, 193, 229
humor, 45, 250–51
hunger, 90–92
Hussein, Saddam, 221–22
hypnosis, 219–20

"I Was a Teenage Werewolf," 40–42
iguanas as pets, 65–66
Imislund, Clancy, 26–28
Independence Day, 128

International Sex Worker Foundation for
    Art, Culture and Education, 68
intolerance, 56
Iraq, 220–22
Italy, 158
ivory Eskimo rock, 172–74

Jack London Square, 254
Japanese tourists, 180–81
Jefferson, Thomas (statue of), 128
Jeffrey (grandson), 111–13, 135–37
"Jigsaw John," 14
jokes, 249, 250
Jones, Allan, 124
Jones, Gene, 210–211
Jones, Lucy, 199
Jones, Natalie, 210
Joshua (grandson), 140–42
journalists
    admitting occupation to customs
        officer, 152–53
    Danny Pearl, 227–29
    Herb Caen, 253–55
    Jack Smith, 254–55, 256–58
    Jerry Belcher, 227–28, 237–39

Kaminsky International Kazoo Quartet, 54
Kansas, tourist from, 189–92
Katana, 48
Kaufman, George S., 262
Kazan, Elia, 35–37
kazoo salesman, 52–55
Kerkorian, Kirk, 11
Kerrey, Bob, 230–32
Ketlin, Hank, 189–92
kidney donor, 22–24
Kight, Morris, 14–17
King, Don, 13–14
King, Martin Luther, Jr., 81
King, Rodney, 132
Knoxville, Tenn., 38
Knutson, Beverly, 123, 124
Korean War
    deaths and memories, 211–15
    gunnery sergeant and ideology, 106
    husbands leaving for, 217
    memories of friends, 223–24

Private Ex, 218–20
truth and lies, 230–32
veterans and widows visiting
    Korea (1993), 163–65
Korean War Memorial, 212–15

L.A. Fashion Institute of Design and
    Merchandising, 58
Lance, Al, 86–87
Landon, Michael, 40–41
Langley, Jeff, 31–33
Langley, Karen, 32
Lansky, Sophia, 59
Larkin, Bill, 250
Larrogoite, Alfonso, 158, 161
Larrogoite, Claudio, 162
Larry (cancer patient), 202–3
Lesaca, 161–62
lies, 230–32
Linda (daughter), 124, 139
Linebager, Jeremy, 124
lint, 116, 143, 256
lions, 152
Lolatte, Kristina, 41–42
Los Angeles
    existence of, 183
    foreign impressions of, 155–56
    journalism, 255
    perspectives on, 166–67
Los Angeles County Museum
    of Art, 195–96
Los Angeles Regional Foodbank, 90–91
Los Angeles Times, 78
Lourdes, 160
Louzshkov, Yuri, 58–59
loyalty oath, 36

magic, 112–13
Mammaril, Pete, 212, 215
"The Man Who Came to Dinner," 262
Marin County, 76
Marine training exercises, 225–27
Marr, Sally, 60–62
marriage, 116–18
Martinez, Al
    as "Elmer," 136
    helping with homework, 135–37

marriage, 116–18
military service, 106, 163–65, 211–15,
     218, 226–227
running away from home, 134
searching for roots, 156–62
surgery, 118–20
Martinez, Joanne Cinelli
adventure travel, 168
and Barkley the dog, 66–67
home from vacation, 167
Jack Smith tribute, 256–58
and Jeffrey's homework, 135–37
marriage, 116–18
ordering in restaurant, 55
searching for roots, 157–62
Martinez family
ancestry, 156–62
Emily, 132–34, 170, 198
Jeffrey, 111–13, 135–37
Joshua, 140–42
Linda, 124, 139
Marty and Lisa moving, 142–44
Mary, 134
Nicole, 121–22, 125–27, 130–32, 133,
     142–44, 244
Shana Lee, 113–16, 125–27, 133
soldiers in, 214–15, 216–17
Travis, 123–25, 127–29, 133, 137–40
Mary (sister of Al Martinez), 134
Matteo's restaurant, 266
Mauldin, Bill, 218
"Max" (kidney donor), 22–24
Mazzeo, Lauren, 124
McCarthy era, 36–37
McMahon, Ed, 239
medals (war), 221, 231–32
mental incapacities, 28–30
Midnight Mission, 26–28
Miller, Henry, 216
Mills, Christopher, 259
Mirken, Bruce, 78
Miss Universe contest, 62–64
Monroe, Eason, 35–37
monuments, 128–29, 212–15
Moore, Ceola, 95–97
Moore, James, 95–97
Morrison, Herb, 193

mothers of celebrities, 60
mothers of men on death row, 88–90
motor home accident, 24–26
movie producers
Elia Kazan, 35–37
Gene and Natalie Jones, 210–11
Sam Arkoff, 40–42
Steven Spielberg, 219
movies
"A Face of War," 210–11
"I was a Teenage Werewolf," 40–42
"Saving Private Ryan," 218–19
moving, 142–44
Multiple Chemical Sensitivity, 75–77
murder
Black Dahlia, 240
child abuse, 113–16
Danny Pearl, 227–29
drive-by shooting, 95–97
Hollywood beauty queen, 240–42
horror of, 100–102
police officer shot, 242–44
Skid Row Slasher, 27
Murrietta, Detective Al, 240, 241–42
museums
art, 165–66, 180–81, 194–96
sex, 68–69
music, 119, 265–68
My Lai, 231–32

Nagdimon, Jay, 259
name-dropping, 70–71
Nathan, Robert, 123
National Sandwich contest, 77–79
Neal, Ryan, 124
neckties, 58–59
negativity, 137–40
New York, 104, 125–27
news coverage, 77–79, 131
Newton, Byron, 125
Nicole (granddaughter), 121–22, 125–27,
     130–32, 133, 142–44, 244
Nimoy, Leonard, 79
9/11, 102–4
911 Force, 226
noise, 48–49
North Korea, 223

Oakland, 17–19, 254, 267
ocean, 121–22, 189–92
Olympics, 228–29
Orsini, Ciro, 61–62, 241
Oscars: Lifetime Achievement Award, 35

painters, 33–35
Panama, 168–70
paramedics, 31–33
Paris, flea market in, 174
Parks, Rosa, 15–16
patriotism, 221
peace, 77–78, 86, 141, 222
peace movement, 210, 220–22, 247
Pearl, Danny, 227–29
perestroika, 58
perfume/cologne, 75–77
Phelps, Joey, 113–16
photographers, 64
plane crash, 192–94
poets, 7–9, 123, 125, 253
Point Barrow, Alaska, 172–74
police
    car chases, 83–85
    officer shot, 242–44
    society's demands on, 243–44
political activism. See activism
politicians, 221
Pompeii, ancient art, 174–75
pope, statue of, 170–71
pornography from Pompeii, 174–75
Port Hueneme, 192
praying for family, 132
presidents, 163, 221
Private Ex, 219–20
prostitution, 33–34, 67–69
protest demonstrations, 78
protesting, 99

Quinn, Sgt. Thomas, 226
Quinn, Tom, 18–19
Quirky Quake, 197, 199

race, 39
Ragaway, Martin, 249–51
rain, 186, 187–89, 199–201
rain forests, 168–70

reasoning, 135–37
Red Dog Saloon, 12–14
Redwood 2nd Street Saloon, 12–14, 238
reporters. See journalists
responsibility, 231
restaurants
    dining with vegetarians, 55–57
    in Europe, 159–60, 176–78
    hip, 47–49
rights
    abortion, 106
    free speech, 60–62
    gay, 14–17
    McCarthy era, 36
Ripston, Ramona, 37
Rodat, Robert, 219
Rojas, Jose, 100
Rome, 170–71, 176–78
"Roots," 38–39
roots, searching for, 156–62
Roselli, Giuseppe, 9–11
Rubin, Jerry (ex-Yippie), 246–48
Rubin, Jerry (Venice peace activist), 77–79,
    247–48
Russell, Kurt, 70
Russians, visiting L.A., 57–60

salesmen
    of coffins, 73–75
    Jerry Rubin, 247
    of kazoos, 52–55
Sammy the Syrian, 69, 71–72
San Francisco, 253, 254, 255
San Francisco Bay, 193–94
Sandburg, Carl, 5
sandwich contest, 77–79
Santa Ana winds, 202
Santa Monica mountains, 185–86
Santisaranyu, Aanont, 124
satellites, 18–19
"Saving Private Ryan," 218–19
schizophrenia, 28–30
Schneider, Robin, 105, 106–7
school, 123–25, 265
school lunches, 189
Schopenhauer, 198
Schwartz, Jeremy, 124

Scott, George C., 51
See, Carolyn, 251, 252–253
September 11th, 102–4, 221
sex museum, 68–69
sex workers, 67–69. See also prostitution
Shabani (African driver), 153–54
Shakespeare, William, 104
Shana Lee (grandaughter), 113–16,
    125–27, 133
Shanghai, 155
Sheen, Martin, 79
shootings, 95–97, 242–46
Short, Elizabeth, 240
Sideways Sidney, 14
Siegel, Benjamin "Bugsy," 13
Silvas, Ray, 73–75
Sims, George, 39
Sinatra, Frank, 265–68
Six Flags Magic Mountain, 133–34
Skid Row, 26–28
sleep, 197
Smith, FrancEyE, 7–9
Smith, Jack, 254–55, 256–58
snow on the Great Wall, 154–56
Sounes, Howard, 7
Southern California Earthquake
    Preparedness Project, 197
space shuttles, 268–70
Spain, 158, 159–62
Spann, Johnny, 209–11
Spielberg, Steven, 219
squid, 159–60
St. John, John, 14, 100
Stallone, Sylvester, mother of, 60
Stone, Hal, 241
storytellers, 38–39
Sturken, Marita, 87
success, 33
suicide, 27, 34, 258–60
sunsets, 152, 185, 192–93
surgery, 118–20
survival, 22–24, 231
symbols, 127–29

Tangco, Eda, 124
Tanzania, vacation in, 151–54
tattoos, 34–35

taxi drivers, 172–74
Taylor, Alan, 32–33
teachers, 136
teenagers, suicide of, 258–60
television
    actress from "Happy Days," 261
    "America's Dumbest Criminals,"
        10–11
    attempted rescue of child, 84–85
    comedy writer, 249–51
    earthquake coverage, 198
    live car chases, 83–85
terrorism, 102–4, 216, 221–222, 225
Thanh Phong, 230–32
Thanksgiving, 49–52, 92
Thayer, Brynn, 106
Thayer, Michael Alan, 83–85
Thurber, James, 45
time, 235
Timeless Educators Inc., 265
Topanga, flooding in, 202–4
Topanga Canyon Boulevard, 24
Topanga State Park, 31
Torres, Evelyn, 100
Torres, Massiel, 100
Torres, Sebastian, 102
Toulouse, 159
tour guides, 176–78
tourists in Southern California, 189–92, 199
Trace, Al, 54
traveling
    in Africa, 151–54
    behavior changes during, 179
    buying trinkets, 170–75
    Great Wall of China, 154–56
    Japanese tourists, 180–81
    in Korea, 163–65
    in Panama, 168–70
    Rome, finding one's way around,
        177–78
    searching for roots, 156–62
    in Vienna, 165–67
trinkets, 170–75
Truman, Harry, 163
truth, 229, 230–32
Tsangarakis, Chris, 124
turkey, 49–52

2-year-olds, 137–40

underwear, 188
unicorn (drawing), 33–35
unions for sex workers, 69
Uribe, Jose, 124

Van Gogh exhibition, 194–96
Vatican City, 170
vegetarians, 49–52, 55–57
Velazquez, Christian, 123
Venice beach, 189–92
veterans, 86–87, 163–65
Vienna, 165–67
Vietnam War, 85–87, 217, 230–32
violence. See also murder; war
        and car chases, 83–85
        in neighborhoods, 95–97, 131
        and suicide, 259
        televised live, 83–85

waiting, 202–3
waitresses, 12–14
war. See also peace movement
        and 9/11, 104
        brutalities, 215, 230–32
        coming home from, 214–15
        defined, 210
        discussing with grandson, 129
        heroes, 209–11
        human face of, 209–11
        Iraq, 220–22
        isolation of spirit, 220
        journalist's death, 227–29
        Korea, 106, 163–65, 211–15, 217,
                218–20, 223–24, 230–32
        leaving for, 216–17
        memories of friends, 223–24
        Oscar Wilde on, 207
        reality, 221, 230
        reasons for/instincts, 141
        training Marines for, 225–226
        truth and lies, 230–32
        Vietnam, 85–87, 217, 230–32
weather, 185–87, 199–201, 202–4
Weatherwax, Jill, 240–42
Weiland, Don, 215

werewolf movies, 40–42
whale-watching, 121–22
whiners, 257
Whole Foods Market, 90
"Why?" (child's question), 111–13
Wilde, Oscar, 207
Winchell, Walter, 14
Winnie the Pooh, 121
Wives, Families & Friends, 88–89
wonder, 190, 191
"Wonder Woman," 262
words spoken per day, 188
work, 27–28
World Boxing Hall of Fame, 9, 11
World War II, 216, 218–19
writers
        comedy, 60–62, 249–51
        journalism (See journalists)
        "roter" in Africa, 151, 153–54

Yippies, 246–48

Zimbalist, Stephanie, 147

DRAWING THE LINE
by Paul Conrad
Two hundred drawings, spanning the period from the late 1960s to President Clinton's impeachment trial, from America's premier political cartoonist. $25.45

ETERNALLY YOURS
by Jack Smith
Who can forget Jack Smith, the Los Angeles Times' columnist for nearly 40 years? When he died in 1996, we all lost a treasure. But at least his words survived. Here, Jack's widow, Denise, and his sons, Curt and Doug, have collected some of their favorite columns. $16.95

CURBSIDE L.A.
An Offbeat Guide to the City of Angels
by Cecilia Rasmussen
Enjoy a truly eclectic tour of Los Angeles. Explore the L.A. you've not seen with enticing excursions into the city's peerless history and diversity. $19.45

DAY HIKERS' GUIDE TO SOUTHERN CALIFORNIA
by John McKinney
Walks in Southern California, from the simply scenic to the challenging, as described by *Los Angeles Times* hiking columnist and author John McKinney. $16.45

52 WEEKS IN THE CALIFORNIA GARDEN
by Robert Smaus
How to make the most of your garden by the foremost authority on gardening in Southern California. $17.45

ANSWERS FOR CALIFORNIA GARDENERS
by Robert Smaus
Expert advice in an easy-to-read Q&A format from the foremost authority on Southern California gardening. An excellent companion to Smaus' *52 Weeks in the California Garden.* $21.45

IMAGINING LOS ANGELES
Photographs of a 20th Century City
Foreword by Ray Bradbury
Collected here are some 175 photos from more than a dozen Southern California archives that tell the tale of men and women from all over the world who hoped and dared on a grand scale and who turned Los Angeles into the quintessential 20th century city. $28.95

L.A. UNCONVENTIONAL
by Cecilia Rasmussen
Where some people see roadblocks, others, such as the men and women in this volume, see possibility, opportunity and excitement. $30.95

THE SAN FERNANDO VALLEY
America's Suburb
by Kevin Roderick
Valley native Kevin Roderick recounts the area's vibrant past, from its Native American residents through the Spanish, Mexican and American settlers, spinning along the way the tales that give the Valley its unique history and culture. $26.45

SUNSET BOULEVARD
Cruising the Heart of Los Angeles
by Amy Dawes
A guide to the sights, experiences and lost legends of Los Angeles' most famous boulevard. Loaded with photos, maps and tips on where to dine, party and shop. $28.45

ICONIC L.A.
Stories of L.A.'s
Most Memorable Buildings
by Gloria Koenig
The architecture and drama behind 13 of Los Angeles' most recognizable landmarks, including the Bradbury Building, the Getty Museum, Walt Disney Concert Hall and the LAX Theme Building. With an introduction by Frank O. Gehry. $29.95

LAST OF THE BEST
90 Columns From the 1990s
by Jim Murray
The best of Jim's columns from the last decade of his life are included in this paperback volume compiled by *Los Angeles Times* Sports Editor Bill Dwyre and featuring a foreword by Dodger legend Tommy Lasorda. $19.45

THE GREAT ONES
by Jim Murray
The top men and women of the sports world written about as only this late, great sports columnist could. Foreword by Arnold Palmer. $24.45

PLASCHKE
Good Sports, Spoilsports, Foul Balls and Oddballs
by Bill Plaschke
Nearly 70 articles from the award-winning sports columnist that will leave you laughing, crying and wishing for more. $23.95

SURVIVING SUBURBIA
The Best of the Guy Chronicles
By Chris Erskine
Suburban life, complete with a mini van and three–oops four!–kids is mined for laughs on the edge of America's edgiest city. $21.45

LOW-FAT KITCHEN
by Donna Deane
From the pages of the *Los Angeles Times* Food section come more than 110 recipes that use fresh food flavor, not fat, to satisfy your taste buds. $20.45

THE LOS ANGELES TIMES' MODERN CALIFORNIA COOKING
Staff of The Times' Food section
A sequel to the 1981 bestseller *California Cookbook, Modern California Cooking* offers more than 300 recipes that reflect the cutting-edge, international cuisine for which Southern California has become so famous in recent years. An ideal companion to the 1981 volume. $22.45

SOS RECIPES
30 Years of Requests
by Rose Dosti
This bestselling hardcover book offers hundreds of tried-and-true recipes for all-time favorite dishes that literally range from soup to nuts. $19.45

DEAR SOS
Favorite Restaurant Recipes
by Rose Dosti
Rose Dosti has culled her perennially popular column in the *Los Angeles Times* Food section to handpick 225 of her all-time favorite recipes from restaurants throughout the country. $22.45

To order, call (800) 246-4042 or visit our Web site at http://www.latimes.com/bookstore